# Emotions and Migration in Argentina at the Turn of the 20th Century

History of Emotions

**Series Editor:** *Peter N. Stearns*, Professor Emeritus in the Department of History at George Mason University, USA and Susan J. Mat, Presidential Distinguished Professor of History at Weber State University, USA.

The field is predicated on the understanding that human feelings change over time and that they are the product of culture as well as of biology across all major world regions. With a commitment to expansive thematic, geographical and chronological breadth and to interdisciplinary analysis, the series will offer new and innovative titles which convey the rich diversity of emotional cultures.

**Published:**
*Fear in the German Speaking World, 1600–2000,*
edited by Thomas Kehoe and Michael Pickering (2020)

**Forthcoming:**
*Emotions in the Ottoman Empire,* Nil Tekgül
*Feelings and Work in Modern History,* edited by Agnes Arnold-Forster
and Alison Moulds
*Feeling Dis-Ease in Modern History,* edited by Rob Boddice and Bettina Hitzer
*The Business of Emotion in Modern History,* edited by Andrew Popp and
Mandy Cooper
*The Renaissance of Feeling,* Kirk Essary

# Emotions and Migration in Argentina at the Turn of the 20th Century

María Bjerg
Translated by Gerardo Gambolini

BLOOMSBURY ACADEMIC
LONDON • NEW YORK • OXFORD • NEW DELHI • SYDNEY

BLOOMSBURY ACADEMIC
Bloomsbury Publishing Plc
50 Bedford Square, London, WC1B 3DP, UK
1385 Broadway, New York, NY 10018, USA
29 Earlsfort Terrace, Dublin 2, Ireland

BLOOMSBURY, BLOOMSBURY ACADEMIC and the Diana logo are trademarks
of Bloomsbury Publishing Plc

First published in Great Britain 2022
This paperback edition published 2023

Cover design: Terry Woodley
Cover image courtesy of Argentina Archivo General de la Nación

A catalogue record for this book is available from the British Library.

ISBN:   HB:      978-1-3501-9394-9
        PB:      978-1-3501-9416-8
        ePDF:    978-1-3501-9395-6
        eBook:   978-1-3501-9396-3

Series: History of Emotions

Typeset by RefineCatch Limited, Bungay, Suffolk

To find out more about our authors and books visit www.bloomsbury.com
and sign up for our newsletters.

*For Tobías, my favorite violinist*

# Contents

# Acknowledgments

This is an extended and revised version of *Lazos Rotos. La inmigración el matrimonio y las emociones en la Argentina entre los siglos XIX y XX*, published in 2019 by Editorial de la Universidad Nacional de Quilmes. Many people have contributed to making the publication of both the Spanish- and the English-language versions of this book possible. I would like to express my gratitude to Anna Mónica Aguilar, María Angélica Corva, Nancy Calvo, Osvaldo Gerschman, Noemí Girbal, Ana María Saucedo, Alejandro Villar, and to my colleagues from the Centro de Estudios de Historia Cultura y Memoria at Universidad Nacional de Quilmes. I am deeply grateful to Javier Moscoso, who saw something of interest when he read *Lazos Rotos* and encouraged me to publish it in English. Marcelo J. Borges deserves a special mention because he read the entire manuscript and made insightful comments. I would also like to thank Maddie Holder and Abigail Lane, who have been extraordinarily supportive editors.

Access to public archives and libraries was crucial for this research. I owe special thanks to the staff of the Archivo Histórico de la Provincia de Buenos Aires, Archivo General de la Nación, Sección Histórica del Departamento Judicial de Dolores, Biblioteca Nacional Mariano Moreno, and Biblioteca de la Universidad Nacional de la Plata.

I gratefully acknowledge the financial support received at Universidad Nacional de Quilmes. Equally crucial for this project was the generosity of the German Academic Exchange Service (DAAD) that financed my stay at the Center for the History of Emotions at the Max Planck Institute for Human Development. I thank Ute Frevert for hosting me there.

# Introduction

At the dawn of the twentieth century, on the platform of a southern Italian train station, amidst the bustle, women and children in tears crowd together to say goodbye to travelers. The travelers are young men who are undertaking the first leg of the journey to South America, husbands who have promised their wives that the separation will be temporary. Some intend to return and plan to meet their families again when they too cross the Atlantic. Both those who leave and those who stay behind will have to get accustomed to a transnational life that involves new roles and responsibilities, as well as the challenge of preventing migration from dissolving their affective bonds. When men leave, their real presence becomes an imaginary closeness, and the daily and oral dynamics of the marital relationship turn into fixed words on a piece of paper where expressions of love, recriminations, and suspicions, as well as news, advice, and information, converge, creating a "singular transnational space."[1]

The man's fear of his wife's infidelity, the woman's fear of being abandoned by her husband, the need for money, the administration of remittances, the advice on the household management, and children's upbringing were common topics in the epistolary exchange through which the marriage relationships transformed by the migration were sustained.[2] Letters certainly had the capacity for shaping a sense of imaginary co-presence by transporting thoughts, objects (a photograph, money, a dried flower), and emotions.[3] Nevertheless, it is also true that the migratory experience was disruptive, as distance weakened the bonds, and the passing of time eroded the longing for reunion. If thousands of married couples separated by migration managed to reunite because husbands returned to Europe or wives and children crossed the Atlantic to join them, thousands more were unable to fulfill the promise of family reunification made upon departure. On some occasions, women refused to emigrate when they were called by their husbands. In others, it was the men who, attracted by the novelty of the big cities or immersed in the intense mobility of internal migrations—which used to follow overseas ones—discontinued contact with their families, broke the promise of returning, formed new couples, and even got married again.

But the breaking of marital bonds resulted not only from a definitive separation, since the reunification of husband and wife did not always entail the resumption of a harmonious and loving relationship. The dissimilar impact that the experience of migration had on the feelings among spouses, or the different expectations the migratory project generated on them, used to turn the reencounter into a motive for disappointment and bitterness rather than a source of joy and pleasure. Eroded by long separations, the couples failed to reestablish the common languages of affection and intimacy. Although more unusual, it used to happen that the period of separation was so brief that it lasted months instead of years, and even that the family traveled together. But none of these circumstances ensured the integrity of the marital bond. When the expectations of material progress remained unfulfilled or when the man and woman's experience of adjustment—which never were identical—diverged, conflict and mistreatment ended up taking over the relationship. Then the shared project that had motivated the transatlantic venture would lose its meaning and become a reason for reproaching and regretting. In these cases, the bond between husband and wife deteriorated until it finally disappeared, even if its legal dissolution was banned.

At the intersection of the history of migration and the history of emotions, this book tells small stories with unfortunate denouements, which reveal how migration transfigured the anatomy of the marital bonds—unions of a fragile nature unable to resist the ravages of distance, time, and frustration, and in which the affection ended up being colonized by anxiety, indifference, resentment, contempt, and rage. These stories reveal the heavy emotional toll of migration, and at the same time, expose the flip side of a historiographical account that evokes the image of men and women who got accustomed to the transnational life, who could imagine themselves together when they were separated, and who were able to sustain the fluidity of the epistolary dialogue even though they often could hardly read and many times needed someone else to write for them. These were couples capable of mending the marital bond by correspondence, and who, after an intense "work of waiting"—which entailed distress, anxiety, and sorrows—reunited on the other side of the Atlantic Ocean to resume a relationship that had been on hold for several years.[4] In effect, all of these situations took place, but at the same time, in the lives of thousands of men and women the migratory experience caused a tear through which oblivion, betrayal, disappointment, and violence slipped in.

The book focuses the lens on critical circumstances of the married life in which it was no longer possible to mend the bond, and the marital conflict ended up aired in the criminal courts. The judicial record is the primary source of this research, a kind of document which, although it has been widely used by historians interested in crime, punishment, social control, and subaltern agency, still remains little explored in relation to the history of migration.[5] Mine is only an initial approach that deals with criminal proceedings held in the city and the province of Buenos Aires in the late-nineteenth and early-twentieth century involving Italian and Spanish immigrants. The spatial and ethnic delimitation is a choice that obeys the demographic impact these migratory groups had on the two territories, an impact that is reflected in the court records as, in the vast majority of cases, plaintiffs and defendants were Italian, with Spaniards following closely behind, while French, English, and Germans immigrants were barely represented.[6] The selection by origin is also based on the abundance of bibliography on migration from Italy and Spain that recreate the contexts—both of origin and of arrival and insertion—where I was able to find the clues to unravel some of the problems posed by the sources.

In particular, the corpus encompasses bigamy lawsuits filed by women against their husbands, complaints of adultery submitted by men against their wives, lawsuits for domestic abuse, and trials for uxoricide (wife killing) in which the wife's infidelity—real or supposed—and the husband's insanity intermingle.[7] However, rather than being the primary objects of research, bigamy, adultery, marital abuse, and uxoricide are pretexts to illuminate the emotional life of the transnational family. In the voices of plaintiffs, defendants, and witnesses, the judicial proceedings uncover the emotional costs of the migratory experience, and at the same time expose the persistent trace of atavistic attitudes, emotional standards, languages, and practices rooted in the societies of origin of the immigrants.

Some years ago, in a pathbreaking article, Loretta Baldassar and Paolo Boccagni pointed out that even though mixed and contrasting emotions and feelings such as hope and nostalgia, guilt and ambition, affection and disaffection were an integral part of the life experiences of migrating, the emotional side of the migrant condition is still relatively understudied.[8] Although this assertion holds true, several historians of migration have already undertaken the initiative to approach mobile lives to observe the emotions, not only of those who were leaving their family but also for the ones who were left behind. The migrants' emotional languages expressed in their personal narratives have been the privileged focus of analysis, and their correspondence the most relevant source.[9]

Letters reveal several dimensions of the affective bonds, uncover emotional repertoires, and reflect the standards that regulated the expression of feelings in different geographies and historical moments. These narratives, in which the correspondents created representations of themselves and the world around them connecting the individual and the social, provide entry points into the subjective dimension of the migratory experience. Nevertheless, not all the immigrants were part of the literate culture, and usually, they had to turn to third parties to sustain the epistolary relationship with their loved ones.

This circumstance affected the fluidity of communication across the Atlantic as the mediation of someone who wrote or read the letters restricted the intimacy to express the emotions. The high illiteracy rates of the immigrants from the south of Europe who arrived at the port of Buenos Aires at the turn of the twentieth century conspired against the ability to maintain a transnational marital life.[10] No doubt correspondence provided a vehicle to keep families connected, but it only represents the experience of those who had the necessary cultural, emotional, and material resources to nurture the bonds and reaffirm the validity of the migratory project. Immigrants not only had to know how to read and write—or have someone who did it for them—but they also had to get accustomed to a new form of communication, learning how to dialogue with somebody who was absent.

Mail delays or misplacements, and intermittences caused by changes of address, shortage of money, or lack of paper and pencil, conspired against the continuity of the epistolary dialogue. For example, it was not unusual for the immigrants to justify the briefness of their letters or the temporary interruption of the epistolary contact by arguing that they had been busy searching for employment, that they did not have a dime, that they wrote with the last bit of pencil or that they had moved from the city to the rural interior and there was no post office nearby.[11] In addition to the material hindrances, the ambiguity and the misunderstandings present in epistolary communication also played a role. Letters used to become a terrain traversed by claims, misunderstandings, and bitter disputes that ceased when one of the parties discontinued the epistolary exchange in a gesture of annoyance.

The protagonists in the stories presented in this book were not able to maintain an artifice of closeness that let them preserve the ties of affection. Many of them ended up turning the temporary separation into a rupture, which induced men to equate the long silence and the lack of news from their wives with widowhood or with a sort of informal divorce that enabled them to behave as if they were single. But the prolonged separation and the irregular communication also cooled the love of the women and encouraged adultery. Sometimes infidelity occurred in the place of origin when migrant husbands abandoned the wives, and they "forced by necessity fell into the arms of another man."[12] Nevertheless, adultery could also be an unwanted consequence of the couple's reunion. It did not matter if the separation had eroded the bond, or if the marital relationship already showed signs of breakdown before the husband's departure. When a husband called his wife, it was not easy for her to refuse to migrate. And although some women—as we will see further on—disobeyed the mandate of "following her husband wherever he takes up residence", others crossed the Atlantic to reunite with a man they no longer loved. For example, remaining in Italy as a "white widow" (a married woman whose husband had emigrated) would restrict her rights since even for the most trivial official procedure an *autorizzazione maritale* (marital authorization) was needed.[13] In Spain, instead, the law provided for the wife's right to request an exemption to the article of the Civil Code that obliged her to live with her husband when he moved the residence overseas.[14] Nevertheless, it is likely that the economic dependence and the socialization in a culture that valued female submission, and had enshrined it as a duty in the Civil Code, might have led the majority of wives to comply with their husbands' call.

The frustration of women's hopes, the confrontation of illusions with a reality that replicated the material hardship of the places of origin, the disruption of the sense of belonging, and the high emotional cost of uprooting caused domestic violence. Oftentimes, however, the abuse was not new to the couple and was rather simply replicated in another context; notions of authority and obedience that had regulated the distribution of power within the marriage before migration remained intact. The assiduity of quarrels, and the vicious circle of bodies that scarred only to be injured again, used to have tragic endings when, driven by a fit of rage, the husband took the life of his wife.

These experiences made up of silences, forgetfulness, and abandonment, or of reunions torn by infidelity, frustration, insults, and physical aggression, were also part of migration. However, this dimension is difficult to glimpse in letters, diaries, memoirs, and autobiographies, to which historians have resorted to illuminate the emotional experience of migrants. More restrained than the intimate accounts, formalized, and with scarce dialectical and linguistic nuances, also the criminal records uncover personal motivations and emotional standards, repertoires, and languages.[15] These sources have the additional advantage of presenting a heterogeneous array of social actors whose relations are mediated by state power. Whereas in personal narratives, individuals may have sometimes written to conform to norms and rules, other times they wrote in defiance. In the court, however, they were prompted to comply with the conventions regulating the expression of emotions. Hence, judicial records allow us to explore the intersectionality of emotional standards and the ways in which individuals displayed and navigated their feelings in a public context characterized by asymmetrical power relationships.

The daily life of most immigrants took place in social spaces like the *conventillo* (tenement house), the neighborhood, or the workplace regulated by atavistic practices and ethnic emotional styles. Nevertheless, this fact did not prevent them from resorting to the judicial system to settle private matters, even when during the trial it would be necessary to give up traditional behaviors. In the solemnity of a courtroom where trials were conducted in a foreign language—at least for the Italians—plaintiffs, defendants, and witnesses had to adapt to new emotional standards and conform to the prescription that regulated the emotional expression in the Argentine judicial system at the turn of the century.[16] Despite their opacity, the court records reveal, on the one hand, how the immigrants managed their emotions and languages to accommodate them to the emotional standards and styles current in the Argentine courts at the turn of the century, and on the other, how the judges, prosecutors, and lawyers construed the verbal and gestural expressions of individuals who were foreign to them not only for their nationality but also for their social origin.

How to unravel the stories behind the narrowness of the legal typification of bigamy, adultery, injuries, and uxoricide *cases* that the law ascribed to them? There is no doubt that criminal records labeled with the same heading (bigamy, adultery, uxoricide, homicide) share similarities derived from the standardization of the procedures and formulas that regulated the testimonies of defendants and witnesses, the statements of the defense, the requests of the prosecutors, and the sentences. As the judicial system, I also treated them as *cases*, although to me their interest lies neither in the crime nor in the evidence. From my perspective, each file constitutes a singular *case* that I treat as a commentary on how migration affected emotions and marital bonds. It is from that singularity that I read the sources and narrate the stories.[17]

The judicial record is a closed universe, beyond which the protagonists disappear, making it difficult for the historian to follow the course of their lives forward, after the trial ends, and backward, before the destabilizing event that tore the fabric of married life occurred. Therefore, to contextualize the behaviors and motivations of these individuals caught in dramatic personal circumstances and to tell their stories, I supplemented the court files with a variety of secondary sources. Firstly, I used the civil and penal codes and the legal doctrine of the period. The legal codification is the compass that guides the reading and interpretation of the criminal record as a legal instrument. In turn, the jurists' ideas, and concepts about some of the crimes addressed in the following chapters—like adultery, for example—shed light on the cultural atmosphere of a period of intense parliamentary debate and academic production triggered by the approval of the Penal Code of 1886, the Project of Reform of 1891, and the Laws of Reform of 1903 and 1906, respectively. Although this academic production did not compel lawyers or judges to adhere to it, for its contents did not translate into mandatory norms, the opinions of the jurists were echoed in the legal circles, not least because most of them were professors at the schools of law where court officials were trained.

To interpret the cases beyond the borders of the law, it is also crucial to recreate the contexts of the plaintiffs, defendants, and witnesses, for it is there where we may find the answers to questions posed by the historian that, as Carlo Ginzburg noted, often differ from those made by the judges.[18] Since the historical actors involved in the judicial proceedings were immigrants, the evidence from the immediate context of the trial alone does not suffice and, therefore, it is necessary to go back to the origin to trace—as far as scant information allows— their lives before migration.[19] But, in addition, these men and women who exposed their marital conflicts in the court continued their lives, in freedom or in jail, after the trial ended. The rest of their stories are often found in the little details, in the blurry line of the path followed by individuals whose lives were torn apart. To delve into both ends of the personal paths of plaintiffs and defendants, I resorted to church and civil records from the places of origin and destination, as well as to population censuses and local histories. The newspapers of that epoch were another valuable resource since most of the episodes of domestic violence reported in the police news—in particular, the uxoricides— allow us to recreate the social atmosphere that surrounded those dramatic events, as well as to contrast the emotional languages used by the press and the law to make their judgments about crimes that challenged current notions of family and marriage, male honor and female decency, reason, and passion.

Narrating a case by linking it with the context demands an arduous work of searching —slow, unrewarding, and artisanal. Sometimes, the information is so meager that it was not possible to trace the historical actors outside the courtroom. In that case, the research proved fruitless, and I had to settle for the content of the criminal record, a blurry photograph of a dramatic moment beyond whose outline there is only darkness. But on other occasions, I managed to track the people to the origin and follow them after the end of the trial. For that reason, the reader will notice that each chapter tells only a handful of stories: those of individuals who left traces in other sources that help me solve the little mysteries of their lives. However, those for whom the trial was their only exit from anonymity also played their role, since although I could not recreate their life trajectories, their complaints, declarations, and testimonies give access to reasons, expectations, agency, and emotional languages. If only the ones who could be followed up provided narrative density to the stories, both groups of cases contain the singularity from which to make inferences about the broader social and cultural problems.

The book begins with the stories of bigamists and their legitimate wives filing lawsuits against them in the Argentine courts. Upon hearing rumors that their husbands had got married again, or that the second marriage was imminent, some women crossed the Atlantic to confirm the betrayal with their own eyes. Others, who had spent years without any news from their husbands, traveled to try and look for them, and they learned of the bigamy after arriving in Argentina. Whichever the case, they had to circumvent legal restrictions to emigrate, since both in Spain and Italy, a married woman could not get a passport without marital authorization. Accompanied by their brothers or fathers, these women usually appeared before the migratory authorities asking for exemptions from the norm that would allow them to travel. When their requests were denied, they reiterated their petitions, to which they used to add pleading letters describing their misfortunes and assuring that they counted with the money to pay for the journey and relatives in Argentina who would accommodate them. In her study based on the records of the prefecture of Potenza, Victoria Calabrese shows that the bulk of the passport applications submitted without *autorizzazione maritale* was rejected (which seems not to have been the case among the wives of the bigamists I study here). Nevertheless, the analysis of the letters they attached to them reveals that the applicants resorted to strategies of manipulation of the law based on emotional languages in which they victimized themselves looking to get the compassion of migration authorities.[20] Moreover, they also reveal that going through all these legal procedures, women learned how to interact with state officials, an experience they might have profited from to sue their bigamous husbands.

But not all wives reacted the same way to the desertion of their husbands. Driven by affection or necessity, some of them started intimate relationships with other men, cohabited, and had illegitimate children. An example of this response to destitution and solitude is the story of Felisa Castellani, told in the third chapter and dealing with adultery. But this crime, that tarnished the husband's honor, was not always an answer to abandonment. Sometimes it was an unwanted consequence of the marital couple's reunion and the result of frustration, misery, and domestic violence. Moreover, it was not unusual—as it is shown in the fourth chapter—for the abusive husbands to sue for grievous bodily harm, attempting to conceal a story of marital violence, declaring in court that the crime was the response to their wives' infidelity.

The marital conflict that aroused a whirlwind of opposite feelings sometimes ended in a tragic event: the uxoricide (typified as homicide when the couple cohabited but was not legally married), to which I devote the last two chapters. The murderers, submissive and fearful or defiant and shameless, made up accounts of stormy marital relationships and alleged mitigating circumstances to fight against the severity of the sentence. Usually, these accounts relied on the prescriptive language of the patriarchal family, thus wives' disobedience and adultery were put forward by husbands who claimed to have killed their wives with "the reason clouded by the passion of jealousy." However, albeit exceptionally, the murderers introduced in court—or intended to do so—the language of romantic love to justify the crime, by depicting themselves as individuals dejected by the sorrows of unrequited love. But regardless of the emotional lexicon and the fact that all migratory projects were indeed marked by the unpredictable, few migrants might have imagined that theirs would end up in such a tragedy.

1

# The Land of Prosperity

Between 1880 and the outbreak of the First World War, Argentina received 4.2 million immigrants. The expansion of this flow, which reached its historical peak at the beginning of the twentieth century, suffered an interruption during the first half of the decade of the 1890s. Between 1881 and 1890 the number of immigrants was over one million, with some 650,000 settling permanently, a notable number in a country whose total population was approximately two million people. However, after the economic crisis of 1890, immigration declined, and immigrants who returned to their home countries exceeded the number of those arriving.[1] The former migration flow patterns were reestablished in the first decade of the twentieth century, when the positive balance of arrivals versus returns surpassed one million.[2]

Around 80 percent of immigrants came from Italy and Spain.[3] Most of them were young men, unskilled day laborers from rural backgrounds who arrived through the mechanism of chain migration looking for a job in a country that was experiencing a formidable economic boom due to the expansion of agriculture and livestock exports. The relevance of migration chains may be noted in the regional traits of the migration process. For example, most of the Italians came from the South and Central regions of the peninsula, especially from Sicily, Calabria, Basilicata, and the Marches. Whereas more than half of Spaniards were from A Coruña and Pontevedra provinces, whose crowded settlement in Buenos Aires transformed the city into a "Southern Galicia."[4]

The engine of economic expansion was set in the countryside, where Sarmiento—one of the mentors of Argentina's modernization and president of the country in the period 1868–1874—had imagined a landscape dotted with agricultural colonies. His discourse evoked bucolic images of a country of farmers where the sown land displaced the loneliness of the *estancia* (cattle ranch), and industrious European immigrants contributed to eradicate barbarism.[5] Even though the agricultural colonization projects were successful in some provinces of the littoral, like Santa Fe and Entre Ríos where Italian,

Swiss, German, and Jewish farmers settled, by the turn of the century, most immigrants lived in cities, towns, and villages. Two factors discouraged the settling of the newcomers in rural Argentina. On the one hand, the most intense demand for labor lasted only a few months per year and it was reduced to the harvest season. And on the other hand, the concentration of land in large agricultural and livestock ranches—especially in the province of Buenos Aires— and the steady increase of land prices hindered immigrants' access to purchase. However, the continuous expansion of agriculture since 1890 allowed immigrants with little capital at their disposal to rent a piece of arable land as sharecroppers.[6]

Cities and towns did not secure permanent employment for everyone either, but they offered a wider variety of opportunities. The industrial economy sector, which grew in consonance with the rhythm of the agrarian one, employed many laborers in meatpacking plants and flour mills that produced goods both for export and for the domestic market. Other industries, such as textiles and food processing, supplied products elaborated with local primary material, while a network of workshops, generally owned by better-off immigrants, supplied the rest of the domestic market.[7]

Turn-of-the-century Argentina was a country under construction that grew at a frenzied pace, thus the expansion of the urban grid also created new job opportunities. Cities were expanding, new towns were being founded, luxurious urban mansions, sumptuous public buildings, and working-class houses were being built, and new railroad lines were extended (from 2,300 kilometers in 1880 to 16,700 in 1900).[8] The ruling class made use of all this evidence to celebrate the success of their modernizing project and resorted to images of a thriving country to promote Argentina abroad, trying to attract new settlers and foreign investors.[9]

Among the Argentine ruling class and intellectual elites, cities were regarded as the privileged tools to lead the modernization of the territory, and not as the consequence of modernization itself. This conception of modernity had its most audacious expression when Dardo Rocha—governor of the province of Buenos Aires—set out to create a city from its foundations. In 1880, the province had to accept the transformation of the city of Buenos Aires into Argentina's federal district and was forced to find a place to set its own capital city. Rocha rejected outright any possibility of establishing it in some preexisting town and committed himself to founding La Plata. *Lomas de Ensenada*, the site chosen for the new provincial capital, was humid and swampy but had the advantage of being close to the shore of the Rio de la Plata and the Ensenada natural harbor. On a suffocating morning in mid-November 1882, the groundbreaking ceremony took place, and from then, the place became the scene of a feverish activity led by legions of masons, bricklayers, carpenters, and laborers who built the city at an amazing speed. Stylish buildings inspired by European metropolises transformed the landscape day after day to make Rocha's utopia come true. As some sort of Peter the Great from the Pampas, he had decreed that a great city would be erected in *Lomas de Ensenada*. In the following years the governor's residence, the building of the Provincial Legislature, the city hall, the courthouse, and the train station were opened. Meanwhile, tram rails were laid, streets paved, and schools and private houses built. When the decade of the 1880s was coming to an end, La Plata already had 6,000 inhabitants and had been awarded a gold medal for modernity at the 1889 Paris Exhibition.

The broad boulevards and diagonals of the brand-new provincial capital—whose design is said to have been inspired by Jules Verne's harmonious urban community of *France Ville*—as well as Buenos Aires' avenues, which were lined by elegant mansions and *petits hôtels*, nurtured the Parisian daydreams of the local ruling class, and forged the collective imaginary of Argentina's indefinite progress. However, this open and promising new country still was a magmatic emergent society in which job instability frustrated the expectations of upward mobility, prompting many immigrants to return to their home countries. Even though the rates of return migration differed by decade (for example, they were higher in the decade of the 1890s, due to the financial crisis) and national group (Italian immigrants tended to return home more often than their Spanish counterparts), between 1880 and 1910, 36 percent of immigrants headed back to Europe. Nonetheless, this figure encompasses not only those who returned permanently, but also the contingents of the temporary day-laborers known as *golondrinas* (swallows) who, profiting from cheap fares and relatively high local wages, traveled annually from the South of Europe (in particular, from Italy) to the *Pampa Húmeda* for the harvest.

The national population censuses of 1895 and 1914 provide two eloquent pictures of the impact of immigration and its uneven distribution throughout the country. In 1895, one out of four inhabitants was an immigrant, while in 1914 that figure had climbed up to one out of every three. Among the foreigners, there was a larger number of young people—between the ages of 20 and 40—than among the native population, and men far outnumbered women.[10] The impact of the immigration flood upon the preexisting population was the highest in the world (around 25 percent in 1895, and 30 percent in 1914).[11] Most foreigners settled in the city and the province of Buenos Aires and in the towns of the littoral, contributing to accelerating the pace of urbanization. In 1895, 37 percent of the Argentinian population lived in urban areas, and by 1914 that number had climbed to 51 percent.[12] Buenos Aires—both the Capital city and the province—Santa Fe, and Córdoba were the fastest growing areas,[13] whereas most of the other provinces (the so-called *el Interior*), whose productive profile did not fit in with the model-based agricultural and livestock exports, were excluded from the benefits of progress, lagging far behind the splendor of the "modern" Argentina.[14]

In the decades of the 1880s and 1890s, along with immigrants from Italy and Spain, also French, British, Germans, and Scandinavians arrived at the port of Buenos Aires. These were European and Christian minorities who adapted quite smoothly to the social and cultural dynamics of the country. Nonetheless, at the turn of the century, the migration flows began to show a novel religious and cultural profile. In addition to the typical southern Italians and northern Spaniards, Jewish, and Arabic-speaking immigrants from Greater Syria began to reach the shores of the Río de la Plata. The "exoticism" of the "Russians" and "Turks" (as the local population referred to the Jews and the Syrian-Lebanese) became a matter of concern for the ruling class, which sought to amalgamate the multiple identities that coexisted in the country into a homogenous cultural landscape.

Far from cultural unity, towards the end of the *Belle Époque*, the urban areas of Argentina had become a cosmopolitan world, where many languages were spoken, different religions were practiced, and an intense sociability charged with ethnic meanings was taking place. The country had been modernized—in a partial, but undeniable way—and immigrants and their children were experiencing upward mobility by entering the universe of the middle-classes. A house of their own, either as an aspiration or as a reality, was regarded as the most telling symbol of upward mobility both in the rhetoric of the ruling class and the hopes of thousands of immigrants. From the perspective of the country's political leadership, a family home could shape the workers into moral and cautious individuals and contribute to their integration into the host society. While for the immigrants, owning a house gave way to greater stability and better living conditions in "decent" neighborhoods, which used to show distinctive ethnic marks because of the influence of chain migration.[15] In these small worlds of countrymen, relatives, and acquaintances, the language and the traditions of the regions of origin were preserved. Nevertheless, their inhabitants could not stay away from the cosmopolitan dynamic of the city and had to adapt to the frenzy of modern life, and to the emotional and cultural standards of the *fin-de-siècle* Argentine society.

In the daily life of the ethnic neighborhoods, the preservation of the immigrants' cultural traits and habitus through maintenance of homelands' dialects, culinary traditions, clothing styles, and emotional standards was reinforced by an intense associative life based on the plethora of formal institutions, most of which adopted the form of mutual-aid societies. Founded in both big cities and small provincial towns, these associations channeled the integration of immigrants to the host society by offering health services to their members and acting as intermediaries in the incorporation of newcomers to the labor market. However, they also played a crucial role in the immigrants' social lives. The observance of national holidays of the homeland, the balls and the dances, and the concerts and plays performed in the mutual aid societies' halls, were usually attended by a large audience of ordinary members and leaders, who despite social class differences, came together in the same imagined community. In these events, the leaders publicly reaffirmed their status as an ethnic elite, their symbolic capital, and their role as promoters of myths that shaped the group's identity. Instead, the reasons for ordinary members were usually more prosaic. Laborers, craftsmen, clerks, and commercial employees would attend a dance or a concert to socialize with countrymen, hear news of the homeland, exchange information about jobs and wages, wear a brand-new suit, or court a good-looking female compatriot. Many of the endogamous marriages that reinforced the sense of belonging to the ethnic community could be traced back to courtships initiated in the social events organized by the mutual-aid societies.

Even though unmarried immigrants who left their fiancées behind used to return home after some time to marry them or got married by proxy, it was not unusual that marriageable women left Europe—generally accompanied by a close male relative—because their chances of getting married declined as young men increasingly left for the Americas. The migration through dense webs of social networks encouraged the incorporation of those newly-arrived young women to the social life of the ethnic communities, where most of them eventually met their future husbands.[16] Although a significant number of laborers who disembarked year after year in the port of Buenos Aires stayed briefly in the country and then returned to Europe, the majority of them ended up integrating into Argentine society and attaining at least some success in the venture of social mobility. While in urban areas such success consisted of achieving homeownership, or running a small business or a workshop, in the countryside, during the years of the great agricultural expansion between 1890 and the beginning of World War I, rental of land paved the way to upward mobility.

Obtaining free access to education for their children, which had generally been denied to the immigrants in their home countries, was an additional confirmation of the success of the migration project. Education not only allowed the second generation to break down the barriers of language that segregated their parents from the host society but also to get a respectable and well-paid position. However, not every immigrant who stayed in Argentina enjoyed the benefits of modernization and progress that the ruling class promoted to attract a foreign labor force. Many of them remained among the mass of unskilled workers whose lifestyles had little to do with the middle classes that were regarded as the essence of the Argentine society.

## The dark side of progress

The emergence of a middle-class family model by the end of the nineteenth century is regarded by social historians as one of the milestones marking the transition from the Argentina *criolla* (creole) to the modern country.[17] Immigrants' high marriage rates—compared to those of the Argentine population—working-class access to homeownership, the spread of the nuclear households, the social concern with upward mobility, economic welfare, and education would prove that the arrival of Europeans prompted a transformation of family patterns, social values, and cultural standards. However, the harmonious universe of women confined in the household, hard-working and thrifty husbands, and educated children dreamt by the ruling class had a dark side made of scarcity, poverty, child labor, neglected childhoods, squalid tenement houses, alcoholism, prostitution, and crime which contrasted with the promises that lured millions of migrants to "the land of prosperity."

One of the most powerful expressions of the other side of progress can be found in the difficult living conditions of the popular classes. The flood of immigrants caused housing problems in Buenos Aires—a city transformed in just a few decades into a global metropolis—but also in many other cities of the littoral. Renting a room in a *conventillo* was a solution for the newly arrived immigrants, whose average wages were low and barely enough to feed and clothe their families. By the middle of the 1890s there were more than 2,000 tenements in Buenos Aires, housing twenty percent of the city's population. Most of them were located downtown and in the southern neighborhoods (La Boca, Balvanera, San Telmo, and Monserrat) where port activity, factories, and workshops were concentrated.[18] In the last decades of the nineteenth century, living near the workplace was crucial since transportation was still scarce and expensive.[19]

Tenement houses used to be old mansions that the elite families had abandoned to move to the north of Buenos Aires when, in 1871, a plague of yellow fever epidemic ravaged the city. Nevertheless, the explosion in the demand for housing, caused by the massive arrival of immigrants,[20] stimulated the construction of new tenements, some of which could accommodate more than a hundred tenants.[21] In many cases, the owners were also immigrants, Italian, Spanish, and French builders and bricklayers who had arrived in the country with a small amount of capital a few years before the start of mass migration.[22]

A typical *conventillo* consisted of several small rooms (no more than 4 square meters each) arranged on two floors connected by a narrow and shaky staircase, and a communal courtyard at the back of which the laundry sinks, showers, and the latrines were located. Overcrowding and deficient sanitary conditions were its most salient features. The gloomy and poorly ventilated rooms were barely furnished: a bed, a table, a couple of chairs, a trunk, and occasionally a small picture of a Madonna or a king hanging on the damp and peeling walls.[23] The tenement house was one of the most conspicuous undesirable side effects of modernization and constituted a social, sanitary, and moral problem. In the eyes of the hygienist physicians of the time, tenements were a source of infectious disease and contagion that threatened the health of the whole society. For the upper classes, which enjoyed the pleasures of progress in their comfortable mansions in the north side of the city, the tenement houses were dumps where vice and moral depravity proliferated. Nevertheless, none of those pessimistic diagnoses solved the popular class housing problem. Between the decade of 1880 and the beginning of World War I, the *conventillos* continued being the only option—at least temporarily—for thousands of immigrants.[24] While it is true that most of the newcomers were already used to living in crowded places, where privacy and discretion barely existed, in the tenement houses they had to get used to living with strangers. Sharing the bathrooms—if indeed there were any—the cooking area, the sinks, and the clothes lines caused disputes among the neighbors and turned the courtyard into a scene for daily life scandals. But the tenement was also a workplace for some of the residents, especially for women. Seamstresses, laundresses, and ironers worked at home profiting from the common facilities, which usually turned into a source of tension because those women violated the house rules, and the landlord usually fined the laundresses for the indiscriminate use of water, or the seamstresses for bringing their sewing machines out in the courtyard in search of daylight.

Prying eyes and gossip used to transform daily life into a nightmare. As we will see over the next chapters, the fact that witnesses who testified in cases of adultery, marital abuse, and homicide exposed before the prosecutors and investigating judges the intimate details of their neighbors' lives reveals the absence of any notion of privacy. Whatever happened in one room was heard by the next-door neighbor, and it would quickly become a rumor and the source of communal gossip. Since no one could preserve privacy, everyone ended up being indiscreet.

One among the numerous examples of that lack of intimacy may be observed in the testimonies of Anita Grandi's neighbors when in 1897, her husband, an Italian machinist named Mauro Stella, denounced her for adultery. They had been married for a little more than ten years and, since then, they had lived in a *conventillo* in San Telmo neighborhood. While her husband was working in a turnery, she betrayed him to José Berreta, a friend of the couple. When fifteen residents of the *conventillo* were summoned to testify in court, they did not spare any detail of the sexual encounters Anita had with her lover. Each added a new colorful detail to the story of an "illicit relationship" that had begun in the spring of 1896, when the tenants noticed that, in the absence of Stella, Berreta sneaked into the room to visit Anita. The noises and the voice tones that could be heard from the next-door room led one of the witnesses to believe that "it was something more than just a visit," which was finally confirmed when "one afternoon, as Berreta left the room, a neighbor who was crossing the courtyard glimpsed Anita naked through the half-open door."[25] When rumors about the affair started, the lovers began to meet outside of the tenement, in an adjacent empty lot. However, the neighbors managed to "spy on them over the dividing wall just to confirm the betrayal before telling Stella about it." According to the voyeurs, the couple had sex leaning against a tree. Anita lifted her skirt, Berreta had his pants unbuttoned and caressed and kissed her entire body, and both moved a lot during the sexual act.[26]

For the popular classes that lived in the crowded and narrow rooms of the *conventillo*, deprived of intimacy and quiet, the streets of the city became a place of relief, leisure, and sociability. Although women also went out, the streets were the domain of men and children. In the discourse of hygienist doctors, criminologists, and politicians, the image of poor, vagrant, ragged, and thieving children became part of a repertoire of allegories for the social decadence brought about by modernity. Numerous photographs of daily life in Buenos Aires published in newspapers, periodicals, and tabloids show groups of unsupervised children wandering around the city. The pictures display them playing on the sidewalks, climbing up trees on the riverbank, selling newspapers, fruits, and vegetables, and shining shoes. Although the elite, the ruling class, and the police did not look kindly on these "loose children" left to roam free by their parents, admittedly, being on the streets kept them away from the unhealthiness of the gloomy tenement rooms,[27] and from violent homes where abuse and drunkenness were almost everyday occurrences, while also allowing them to earn a daily wage that could contribute to the family's meager incomes.[28] An official report on the living conditions of children from the popular classes pointed out that the street had turned into:

> An extension of the tenement house, where minors are constrained by rows of tiny rooms and by stacks of all sorts of objects without enough space to move and play ... [children] are exposed to the constant comings and goings of tenants, but mostly to the threats and intolerance of the adults who can only regard them as annoying guests whom they chase away.[29]

In 1894, the Argentine Congress enacted a Common Education Law, which established secular, public, free, and compulsory education for every child between six and fourteen years old. The law was based on the premise that schooling was an essential requirement to consolidate modernity and preserve the social order to which the ruling class aspired. However, the relationship of poor children to school was ambiguous and erratic. Eleven years after the enactment of the law, the second national census of population recorded over 117,000 school-aged children in the city of Buenos Aires, of which only 57 percent attended school. Nonetheless, 26,000 of those who did not receive education had acquired some elementary reading and writing skills, indicating that at some point they had dropped out of school. In 1904, two decades after the enactment of the law, the municipality of Buenos Aires conducted a census that revealed the percentage of children who did not attend school had decreased to 22.5 percent, although 15 percent of the minors were still illiterate.[30] In the neighborhoods with the highest concentration of immigrant families, the dropout rates were higher than the city average.[31] As a result of the demographic boom brought about by massive immigration, the school population was growing at a faster pace than the state's ability to build or remodel schools, and to train teachers. These constraints converged with the fact that poor, illiterate, and semi-illiterate immigrants often valued their child labor over their literacy, thwarting the realization of the goal of universal education. Beyond the dreams and ambitions of the ruling class and the intellectual circles, the working child ended up prevailing over the student child.[32]

Just like children, adult men were also lured by the street. Once the workday came to an end, the bars, coffee shops, and drinking establishments that proliferated in the city became an alternative to the narrowness and seclusion of the tenement house room, but also a source of temptation. Those bustling places became spaces of male sociability in which it was easier to keep secret or share a personal or intimate matter, than in the domestic world where the walls had eyes and ears.[33] Going to bars was an opportunity for single men to meet with a friend or build new relationships. They were also a favorite pastime for many married men, although among couples this escape route from domestic overcrowding often became a source of marital conflict. Women used to complain about their husbands coming home drunk, gambling their wages away, and leaving them alone in an unfamiliar city.

In addition to providing spaces for male socialization like bars, the street had another appeal: women selling sex. As Donna Guy noted, just a small number of prostitutes worked inside the legal brothels of turn-of-the-century Buenos Aires; the majority sold sex in public spaces or in clandestine brothels.[34] Although there is no agreement among historians about the magnitude of the sex industry in the city, the prevalence of young men living alone or sharing their living spaces with other men might have stimulated the demand for prostitutes. Pablo Ben has pointed out that the feuilletons that were sold in the streets of Buenos Aires targeted at readers from the laboring class uncover the existence of a sexual culture that challenged the patriarchal notions of marriage and family.[35] The feuilletons were publications with a few pages that featured brief illustrated stories, simple rhyme poetry, and jokes that presumably were read out loud in bars and cafés. Although the authors who wrote there did not openly agree with the moralistic view of the elite—that enshrined the archetype of a virtuous female confined in the household—they displayed an ambiguous attitude towards women selling sex. They represented popular class manliness through provoking images of men harassing women in the streets, paying for sex, and sharing their sexual conquest with their drinking partners. However, feuilletons also featured stories with morals with the intention of instilling in working class men the ideal of a methodical living and discouraging them from wasting their money on fallen women.[36]

In some of the cases of adultery analyzed in this book, the defendants declared that their husbands had forced them into prostitution to get the family out of poverty.[37] Although resorting to the image of the prostitute may have been a defense strategy, its invocation reveals that the sale of sex (casual or professional) was a widespread practice among the popular classes. Yet, these women had also been exposed to the moralistic rhetoric of the elites, who saw prostitution as a threat to the female ideal of domesticity, monogamy, and reproduction. When the adulteresses presented themselves in court as victims of the exploitation of their husbands—who had pushed them into a profession at odds with female virtues—

they probably expected a gesture of sympathy from the judges, despite the fact that within their social circle, buying and selling sex was an activity largely devoid of the connotations of vice and indecency that the elite attributed to it.

In the early twentieth century, the anxieties of the ruling class and the intellectual elite about the alleged moral deviation of the lower classes not only sparked heated political debates about social control but also resulted in a dense corpus of academic treatises on medicine, criminology, and psychiatry.[38] Immigrants were no longer regarded as hard-working classes essential for carrying out the modernization of the country—like the mentors of the nation had imagined in the mid-nineteenth century—but rather began to be perceived as a "dangerous class," responsible for the rise in crime rates.[39] This new perspective was based, among other sources, on official police statistics that showed a sustained increase in crimes against property and people perpetrated by foreigners.[40] According to experts in criminology, the Italian and Spanish origin of the majority of the immigrants was the factor that explained this negative tendency. Echoing the premises of Italian positivist criminology, Argentine criminologists maintained that a natural tendency to commit homicide was the prevailing feature of "the Latin race."[41] For example, in 1905, Cornelio Moyano, a law professor at the University of Córdoba, argued in one of his books that Spain and Italy displayed "the highest crime rate on earth," and that it has been proved that people with such a "racial" origin had a propensity to commit blood crimes.[42]

The idea that crime had grown because of the extraordinary transformation of society caused by mass immigration circulated among the general population through newspapers, tabloids, and feuilletons. As Argentina turned into a cosmopolitan society, and cities and towns expanded in an unorderly fashion at the pace of the rapid population growth, police news began to occupy a more prominent space in both national and ethnic newspapers. Blood crimes, such as the crimes of passion and romantic suicides that were usually reported with much detail, must have aroused the concern and morbid curiosity of the readers. But the press would also inform about a myriad of violent episodes that did not involve death. Police news reported daily about fights in the tenement houses that escalated from insults to blows and small wounds, domestic abuse, child maltreatment, men who harassed women on the streets, and thieving children who roamed the city. Such news occupied few lines, and usually the journalists did not reveal the identities of the persons involved in the events. Although if they were foreigners, on most occasions their national origin was mentioned. This practice contributed to solidifying the idea of the disorderly foreigner.

The arrival of millions of immigrants fueled the spectacular economic growth and the profound social and cultural transformation that Argentina experienced between 1880 and the onset of World War I. However, this transformation—that led the poet Rubén Darío to devote to the country's cosmopolitan character and extraordinary accomplishments the pompous poem *Canto a la Argentina* (Song to Argentina)—was not free from contradictions and undesired consequences. The coexistence of a celebratory image that portrayed Buenos Aires as "the Paris of South America" with another that despised it as "the city of sin" illustrates the contradictions of modernity and the tensions of a society under construction that was being remade in large part by the influx of immigrants. This paradox provides the backdrop to the dramatic stories that unfold in the next chapters.

2

# Promise, Wait, and Betrayal

Although at the turn of the nineteenth century most immigrants arriving at the port of Buenos Aires were young single men, I will now only focus on married couples who agreed a migratory strategy based on the promise and the wait. Husbands departed first, and their wives, with young children and sometimes pregnant, remained in Europe waiting for their spouses to return home or, when the material conditions were favorable, for their call to join them in South America. The conjugal relationship was drastically affected by migration and faced the spouses with the challenge of re-signifying a bond made of closeness and shared everyday life into a translational relationship supported by two fragile paper bridges: letters and remittances.

In the new anatomy of the marital bond, women acquired a certain degree of autonomy because, even though their husbands tried to control their daily lives from afar giving instructions and suggestions by correspondence, in practice they were the ones who assumed the daily management of home and family. The absence of men created a space for female freedom. At the same time, women continued to depend on the money sent by their husbands to ensure the subsistence and to carry out the variety of activities and projects that shaped the migration strategy. In this new family dynamics, the promise was the ordering factor of the future, from which a "moral economy of waiting" was configured.[1] That promise had a double meaning: it was affective and material at the same time. Although migration separated the couple's bodies and put love and intimacy on hold, the spouses agreed to the reunion, and the husband's absence was understood as the cost of shared expectations of economic progress.

The epistolary exchange created a sense of imaginary co-presence, driving off the ghost of oblivion, nurturing the longing, and alleviating nostalgia. More prosaic, the remittances validated the migratory strategy that had resulted in the family's transnational existence and, like correspondence, reassured the persistence of marital love. The work of waiting demanded a delicate and difficult handling, for which many of these men and women were not well prepared, not only because, as we have already pointed out, a large part of them depended on vicarious writers or readers to maintain the epistolary communication, but also because with migration, the subjectivity of both spouses suffered profound changes that conspired against the continuity of the family migratory project and the marital relationship.

The stories of bigamy presented in this chapter started with a promise and ended with a betrayal. For the sake of the economic betterment of the family, wives and husbands agreed to a temporary separation that would oblige women to wait and men to reassure their love for the wife and the commitment to the migratory strategy by sending money and letters from abroad. Although these couples imagined a common future—the realization of which depended on the return of the husband to Europe or on the reunification of the family—women's work of waiting ended up being fruitless when the temporary absence of their husbands turned into oblivion and abandonment. Over the years, however, the neglected wives decided to follow the faint trail of their lost spouses and appeared in Argentina to claim what they had been promised. Although upon departure some of them knew that the reason behind the disappearance of the husband was a second marriage, others discovered it after their arrival. In both cases, these women who migrated in such stressful circumstances were compelled to start their lives in the new country while coping with cumbersome procedures to get the documents that proved they were the legitimate spouses of the bigamists.

After a long wait that must have involved anxiety and distress, the copies of their marriage certificates finally arrived, enabling the betrayed women to sue their treacherous husbands. The stamps on the margins and the backs of these documents (issued by local parishes, civil register offices, the Ministry of Justice and Worship, and the Ministry of Foreign Affairs of both the country of origin and of Argentina, and by consulates, public translators, and court officials) uncover the intricate circuit followed by these certificates that would have remained inert, covered by dust, and smelling musty in a church or in a state office had they not been claimed as evidence of a crime. Instead, the marital conflict set them in motion, transfiguring them into emotional objects, bearers of the feelings entailed in the transit from love to disaffection, from communion to disunion, from longing to oblivion.[2]

Second wives sometimes also filed complaints and requested the nullity of marriage, resulting in the bigamist being sued twice. Cases of forgiveness by one of the wives also occurred, as it happened to José Serafín.[3] At the beginning of

1873, Rosa Unzueta married José, a Neapolitan immigrant, in the parish church of Dolores—a small town in the province of Buenos Aires—after two fellow countrymen of his certified that he was single. But when, a few years later, Magdalena and Domingo, the legitimate wife and the son of the bigamist, arrived from Italy, José abandoned Rosa to reunite with his family. So, Rosa sued him. Magdalena had been living in the town only for a month when she was summoned to testify in court. As she did not speak Spanish, the judge allowed her to have a countryman act as interpreter. Magdalena declared that although Serafín was the father of her child, they were not legally married, but "since before he [Serafín] left Italy about eight years ago she cohabited with him."[4] Her testimony did not satisfy Rosa, who appeared in court again arguing that the interpreter had distorted Magdalena's testimony because he was a close friend and accomplice of the bigamist. The plaintiff asked for the first wife to be summoned again and proposed the names of two "impartial and honest" interpreters, but as the Italian woman failed to appear in court, the judge ordered the police to find her whereabouts. A few weeks later, a letter arrived in the court stating that "Mrs. Magdalena Carbone and her son have been taken by Mr. José Serafín, their destination and place of residence being unknown."[5] This was the last page of a brief court record beyond which the trace of Magdalena and the bigamist vanishes. However, the baptism records of the parish church of Dolores shed light—albeit faint—on Rosa's path after her failed attempt to punish her treacherous husband. Four months after the police abandoned the search for the key witness of the trial, Juana, "natural daughter of Rosa Unzueta," was baptized in the same parish where her mother had married José Serafín believing him to be single.[6]

The cases of other immigrant bigamists left more traces in the records. In the following pages, I tell the stories of Luis Aldaz, Nicolás Conforti, and Domingo DeBartolo, three bigamists whose wives, after a prolonged separation, came to Argentina following their fuzzy trails and ended up suing them. The selection of these cases obeys to the unusual density of the court records, which encompassed thorough statements of plaintiffs, defendants, and witnesses, the presence of a renowned lawyer, and private correspondence the betrayed wives provided as evidence. But, in addition, these cases give a glimpse of the state of the marriage relationship before migration, shedding light on the reasons why these—and other—immigrants broke promises, betrayed their wives, and abandoned shared projects. When the bond that united the spouses was already damaged before the husband's departure, migration was tacitly transformed into the substitute for marital rupture. But on other occasions, a tie that looked strong would weaken with the passing of time, making love and longing turn into disaffection, oblivion, betrayal, and rancor.

## The Spanish seamstress, a woman of discreet feelings

In the summer of 1881, Father José Novota, a Spanish priest from Zaragoza, received his compatriot Andresa Barachina and her 11-year-old daughter, Facunda Aldaz, in his parish in the city of Buenos Aires. Andresa brought a letter of recommendation from a relative of Novota living in Pamplona (where the woman and the girl were from), a copy of the document certifying her marriage to Luis Aldaz, and the birth certificate of Facunda. Andresa had traveled from Spain to find out the whereabouts of her husband, with whom she had lost contact for almost a decade.[7]

Luis Aldaz had emigrated in 1871. During his first two years in Argentina, he had corresponded briefly but lovingly with his wife, and then stopped writing. His family never heard from him again nor did they have any news of his fate, except for the rumor that had recently reached Pamplona about his forthcoming wedding to another woman, despite his being still legally married to Andresa.

The first letter Andresa received from Luis was written in September 1871. By then, eight months had passed since his departure. In this letter, Luis explained the reason for his delay in communicating, saying that he had wanted to write to her only when he could confirm to her that he had found a good job. The letter indicated that he was living in the interior of the province of Buenos Aires, where he had started working as a laborer in a railway gang a few weeks before. Luis apologized for not sending "a single ounce since this is my first month here, I could not save," and promised to send some money in the next letter so that Andresa could buy a dress for Facunda, "whom I miss very much . . . her memory makes me cry like a child at night." In the last paragraphs, perhaps to ward off suspicions or ease any jealousy harbored by his wife, Luis added that he did not like Argentine women at all and that he considered them "not so pretty, and very lazy." He ended the letter by saying to Andresa: "You are the woman of my heart, and I never forget you."[8]

Two months later, a second letter arrived in Pamplona. It contained a portrait of Luis and some money:

> To buy Facunda the floral dress, and, added to the money you get as a seamstress, as an aid to cope with the winter . . . do not waste it because is the result of my

sweat, of my demanding work that starts at 4 in the morning and ends at sunset ... that keeps me moving from one place to another changing sleepers in the tracks from Buenos Aires to Lobos and Chivilcoy.[9]

After this letter, there was a final missive, written in February 1873. It consisted of a brief note in which Luis excused himself for not being able to arrange for Andresa and their daughter to join him in Argentina. He explained: "I never forget you and my dear daughter, and I do not lack the will of bringing you here, but I do not have a way to do it, for lack of money, but if you want to come and somebody there pays for it, I will call you as soon as I can."[10]

Upon arriving in Buenos Aires, in addition to those letters and the marriage and birth certificates, Andresa brought the addresses of a handful of countrymen dwelling in the city. Assisted by the priest, she got in contact with one of them, José Goñi, who still was living in Spain when Andresa and Luis got married. It was he who told her that Luis had remarried a short time earlier. After learning of her husband's actions, Andresa decided to sue him for bigamy.

Before the judge, Goñi declared that six years ago, Luis Aldaz had expressed a willingness to call his family, but then "he began to hide the fact that he was married because he was courting another woman with whom I heard rumors he married nine months ago."[11] The witness also provided information on the whereabouts of the bigamist. By mid-August 1881, the justice of the peace of Juárez, a rural town about 400 kilometers south of Buenos Aires City, informed the court that in March 1881, Luis Aldaz, aged thirty-four and at that time a rural police officer, had married Justina Amarante, an Argentine woman aged twenty-one. The couple, however, was no longer living in Juárez but in the town of Bahía Blanca.[12] Three months later, the bigamist was arrested and taken to Buenos Aires.

After such a long separation, the reunion between Andresa and Luis took place in the gloomy setting of a prison, amidst a fateful circumstance. That encounter is an eloquent representation of the rough path through which Andresa entered Argentine society as an immigrant. In those days, thousands of European women traveled to reunite with their husbands, often after long separations. Many of those reunions were the last phase of an experience in which estrangement, anxiety, and misunderstandings were likely very present. Certainly, migration affected all couples, forcing many to re-negotiate their bonds and feelings. Individuals were transformed by a variety of conflicting emotions: fear and euphoria, love and disaffection, pleasure, and anger. Once couples reunited, they needed to recreate their affective bonds, resume a common language of intimacy, and adapt to the changes that each one of them had experienced on account of migration.[13] Nevertheless, for women who arrived responding to the call of their husbands, entering the new society was a less arduous emotional passage than the one experienced by European women like Andresa, who migrated on their own, knowing that nobody was waiting for them, and suspecting they had been deceived. Hurt by the abandonment and the treachery of their husbands, overwhelmed by anxiety, distress, and rancor, these wives were compelled to start their lives in the new country dealing with cumbersome judicial proceedings that forced them to speak of things that would have remained unsaid had a destabilizing event not occurred.

Unfortunately, the judicial record does not provide details of the day when Andresa visited her husband in prison for the first time. What feelings must have assaulted her when she was about to face a man who not only had betrayed her, but who was by then almost a stranger? What emotions did Luis feel on the eve of this encounter? Was he seized by the fear that his wife's spitefulness would be so implacable as to block any chance for him to recover his freedom?

After six months in prison, the bigamist appeared before the judge. Surely his statement did not differ much from the one he had improvised for Andresa in the penitentiary. Although Luis admitted committing bigamy, he argued that when he remarried, he thought his first wife had died.[14] Eager to prove his innocence, and fully aware that his liberty depended not only on his words, but also on the evidence, he presented three letters, dated between December 1879 and January 1881, sent by old acquaintances of his in Pamplona. With those letters, he tried to show that he had written to Spain worried about the lack of news from his wife and daughter. All the answers coincided: Andresa had moved from Pamplona to Zaragoza in mid-1878 because she was ill with tuberculosis, and "here the rumor has it that sometime later she died in the house of some aunt and uncle, where Facunda might be."[15]

Despite Luis' efforts to prove his innocence, the court questioned the authenticity of the evidence. The judge summoned three Spanish immigrants related to the senders of the letters to recognize the handwriting. For his part, the prosecutor was even more suspicious, arguing that even if the letters were not apocryphal, it was possible that their authors had colluded with the bigamist. But none of the hypotheses could be proved because the witnesses did not appear to testify. Nonetheless, it is clear that Luis did not write to Pamplona moved by the intention of reestablishing the contact with his wife, but likely because he was disturbed by the possibility that his decision to marry straddled the thin line dividing legal actions from criminal ones. When he sent the last letter, in January

1881, his wedding with Justina Amarante was upcoming. To get married, he needed some certainty that his first wife had forgotten him, and—although the law said the opposite—that the distance and silence had put an end to their marriage.

Suspecting the letters were apocryphal and that Luis had concocted a hoax, the prosecutor demanded a three-year sentence on the charge that the defendant had committed two crimes: adultery and bigamy.[16] But a few months later Andresa presented a letter addressed to the judge declaring that, after several conversations with her husband in prison, she was now convinced of his innocence because:

> When I left Pamplona in 1878, the word spread that I had died, and the people who told him this, acted driven by that rumor [and] being convinced that it was this mistake that led my husband to marry again and trusting his sincerity and good faith, I drop all charges.[17]

A few weeks later, the defendant was released.

What led Luis Aldaz to commit the crime? I tend to believe that he had no choice but to marry Justina. She was born in 1859 to a *criollo* family long established in the town of Dolores. The Amarantes formed part of a social core of what was then known as "decent people," a people that watched over female sexual conduct, demanded decency and chastity of their women, and valued marriage.[18] In the decades of the 1860s and 1870s, her father, Paulino Amarante, had been a municipal official, Justice of the Peace of Dolores, and Major of the National Guards.[19] He had ties of friendship and godfatherhood with some of the most prominent landowners and military officers in the province of Buenos Aires. The godfather in the baptism of Justina (the only girl among three siblings) was Lieutenant-Colonel Benito Machado,[20] commander of the *Sol de Mayo* regiment, and a figure of national fame because of his performance in the fight against the indigenous population and the expansion of the frontier.[21] Justina was a good catch for an immigrant like Aldaz because the family networks of the Amarante offered him an opportunity for upward social mobility.[22]

How did Justina react to the news that her husband was married in Spain? What happened to her through all the years of the trial? What was the attitude of her brothers and father in the face of dishonor? The judicial record leaves these questions unanswered. Justina was not summoned to testify, and therefore, I cannot assess her reaction.[23] Neither do I know if she remained in Bahía Blanca or moved to Buenos Aires when her husband was arrested. But more than a decade after the end of the trial, her name appears in the national census of population of 1895. She was then living in Buenos Aires and was registered in the census as "Justina Amarante de Aldaz, with fifteen years of marriage and the mother of two children."[24] Her last name clearly connected to that of her husband by the use of the Spanish preposition *de*, following a traditional social practice in Argentina, left no doubts about Justina's status as a legally married woman.

What led Andresa to forgive the bigamist, and Justina to come back to him? To redeem himself, Luis probably gave the two women the same excuse: that he married again convinced he was widowed. The reasons for Andresa's forgiveness are not clear. However, a detail of the court record illuminates the role Justina's family likely played in this decision. At the outset of the trial, Luis presented a pauper's appeal requesting a public counsel. But in the middle of the case, when the prosecutor asked for a three-year prison sentence, Luis fired the public defender. Instead, Aristóbulo del Valle, a prestigious attorney whose fees Luis most likely could not afford, was hired. Moreover, by 1883 del Valle not only had a reputation as an attorney but also as a politician who had been a congressman and Provisional President of the Argentine Senate. It is strange, a priori, to find him defending an immigrant accused of bigamy. Admittedly, that was not a case that would have interested him if Justina's family had not intervened. Their class privilege and social networks afforded Luis the possibility of hiring del Valle. The new attorney was also from Dolores, and his father was among the first settlers of the area, just like Justina's grandfather.[25] Although there is no evidence of a personal relationship between Paulino Amarante and Aristóbulo del Valle, the social and political circle of which Amarante was part had likely allowed him to activate some network of "friends of friends" to access such a reputed attorney.[26]

Soon before this change of lawyers, the prosecutor alleged that Luis was liable to the maximum punishment prescribed by the Penal Code because, besides bigamy, his concubinage with Justina constituted adultery, which aggravated the main crime.[27] Aristóbulo del Valle entered the scene claiming the nullity of the proceedings "because the crime was already prescribed before the start of the trial."[28] The law established a deadline of two months from the date of the second marriage to file a complaint and Andresa presented her claim long after this deadline had expired. In an extensive and detailed plea, del Valle also refuted the prosecutor's argument about the aggravating circumstance because:

> Bigamy belongs to the type of instant crimes since what is considered a crime is entering into a second marriage without legally dissolving a first one; all that precedes (sensuality, deceit, immorality) and all that follows (concubinage) are causes and consequences but do not constitute a crime in themselves.[29]

The appearance of del Valle changed the course of the proceedings and forced Andresa to modify her strategy. Disillusionment and anger may have been the driving forces underlying the decision to sue the man who had disregarded her; however, her intentions to forgive him seemed to hide behind her negative feelings. The several visits paid to Luis in prison at the beginning of the process suggest that she might have been intending reconciliation. However, when a prestigious lawyer took over Luis' defense, Andresa's ability to manage her emotions and to navigate among conflicting feelings came to an end.[30] Although there is no evidence that she had threatened to withdraw the lawsuit, she probably experienced helplessness and fear toward her husband's new in-laws. Obstacles born of class and gender differences as well as her experience of solitude—added to her condition as a foreigner—left Andresa unarmed to proceed with a battle whose end may have originally been to regain love.

An ambiguous figure, resolute and conceding at the same time, Andresa ended up living in a country that she had entered through the heavy door of the judicial system, and where she went through material and emotional deprivations. But over time that very country showed her a kinder face. In 1890, she moved to La Plata, the brand-new capital of the province of Buenos Aires. Her daughter Facunda had married Adolfo Wilcke, a German music teacher. Andresa shared the house with the young couple and made a living as a seamstress.[31]

Andresa decided to withdraw the charges against Luis in solitude, far from Pamplona and her kinship and community networks. The situation of Justina was different because her dishonor damaged the good name of her family. Honor was an emotional imperative deeply rooted in nineteenth-century society, and whose manifestations and meanings differed depending on social class, religion, national belonging, and gender. Although honor was relevant both for men and women, its manifestations varied. For women, honor was linked to sex and sexual behavior. For men, the range of offenses was wider; nevertheless, the most serious was the seduction of a female family member. When a woman's honor was offended, she could not restore it by herself. Even male family members could not redeem it, because when they settled accounts with the offender, they did it to protect their own honor, as the "fallen" woman never got hers back.[32]

The Amarantes tried to keep up appearances by pretending that what had happened was just a misunderstanding, although the argument made by Luis— that he had married in the belief of being a widower—may have seemed foolish to them. To avoid a marital breakdown accepting that Luis' bigamy had been no more than a setback in the life of a man who, in the words of his first wife, "acted in good faith," was likely the less dramatic way to safeguard the family honor.

However, this strategy seemed to be indifferent to Justina's feelings. While Andresa had some margins to navigate between rancor and fear, affection and anger, illusion, and spite, and to manage those emotions according to her aims and the ups and downs of the trial, Justina was excluded from it, most likely at the request of her father and brothers. The culture of honor that guided the conduct of "decent people" like the Amarantes could be very restrictive for women. Justina probably felt betrayed by Luis, and upon discovering his deceit her life was also trapped in a maze of conflicting feelings. Nevertheless, according to the emotional standards and values of her social world, the driving force of her actions was not her feelings, but that the family's honor be safe from public scandal. This required that once the bigamist was released, Justina resumed her marital life, although her love for Luis had probably turned to sadness and resentment.

## A cold marital bed

Sometimes when men were departing, their relationship with their wives was already strained. In these circumstances, it is difficult to imagine how the migration strategy was agreed upon, how each spouse envisaged the reunification of the family, and what was the promise that justified the work of waiting for the return or the husband's call to join him abroad. Perhaps men imposed their will instead of negotiating a family strategy, especially when the conflicts between the spouses were settled through marital abuse and patriarchal authoritarianism.[33] Or maybe they simply left, making elusive promises, but intimately convinced that migration entailed a tacit marital separation.

Although the defendants' statements should be taken with caution—as they weigh up words, and when compelled to explain how the crime came to happen, they fabricate the truth in an attempt to avoid or mitigate punishment—in about a dozen judicial processes I have analyzed how the bigamists alleged that the rupture of the marriage had occurred prior to migration. One of them was Nicola Conforti, who declared that upon his departure, in 1875, he was already separated from Sabina de Ángelis, with whom he "shared the house, but not the bed," because they had been having "marital disagreements" for a long time. According to his words, traveling to Argentina was his individual decision, and so "he left without promising anything."[34] However, his wife gave a different version when, nine years later, she sued him for bigamy.

Sabina and Nicola had married in Castelnuovo di Conza, a small village in Salerno where, in 1871, Maria, the couple's only child, was born. Upon departure,

Nicola promised to come back to Italy in a few years, when he had saved enough money to buy a plot of land. Like many women whose husbands were embarking on a transatlantic crossing, Sabina was left under the care and supervision of her in-laws. But Nicola never returned.

In 1880, Sabina decided to travel to Buenos Aires, where in addition to her husband, one of her brothers lived. It was he who told her that Nicola had married a 17-year-old Italian woman with whom he had a daughter.[35] If Sabina traveled with some expectation of redress, in their very first meeting Nicola made it quite clear that he would not get back with her, and "abandoned [Sabina] for the second time, leaving her helpless in the middle of an unknown city. He did not even take care of his daughter, forgetting his love for the child and his parental and marital responsibilities."[36]

With the help of her brother, Sabina got a job as a maid, and María began to work as a laundress. With few material and intellectual resources—as she was an illiterate peasant woman who barely spoke Spanish—Sabina did not even search for evidence to prove that her husband was a bigamist. Four years had passed since the initial bitter reunion with Nicola when Sabina presented a claim that led to a lawsuit for bigamy and a request for annulment of her husband's second marriage. Although an old rancor must have driven her, the main motivation for her delayed reaction was the defense of the bond with Maria.

At the beginning of 1884, Nicola had claimed the custody of her daughter in the juvenile court, arguing that he could give her a better life than "the poor existence she has with her mother in a miserable *conventillo*."[37] However, behind that claim hid his opposition to the impending marriage of María. The 13-year-old laundress had fallen in love with one of her clients, a 20-year-old bricklayer, also from the province of Salerno. The news that behind his back Sabina had approved the engagement and consented to the marriage, and the fact that she turned to him only because she needed his permission for María to get married, put an end to Nicola's long indifference.

In communities such as Castelnuovo di Conza, male status was linked to the fulfillment of the roles of spouse and father, the ability to protect his material possessions, and his authority over female kin sexuality. Public signs of this system of honor were the woman's expression of respect for her husband and the children's obedience to their father. As we will see further on, transnational migration altered not only this notion of manliness, but also the role of women who, after the departure of their spouses, had to take care of the household and the upbringing of children, work on the family land, and allocate the money their husbands sent them from abroad. Perhaps for immigrants who, like Nicola, arrived in the cosmopolitan and feverish turn-of-the-century Buenos Aires, the moral mandates and the notions of honor and masculinity that ruled the social life of their close-knit communities of origin fell into lethargy in the face of the influence of novelty and urban fluidity. However, a disturbing event could abruptly shake the old social norms out of their slumber. The experience of migration compelled these men to re-signify their identities, but the daily life in the New World retained much of the old one in the social interaction with countrymen in tenement houses, ethnic neighborhoods, and ethnic niches of the labor market. A man's ability to control female sexuality entailed not only his relationship with his wife, daughters, and sisters but also his standing before other men. Sabina's challenge to Nicola's authority exposed Nicola's dishonor in the scrutinizing eyes of his *paesani*, casting shadows on his masculinity. Perhaps the audacity of his first wife caused the moral sanction of his countrymen because, although the context had changed with migration, honor was still a powerful regulator of social life among Italians settled in Buenos Aires.

Sabina's boldness aroused the anger of her husband, who claimed his parental rights before the juvenile judge. In retaliation, his wife sued him for bigamy. But since Sabina did not have her marriage certificate, she appeared in court accompanied by three acquaintances from Castelnuovo di Conza, who asseverated that she was the legitimate wife of Conforti and that they had attended the wedding in Italy. Then, Nicola and his witnesses, two countrymen on whose collusion he had counted to get married for a second time, were arrested. The defense attorney alleged the prescription of the crime, but also argued that the emotions of the bigamist should be considered as a mitigating circumstance because:

> The love that once united the defendant with his wife was finished when he departed from Italy ... the contact between them was infrequent after Conforti established himself in Buenos Aires since they were separated *de facto* before migration.[38]

Although bigamy was proven, Nicola was acquitted because the law in force—which had also been invoked by Aristóbulo del Valle in his defense of Luis Aldaz—provided a time limit for filing the complaint, which—as had been the case for Andresa—Sabina was also unable to meet. But despite the result of the proceedings, she won two battles in the legal dispute against her husband. The court declared the second marriage null and void, and in the winter of 1885, Maria and her fiancé were married in the parish of *Nuestra Señora de Balvanera* with the consent of Nicola.[39]

Behind a banal document in which Sabina de Ángelis and Nicola Conforti were registered as a married couple that, like so many others, authorized and accompanied the nuptials of their minor daughter, laid hidden a stormy story in which love had taken the shape of rancor, and affection that of anger. But not all bigamists were as fortunate as Conforti and Aldaz, for whom resorting to a renowned lawyer or a legal provision recovered their freedom. On the contrary, many ended up in prison, as happened to Domingo DeBartolo, another widower of a living wife.

## An irascible Italian woman in a cosmopolitan city

Shortly before Christmas 1879, Domingo DeBartolo, a 22-year-old day laborer, and Rafaela Fioretto, an 18-year-old peasant, married in the village of Marano Marchesato, in the province of Cosenza, Italy. By 1882, the couple had one child, and Rafaela was pregnant a second time. That year, Domingo left his family in the care of his parents-in-law and emigrated to South America with the promise to his wife that he would return.[40] DeBartolo spent just over a year in Brazil, where he learned of the birth of Carmela, his second child. I do not know the reasons that led him to embark on a new migration to Buenos Aires, where he arrived in 1884, when Carmela had already died. An infectious disease ended the life of the eighteen-month-old child. At that time, Rafaela and her husband still maintained a regular correspondence, but the exchange ceased in 1885.

After fourteen years without any contact with her husband, Rafaela traveled to Buenos Aires with her son, who by then was 19 years old. They arrived in the spring of 1899 and rented a room in the San Telmo neighborhood. For nearly seven months, Rafaela searched for Domingo in Buenos Aires. At first, the vague directions, and perhaps the complicity of Domingo's fellow countrymen, prevented her from tracking him down, until one afternoon in June 1900 when he turned up at the tenement house where Rafaela and their son lived. Confronted with the rumor, Domingo confirmed there was another woman in his life, but negated his second marriage:

> DeBartolo told her that he did not want to live there because it was a *conventillo* and rented a more decent room on Dulce street ... there the husband told his name was 'José Cecilio', and when asked by his wife about that false identity, DeBartolo said that he had a mistress and was afraid she could bother him.[41]

Despite this confession, the couple resumed their married life. Rafaela likely thought it was natural that after so many years of separation her husband had another love relationship, and perhaps felt relieved to learn that it was just a lover and not a wife. However, one month later, Julia Macaya, a 21-year-old Argentine dressmaker, showed up in the tenement house claiming to be Domingo's legitimate wife, with a marriage certificate to prove it. Rafaela's initial stupefaction soon gave way to an attack of fury. The impact of the news and the lack of documents that proved she was married to the same man resulted in a scandalous incident of insults and physical violence. Rafaela's rage was so great that it prompted the neighbors to call the police. She was thus arrested.[42]

Domingo used Rafaela's fury to his advantage to convince Julia, as the record states, that the woman "was not his wife, but a mistress deranged by spitefulness … she [Julia] believed him because at that time Fioretto did not have any document to prove she was also married to DeBartolo."[43] A few days later, Julia accepted Domingo's return to the house they shared. The source remains silent about the reason why Julia decided to ignore a rumor that had reached her at the end of July 1900. It was a month since Domingo had left the house saying that he had to travel to Europe because his mother had died. But an acquaintance of the couple told Julia that Domingo had lied to her because he was married in Italy, his first wife had just arrived in Buenos Aires, and he had moved in with her.

Soon after the incident of rage in the tenement house, Rafaela started what probably seemed like endless visits to the consulate and the courthouse to get the evidence that would allow her to sue her husband. After waiting for several months, the marriage certificate finally arrived from Italy, thus Domingo's clumsy hoax was revealed, and the judicial process began. The bigamist, who had married Julia in 1894 under the false name of Bartolo Di Domenico and had three children from that union, alleged—like Luis Aldaz argued—that when he married Julia, he thought Rafaela had died. He claimed that he had maintained correspondence with his wife and sent money to the family until 1885. In that year, he asked Rafaela to join him in Buenos Aires, but she answered that he should return to Italy as he had promised. Because his wife "refused to obey," Domingo simply stopped writing to her. In 1889—he further declared—he received a letter from a friend of his called Alejandro Morrone, informing him that Rafaela had died. Following this news, Domingo claimed, he wrote several times to his parents-in-law but never received an answer.[44]

The discrepancy between the declarations of the two parties resulted in a face-to-face confrontation in which Rafaela confessed that the letter was a stratagem to make Domingo return to Italy. But the admission of her trick was not enough to mitigate the bigamist's punishment. In June 1901, the court sentenced Domingo to four-and-a-half years in prison, although the Penal Code provided a maximum of three years. In this case, the judge agreed with the prosecutor that the adulterous conduct of the bigamist was an aggravating circumstance of the main crime. However, the sentence was appealed. While in Luis Aldaz's trial, Aristóbulo del Valle's plea was full of technical terms and allusions to foreign jurisprudence concerning adultery as an aggravating factor, Domingo's attorney resorted to emotional language:

> As for the fact of my client having resumed his marital life with his first wife I do not consider it to be an illicit act ... in my opinion, it cannot aggravate the situation of the defendant at the time of his conviction, because, in the face of the unexpected appearance of the wife whom he believed to be dead, it was not in his hands to avoid the emotions of the moment ... and in such circumstance of anxiety and fear, he intended to postpone a catastrophe.[45]

Despite its lack of legal sophistication—compared to del Valle's—the argument presented by the defense attorney was effective, and the court of the second instance dismissed adultery. Domingo got a reduction of his sentence to three-and-a-half years, but he did not get leniency from either of his wives. Rafaela did not forgive him, and soon after the end trial, Julia filed a lawsuit to have the marriage annulled.

The judicial records are fragmented narratives that capture extraordinary moments in which victims and defendants were forced to explain how an incident that tore their lives apart occurred.[46] They are, by their very nature, incomplete, not only as a result of the influence exerted on the participants by fear, lies, and the embarrassment of defendants, plaintiffs, and witnesses, but also because, as noted above, the questions posed by judges often differ from those made by historians. Focused on proving the crime of bigamy, the investigating judge did not ask Rafaela what motivated her travel, why she was still certain that her husband was living in Buenos Aires when so many years had passed without communication, and who guided—or misled—her in the search for Domingo around the city. The answers, at least provisionally, to these questions lay outside of the court file, in small traces hidden in local histories, censuses, and parish and civil records.

The small dimension of Marano Marchesato favored the spreading of information and rumors about what was happening on the other side of the ocean. A close-knit community in the south of Italy, Marano Marchesato had a tradition of migration dating from the 1880s, when the place was home to about

2,800 inhabitants. Devoted to the production of grains, olives, and grapes, the local economy's low demand for laborers and the shortage of farmland had pushed men to cross the Atlantic heading to South America and the big cities of the United States.[47] The vital records of the late nineteenth century repeat a handful of family names—Perfetti, Conforti, DeBartolo, Bartucci, Chiapetti—who were intertwined in tight kinship and social networks.[48] Rafaela likely knew about Domingo's life in Buenos Aires through the news and rumors she got from the Perfetti or the Conforti. Salvatore Perfetti, the son of one of the witnesses at her wedding, also lived in the city. He and Juan Conforti, another Maranesi, were the witnesses to the Domingos' second marriage. Perhaps they were also the ones who, with false clues, disoriented Rafaela in her search, helping the bigamist to delay the outbreak of "the catastrophe."

The migratory strategy agreed by Domingo and Rafaela when the former departed from Italy, and the epistolary controversy they maintained to change its terms, reveal the existence of a notion of marital love in which responsibility and obedience were intertwined. Correspondence and remittances helped keep the affective bonds alive during separations that lasted many years, but also were the way for the husband to show his commitment to the family migratory project. In turn, the wife should manage the money she received with moderation and care.[49] When upon departure from Europe the marital couple agreed that the wife and children would join the husband abroad once he was settled, it was assumed that a married woman had no alternative but to cross the Atlantic once her spouse called her. By obeying and leaving behind her kin, friends, and familiar landscapes, she demonstrated her conjugal love. Instead, if the pact was the husband's return, he had to go back. A change of plans would entail a renegotiation of the family's migratory strategy that could end up breaking the marital bond, as had happened for Domingo and Rafaela.

As we will see in the next chapter, the obedience of the wife to her husband was at the core of the normative notion of marriage. This may explain why Domingo resorted to that argument in his defense. In his view, Rafaela's refusal to emigrate had started a sequence that led him to commit the crime of bigamy. By disobeying, she not only challenged her husband's power, but also resented the foundations of their marriage. For Domingo, presenting his wife as a submissive figure would be an effective resource to mitigate the sentence because Rafaela's rebellion was reason enough to assume that the marital bond had given way to a *de facto* separation. But, regardless of the intentions of Domingo and his lawyer, this case also sheds light on the margins of female resistance to the social and emotional standards of that time. Within a set of specific prescriptions that responded to a particular context in which men migrated, leaving their wives and children under the supervision of parents, brothers, or in-laws, Rafaela first challenged the power of her husband by attempting to negotiate his return, and then, when the marital bargaining proved to be ineffective, she resorted to a lie. Like many women in her condition, she considered that the migratory project should not have to cost her own uprooting. If some women indeed were waiting for the call of their husbands to leave everything behind and set out on the Atlantic crossing, others were expecting the migrants' return and the improvement of the material conditions of the family through the money they had earned in the Americas. Rafaela played her strategy in the interstices of the patriarchal system, but the power relationship continued to lean in favor of her husband, who reneged on his promise, and, unable to impose his will, cut off all communication. Nevertheless, Rafaela took a step further and in collusion with Morrone, concocted a deception, trusting that after learning of her death, Domingo would return to Marano Marchesato. In the end, however, the facts would prove that she was wrong.

## Widowers of the living

As several historians have proved, bigamy was a practice rooted in Latin America's colonial past.[50] However, the focus of some of these remarkable investigations and the questions their authors pose is different from mine.[51] In this chapter, bigamy is a pretext to explore the relationship between gender, mobility, and marital love, and to delve into the emotional landscapes of migration. The experience of unfaithful husbands and their wives, on the one hand, sheds light on the variety of emotional styles that seem to have coexisted in turn-of-the-century Argentina; on the other, it reveals how migration conspired against the bonds that tied families together, leaving an indelible mark on the subjectivity of men who migrated and the wives who stayed behind.

Transatlantic marital relationships and the practice of bigamy itself changed significantly during the era of mass migration. In colonial times, because of the distance and precarious communications between the metropolis and the colonies, it was unlikely for the legitimate wife to learn of the double marriage, and even more rare for her to travel to the New World to sue her husband. However, in the last quarter of the nineteenth century, the modernization of transport, the reduction of fares, and the acceleration of communications, the density of social networks, the multiplication of epistolary exchanges, and the regular circulation of seasonal laborers and return migration, shaped a transnational terrain that kept the Old and the New Worlds in close contact, making it more difficult for the bigamists to hide their treachery and keep them safe from lawsuits.

In a panoramic perspective, a place like Buenos Aires in the early twentieth century appears as a promise of anonymity and discretion. A labile universe brimming with people, the city—as shown in the first chapter—was the scenario of a male sociability which took place in the streets, coffee shops, and bars, where foreigners and locals converged in spontaneous and fleeting relationships.[52] If the arrival of a massive wave of immigrants before the World War I changed the physiognomy to the Argentine society, more than anywhere else, this change was evident in Buenos Aires, where more than half of the population was made up of young male immigrants. Disembarked in an unknown city that deprived them of the physical presence of their families, these men's emotional landscape was pervaded by an unstable and changing morality to which they were certainly not accustomed in their places of origin.[53] However, if we reduce the scale to observe Buenos Aires from the *conventillos* and ethnic neighborhoods where immigrants coming from the same European locality converged, the promise of anonymity of the street relationships vanishes. In the narrow setting of everyday life, where everyone knew each other, it was difficult to avoid prying eyes and gossip.[54] The social control by countrymen could be as stifling in an Argentine cosmopolitan town as in a rural village in Southern Europe. In these circumstances, for the women left behind it was easier than it had been for their counterparts from the colonial period to learn about the moral lapses of their husbands. If they crossed the Atlantic to search for them, they could track them resorting to the social networks that reproduced their communities of origin in the neighborhoods of Buenos Aires.

Among the immigrants settled in the small towns and rural villages of the interior of the province of Buenos Aires, the control exerted by the moral communities of countrymen was even more intense than in the tenements and neighborhoods of large urban centers. Although distance, internal mobility, and interruptions in epistolary communications contributed to delaying the disclosure of bigamy, it was not always easy to maintain secrecy or avoid social scrutiny. The disapproval usually resulted only in gossip, but occasionally the moral sanction was expressed more forcefully when neighbors uncovered the imposture by reporting the crime to the local authorities, as happened to the Italian Nicola Ruperto. At the end of the spring of 1890, Giuseppe Maria Finelli and Alejandro Di Lupo denounced Ruperto's illegal marriage before the head of the civil registry in the town of Balcarce. They declared that they had been his neighbors in Castelvetere in Val Fortore, a township in the region of Campania, and therefore "know he is married, and that his wife, Maria Teresa Bibbo, still lives there."[55] The official filed the complaint with the justice of the peace, and when the arrest warrant was issued Ruperto ran away, leaving his 19-year-old Argentine wife behind. Four years later, the lawsuit was dismissed because the judicial authorities failed to find out the bigamist's whereabouts. In Balcarce, the rumor was that Ruperto had returned to Europe. Unable to travel to Argentina to sue her husband, perhaps it was his legitimate wife who prodded her countrymen to report Ruperto to the local authorities, devising a more sophisticated—or at least more effective—scheme than Rafaela's. A search in the baptismal records of Castelvetere in Val Fortore revealed that in March 1901, María Teresa Bibbo bore Maria Rosaria, the fruit of the reunion with her unfaithful husband.[56] Unfortunately, there is no way of knowing if she colluded with her countrymen from Balcarce to get her husband denounced or, on the contrary, if she was unaware of his love story with the *criollo* young woman and waited for him to return because that had been the marital agreement when he left. Either way, she would have turned into one more of the many "widows in white" that populated the Italian peninsula, had it not been for the report of Finelli and De Lupo.[57]

The stories I have narrated so far reveal the limits—ambiguous and changing—of the transnational affective relationships maintained by millions of people engaged in the artifice of closeness produced by the epistolary conversations and the remittances. Probably the most evident limit was imposed by the daily dynamics of the big Argentine cities. To men like Luis and Domingo, managing in parallel their adaptation to Buenos Aires and their marital life, suspended and awaiting an uncertain reunion, might have not been an easy task. The force of novelty conspired against the bonds that tied them with their families, and the past became blurred in front of the power of the fluid landscape of the urban world. The lure of freedom, the opportunities for casual sexual relations, the temptation waiting at the doors of brothels and bars, and the appeal of prostitutes—all of this awakened new passions.

As noted in the previous chapter, the city was the setting of a new sociability based on spontaneous, occasional, and fleeting relationships.[58] Bars and the streets were more attractive than the miserable room in a tenement house, while a dirty tent by the side of a railroad track, or a shed used as a dormitory for a gang of harvesters, could hardly emulate a home. These experiences must have left a lasting mark on the subjectivity of these men, whose identities and emotions must have changed along with their migration project. In that process, the relation between the migrants' universe of origin, their present, and their expectations changed.

If the bonds of the immigrants with the affective life of origin depended to a large extent on the epistolary exchange, the track of the letters had to follow the extraordinary spatial mobility of the male labor. The phenomenon of "migration inside migration" affected thousands of men who had no fixed residence for a long time. This instability restricted the continuity of the epistolary exchange because the letters got lost along the way or awaited their recipients at the consular offices. It was not unusual that *El Correo Español* and *La Patria degli Italiani*, two leading ethnic newspapers, published long lists with the names of persons whose correspondence was piling up at the consulates of Italy and Spain, urging them to pick it up.

Migration also imposed changes on the lives of women. As noted above, when their husbands emigrated, they assumed productive roles and coped with the requirements of managing a home. Household and extra-household responsibilities, illness—of themselves or their children—death, and alterations in the structure of the extended family imposed challenges and brought change.[59] For example, afflicted with tuberculosis, Andresa moved from Pamplona to Zaragoza when Facunda was 9 years old. It was a long time since her husband had stopped corresponding with her, and she probably had given up hope that he would call for her. But when the rumor that he was about to marry again reached her, she decided to travel. I do not know what happened that pushed her to undertake such an unpredictable venture like that of regaining her husband in another continent. Was she still in Zaragoza? Had she lost the support of their uncle and aunt? Were their parents still alive?

The underlying reasons for Rafaela's decision are not clear either. Nevertheless, there is evidence that a significant change occurred in her life: her parents died shortly before her journey to Argentina. This episode narrowed her affective circle, but at the same time freed her from patriarchal control. It is also possible that her part of the inheritance, in the form of monetary compensation, provided her with the resources to pay for the tickets to Buenos Aires.[60] Until 1885, when she refused to cross the Atlantic, Rafaela regarded her husband's migration as a means of improving the family finances that did not necessarily require the mobility of the whole family. However, fourteen years later, when her son was on the road to adulthood, and her parents had died, her view of uprooting seems to have changed.

A delicate interweaving of unpredictable circumstances and deliberate actions caused changes in women's lives. The promises and the migratory strategies agreed with their husbands at their departure had to be renegotiated or re-signified. In the absence of their husbands, many women remained subject to the patriarchal control of their parents and in-laws, a supervision with which migrants moderated their worries about the sexual behavior and the fidelity of their wives.[61] But paradoxically, migration expanded their spaces of autonomy, either because men entrusted wives with many extra-household tasks, or because, when abandoned, women had to face bigger workloads outside the home to ensure their subsistence.

However, when these women lost track of their spouses, or when they learned that they had been betrayed, it was not so easy to cross the Atlantic and find out their whereabouts; even more challenging was to face unknown bureaucracies and navigate unfamiliar legal systems to file lawsuits against them. Expressions like *esquecidos* (referring to the men who disappeared in the large mass of immigrants), and "widows of the living" or "widows in white" were common in some European regions like Galicia, southern Portugal, and the south of Italy.[62] Although the two last expressions allude to the liminal state between the husband's migration and the family reunion more than to abandoned women, it seems reasonable to ask how many of them would be the legitimate wives of bigamists who did not have the emotional and material resources to face the route followed by Andresa and Rafaela, who could not get a passport without marital authorization,[63] or who simply did not wish to incur in the costs of uprooting, and chose to forget their forgetful husbands. Oblivion, however, has not always taken the shape of resignation, because the widowhood of the neglected women was not a personal choice but a semantic resource with which the communities exerted control over female sexuality. Under the ascetic attire of these abandoned wives, there were young bodies urged by sexual, emotional, and material needs which adultery and concubinage could satisfy, because just like the widowers of living wives, the widows of the living could not remarry either.

## 3

# Breaking the Sacred Vows

The consequences of the loss of population caused by the rise in the number of young men who crowded the ships bound for the Americas at the turn of the twentieth century created debate among the political and intellectual leaders in different regions of Europe. In southern Italy, for example, the liberal sectors supported emigration with the expectation that the remittances and the eventual return of migrants with money would inject convertible currencies into the most backward regions of the peninsula, thus speeding up their transition to industrial capitalism. While the liberal arguments were based on the image of the temporary migrant who after a period of sacrifice, austerity, and savings, came back home with the fruit of his experience abroad, the more conservative sectors considered migration a disruptive factor that would cause moral, social, and cultural deterioration, eventually provoking social chaos. Accordingly, conservatives demanded restrictive policies from the state, arguing a double concern: economic ruin, as migration would undermine the agricultural workforce, and social ills caused by the increase of helpless wives and children. Images of women and children crying on train platforms, and of wives begging their husbands not to leave them on their own, filled the conservative speech. The picture of the abandoned wife left destitute was often evoked to predict a dissolution of the family, and the inevitable fall of women in prostitution, adultery, illegitimate births, abortion, and infanticide.[1]

Although it is true that both the optimistic projections of the liberals and the unfavorable predictions of the conservatives exaggerated the effects of migration because neither did most of the men return with money, nor were all wives deserted, there must have been many women who suffered abandonment and sought in adultery a way to cope with loneliness, poverty, and disaffection. To feel the protection of another man's arms was, however, not only an experience of the wives who remained at home, but also of those who joined their husbands abroad. Once the couple was reunited after a separation that used to last for several years, it was not always possible to reestablish the affective bond and rekindle the language of love and the intimacy of conjugal life. Moreover, many women were frustrated when confronting the gap between their material and emotional expectations and their husbands' meager achievements in the host country. Disillusionment led to recriminations that often turned into heated quarrels and fights that wounded the marital relationship. As in their places of origin, in the new society the repertoire of alternatives was narrow, although it is true that in a society with high rates of masculinity like turn-of-the-century Argentina, there were more arms for women to find refuge. In their Argentine destinations the wives of the immigrants experienced other forms of abandonment, loneliness, and destitution. As in their places of origin, in the new country the repertoire of alternatives for a troubled marital relationship was very limited, since like in Italy and Spain, in Argentina the civil law did not admit the dissolution of marriage.[2]

Between 1880 and the first decade of the twentieth century, the arrest warrants issued by the police of the province of Buenos Aires show that the majority of women who ran away from the marital home were foreigners. Some of them fled alone, like Ana Sissel, a 35-year-old Swiss woman, whose spouse reported her desertion at the police station in the small town of Rauch, or Redegunda Cappioli de Caccia, an Italian woman "aged forty-one, white, pale, and brown-eyed," who abandoned her home in Tres Arroyos after having stolen money from her husband. However, most women deserted their spouses in the company of lovers and often brought their children with them. That was the case with Prudencia Jarreau, a Basque woman, who abandoned her husband taking their sixteen-month-old child with her, and with Lucia Marzorini, a 20-year-old Italian who, according to her spouse, "ran away with our two small sons instigated by a man with whom she has an adulterous relationship."[3]

The police reports, brief and laconic, in which the voice of a betrayed husband has been translated by the police officer who received the complaint, provide just a blurry picture of a critical moment in a marriage. These documents remain silent on women's reasons to escape, on the emotional experiences of both the fugitive wives and the deserted men, and the outcome of the attempt to move away from the husband. A variety of situations may explain their behavior: the couple's inability to recreate a common language of love and intimacy after a prolonged separation, the lack of sexual desire, marital abuse, and emotional suffering, or the existence—beyond the boundaries of the domestic sphere—of margins for the intimate navigation of feelings that turned adultery into an emotional refuge.[4]

Although it is difficult to maintain that infidelity was the reason for all these bold reactions, the regularity of the reports suggests that the practice of home abandonment was more widespread among immigrant women than among their Argentine counterparts.[5] In the following pages, I focus on the crime of adultery and rely mostly on court records for illuminating some manifestations of the dark side of the marital life and uncovering the emotional consequences of migration, long estrangements, and unfulfilled expectations.

## Vengeance

In September 1892, Pedro Lamar, a 37-year-old Italian laborer who had been living in Miramar, a small coastal town in the southeast of the province of Buenos Aires, for five years, appeared at the police station to denounce that:

> Suspecting that his wife was being unfaithful to him with his brother Nicolás Lamar, he hid in the kitchen of the house he lived in to verify his suspicion and confirmed the fact that he is reporting. At about two o'clock of the afternoon of that day he [Pedro] surprised them in *flagrante delicto* on account of which he asks for them to be punished with the penalty provided by law ... At the same time Mr. Lamar asks for the removal of the son he has with that woman to be put in *don* Francisco Azcona's care who is a neighbor of recognized standing.[6]

Felisa Castellani and her brother-in-law, Nicolás Lamar, had arrived in Argentina just two months before Pedro filed the complaint. When in 1886 her husband emigrated from the small Calabrian village of Fuscaldo, Felisa and her three-month-old son were left behind and compelled to move in with her in-laws. As the house was too small to accommodate them, they had to share the room with Nicolás. Like many other emigrants did upon departure, her husband committed himself to send money from Argentina. But, according to Felisa's statement before the court, "he never sent anything with the excuse that the money he earned was barely enough to ensure his own subsistence ... had it not been for the help of Nicolás his departure would have left her in abandonment and destitution."[7]

In turn-of-the-century Italy, emigration brought about economic opportunities and new forms of wealth, but at the same time, the profound social changes caused by the departure of men led to anxiety both in those leaving their families and in those staying behind. Fears about their wife's sexuality made emigration particularly difficult for men. That dilemma was resolved by subjecting women to the patriarchal regime, leaving them supervised by their in-laws. That custody provided material safeguard and ensured the subsistence needs of wives and children, and at the same time, mitigated men's anxiety about their spouses' infidelity. In Italy, honor determined a man's status within the community, and the submission and demonstration of obedience of his wife and children were crucial for a man's social standing. But a man's honor also depended on his reputation as honest, his ability to control female sexuality, and his fulfillment of the role of provider of food and shelter for the family.[8] Although the migrant husband delegated part of this responsibility to the male relatives who remained in the peninsula, this was perceived as just a temporary situation, since he was deemed responsible for sending money to his family back home. When he failed to meet that social expectation, the whole structure of the honor system collapsed.[9] That is likely what happened to Pedro Lamar. In a cultural context in which masculinity was associated with the image of the male provider, the few letters he sent to Felisa in which, according to her statement, "there was no good news but just pretexts,"[10] far from excusing her husband, damaged his reputation. In fact, in the investigation, Nicolás admitted to having had an "illicit relationship" with his sister-in-law, but defended himself alleging that "since he could not let them live in misery, he took care of Castellani and her son, Domenico, helping them as much as he could with food and money and, eventually, took the place his elder brother left empty."[11]

Also, Felisa acknowledged the crime and her excuse did not differ much from that of Nicolás. She described Pedro as a man without responsibility, who did not keep his word and neglected her "in an extreme circumstance that first forced her to accept that Nicolás would provide for her and her son, until she later let him visit her at night and ended up breaking the marital vows."[12]

In those days, stories conjuring up images of female adultery, of migrants' wives and minors mired in hardship, of abandoned women who ended up making their living through prostitution, and of husbands who, on their return home, discovered the unfaithfulness of their wives and murdered the lovers, were widespread in the Italian public consciousness.[13] In line with the conservative speeches about the high price that Italian society paid for the massive departure of men, journalists used to show sympathy for the perpetrators of what were usually regarded as "honor crimes." The observers and commentators of that period also frequently alluded to another sequel of the migratory fever: the illegitimate children, symbols of the double offense to masculinity—adultery followed by pregnancy. But unlike the protagonists of the stories in the peninsular press, Pedro Lamar did not return to Italy. It was in Argentina where he discovered the infidelity of his wife, and soon after learned that she was pregnant and that the child she was expecting belonged to Nicolás.

The court record does not shed light on the motives that brought Felisa and her brother-in-law to Argentina. However, it is likely that it was Pedro who called his wife since, in his statement in court, he declared he had promised Felisa he would bring her to Argentina when he saved the money to pay the fare. Maybe it was she who persuaded Pedro to have Nicolás escort her, arguing that crossing the Atlantic was risky for a woman alone with a small child. But it might also be the case that her pregnancy hurried their departure from Italy, where the arrival of an illegitimate child would threaten the Lamars' honor within the community. If Felisa managed to get to Argentina on time, the child would be recognized by her husband, who would never find out that it was the fruit of adultery. Certainly, Felisa's in-laws must have been aware of the woman's "illicit relationship" with Nicolás, but they probably handled it with secrecy to protect themselves from the community's scrutinizing gaze and gossip. However, pregnancy would bring adultery to light, uncovering a chain of complicities and family disloyalties. Recognizing themselves incapable of watching Felisa's moral conduct would dishonor Pedro's father and brothers before other males of the community. In the light of this intricate situation, the unfaithful wife had to leave before her pregnancy became evident. The crime of Felisa and Nicolás was eventually discovered in a society in which the notions of female fidelity and male honor were not so different from the one that prevailed in Italy. In nineteenth-century Argentina, female adultery was regarded as the result of "an almost insane sensuality ... the consequence of lust expressed in the shape of most brutal selfishness."[14] The misconduct of the adulteress had to be punished because, just to satisfy her desires, she sacrificed the love and reputation of her husband, the stability of the home, and the well-being of children. No matter if she had been tempted by the flesh or moved by anger upon discovering her husband's infidelity, nothing exculpated an adulterous woman. The "sin" of loving a third party was irredeemable, because, in the words of the jurist Escriche y Martín, "adultery destroys the husband's illusion of being the only person in possession of [his wife's] heart, wounds his honor, and makes him an object of contempt."[15]

In this cultural context, it was not difficult for Pedro to have his wife and her accomplice imprisoned. The judicial proceeding lasted about a year, and as we will see later, it was discontinued at the request of the plaintiff. During that time, Felisa and Nicolás remained in the penitentiary of Dolores. When the adulteress was in her seventh month of pregnancy, the prison doctor requested that she be transferred to the hospital. Pedro was notified that his wife's health had deteriorated "being pale and weak from refusing to eat [she] has recurrent fainting fits, a fever and other signs of infection."[16] But the news of Felisa's suffering did not arouse Pedro's compassion. And although the prosecutor suggested that he drop the charges so that Felisa could spend the last months of pregnancy at home, he remained steadfast in his decision to punish her. Six weeks later, Felisa gave birth to a girl, and only then did Pedro withdraw the lawsuit.

The justice system allowed Pedro to inflict on his unfaithful wife a brief but painful retribution. A newcomer who did not speak Spanish, the woman was imprisoned while pregnant and separated from the man with whom she had maintained an intimate relationship over the last few years. Nicolás could not support her emotionally because he too had lost his freedom. Felisa depended entirely on the will of a man who, punishing her, sought to satisfy his thirst for vengeance and redeem his honor. As Robert Solomon points out, vengeance is both an intense emotion and a cool, calculating strategy, because it has its "kernel of rationality" from which the offended articulates the revenge, even if he/she expresses himself/herself with indignation or with a burst of anger.[17] Vengeance is reflective and rational, at least instrumentally, in its search for satisfaction; however, calculation and coldness are not incompatible with the power and the intention of the emotion.[18]

Driven by indignation, in his complaint Pedro asked for "a punishment proportional to this unpardonable offense."[19] In those days, the Penal Code provided a penalty of one to three years' imprisonment for the adulterous woman, and banishment for her accomplice.[20] However, the request for the withdrawal of the charges submitted by the double-betrayed husband to the court ended up releasing the offenders before the sentence. Depriving his wife of her liberty and making her gave birth while she was detained seem to have been enough retribution for the offended husband.[21]

Shortly after their release, the lovers left Miramar. In May 1895—when the second national census of population was carried out—Nicolás, Felisa, Domingo (the son she had had with Pedro in Italy), and Rosalía (Nicola's daughter, whom she bore while in prison) were settled in Balvanera, a neighborhood of the city of Buenos Aires. When the census taker asked Nicolás about his marital status, he stated that he had been "married" to Felisa for nine years.[22] Beyond the framing of that census "photography," which portrayed them as an ordinary family, lay an intricate story of love and disaffection, outrage and retribution, passion and reason. A story of vengeance.

## Shame

A few months after Felisa and Nicolás were released, Domingo Gongeiro appeared at the police station of Dolores reporting that his wife, Josefa Alois, had escaped with her lover, Luis Álvarez, taking with her "all her clothes and also mine in a trunk, and three hundred *pesos* that I had from my savings."[23] He also indicated the exact whereabouts of his wife: "an *estancia* (cattle ranch) in the forests of Tordillo, where Álvarez is *puestero*."[24] Domingo said that he was unaware of the reason for Josefa's wrongful conduct, "because I never failed in my duties as a husband and as *hombre de bien* (honorable man)." However, that was not the first time that his wife ran away. Two years earlier, in the summer of 1891, while they were living in Buenos Aires, she escaped with another man, and although Domingo reported the event, when the police escorted her back to the marital home, he forgave her. But as she committed the same offense again, this time he changed his mind and decided to file a complaint for adultery, which forced him to prove that he was her legitimate husband. Although they had been married for five years, Domingo had neither the marriage certificate nor the means to ask for it to be sent from Spain. The judge then accepted his request to "replace the certificate with testimonies," and the plaintiff presented four Spanish fellow workers as witnesses.

What did the husband feel about finding himself forced to appeal to his countrymen for help? What would the witnesses think of his situation? Did his countrymen know that Josefa had already had a love affair in Buenos Aires? Were they the ones who, fully aware that Domingo had forgiven her on that occasion, advised him to seek redress in the courts this time? What was Domingo's purpose in suing her? Did he want his wife to feel ashamed or to show remorse? Or like Pedro Lamar, did he turn to the law to satisfy his desire for revenge? Although all these reasons appear in different parts of the judicial record, shame is the prevailing feeling. According to Stearns, as an emotion, shame has a core meaning that relates individuals to wider social groups and norms—real or imagined.[25] Thus, shame is a social emotion, activated by the specific needs of an individual or a community to maintain certain values, like honor and reputation, and to enforce desired behaviors. But at the same time, shaming has a deterrence effect, in particular when the sanctions are imposed by friends and family members.[26]

When Domingo forgave Josefa's first affair, what prompted him to save his marriage was probably neither love nor mercy for his wife. Rather the reason for his indulgence seems to have been the shame of being exposed before his neighbors in the tenement house where he had been living since his arrival in Argentina. Behind this action he was concealing marital disagreements and protecting his reputation. It is significant that although Domingo reported Josefa's abandonment of the marital home, he did not turn to the law to punish her and, after her return to the *conventillo*, he intended to maintain the fiction that theirs was a harmonious marriage.

When Josefa was captured in her second escape, she declared that it was not true that harmony reigned in her marriage. On the contrary, ever since they had lived in Buenos Aires, alleging that Josefa had humiliated him, Domingo would beat her and threaten her with weapons almost every day. Josefa confessed that she had an intimate relationship with Álvarez, and that a few weeks before she was arrested, she had moved to Tordillo with him, not because she wanted "to run away from home, but because Domingo had thrown her out of the house after threatening her with a rifle."[27]

The adulteress said that after each beating her body ended up bruised and her face distorted, so she remained "shut up in the house for days, to avoid the embarrassment of being seen in that condition ... which feels worst in a small town like Dolores, where many Spaniards know my husband, than in a big city like Buenos Aires." Among the latter was Álvarez, the man with whom Josefa escaped to Tordillo. This 32-year-old rural worker declared that Domingo had introduced him to his wife. Álvarez also said that, even though his relationship with Josefa was not one of as much trust and friendship as the one he had with her husband:

> About four months ago, one afternoon he stopped by to say hello, but Domingo was not at home. Then, Josefa took advantage of her husband's absence to confide in Álvarez that, moved by an old rancor over an episode that occurred a long time ago, but still embarrasses him, Domingo was threatening to kill her.[28]

Since then, Álvarez had become the "confidant of the poor woman," until one day he found her "by chance" in town, and as she begged him to protect her from her abusive husband, he "decided to take her to live with him." The source does not reveal if Josefa elaborated on the old rancor that Álvarez alluded to in his testimony or if he came to know about her runaway in Buenos Aires. But regardless of whether she opened up to Álvarez or preferred to conceal the details of her past, most likely Domingo's rancor had to do with her first abandonment of the marital home.

When Domingo was summoned to declare, he also alluded to shame. However, this feeling was aroused in him when his wife exposed the intimacy of her relationship with Álvarez by "hugging and kissing with him in public and living in concubinage with her accomplice."[29] Shame was also invoked by the plaintiff's attorney, who, deploring Josefa's "wrongful conduct," noted that:

> Her unseemly conduct humiliates my client's manhood ... by breaking the sacred vows, Josefa Lois de Gongeiro ignominiously tarnished the name given to her by the father of her son through insults and bacchanalian scenes that would

not be decorous to mention here because even my pen refuses to describe those shameful attitudes.[30]

Josefa's "illicit relationship" undermined her husband's social reputation. The decision to forgive her after her first escape in Buenos Aires seems to have been a strategy to save their marriage from the ruinous moral and emotional costs of public exposure of infidelity. Perhaps on that occasion it was easier for Domingo to conceal what had happened. In effect, it was a fleeting episode that took place in a big city where social scrutiny was not so intense as in a small town like Dolores, a sort of parenthesis after which the couple resumed the conjugal routine. However, hidden behind the façade of a harmonious marriage was a painful existence made of disaffection, rancor, and mistreatment. On that occasion, Domingo likely believed that the abuse would have a higher deterrent effect than a punishment imposed by a distant legal authority.

Although the move from Buenos Aires to Dolores does not seem to have altered the dynamics of the marital relationship, it made Josefa more vulnerable to abuse. In court, the public attorney said that the defendant "has no relatives in this town, standing alone to face the brutality of her husband."[31] This might explain why Josefa resorted to the same pattern. Deprived of kin and friends to turn to, Álvarez, a young single countryman whom she saw regularly in her own home, again made adultery the way out of a miserable life. However, the repetition of a behavior that had ended up locking her in a spiral of abuse did not ensure Josefa's (nor the other adulteresses whose stories inform the analysis of this book) emotional liberty. This was so because of the fact that, in most cases, the betrayed husband's dropping the charges did not mean that abuse and emotional suffering would come to an end. In effect, "the happy ending" of the story of Felisa and Nicolás Lamar seems have been an exception.[32] Even if the scant evidence available makes it difficult to track the course followed by these couples after the trial was over, I am led to believe that the runaway from the marital home and adultery were just glints of freedom, fleeting emotional refuges from which the police and the law took women away to return them to their authoritarian and abusive husbands.[33]

William Reddy maintains that emotional expressions—emotives in his terms—are affective utterances that represent an individual's attempt "to call up the emotion that is expressed; an attempt to feel what one says one feels."[34] This means the translation of inward feelings to try and match them with the emotional conventions in a process of navigation. Unlike the analytic perspectives that conceive emotions as socially and culturally shaped, the navigation of feelings recovers historical actors' agency by recognizing their capacity to find a space for the rupture of the hegemonic emotional regime. Emotional norms do not determine entirely the emotional styles, allowing the process of navigation and of emotional work that an individual carries out to find a way to fit in what she or he feels within a given context. The tension between construction and adaptation provokes emotional suffering, but the navigation eventually allows the person to reach an emotional refuge, a space of freedom that provides safe relief from prevailing emotional norms.[35]

Several historians of emotions have pointed out the limitations of Reddy's analytical framework. On the one hand, the critique has focused on his overarching and binary concept of "regime"—tied to state formation and hegemony—which suggests that one set of emotional norms is true for all, except for what the author calls "emotional refuge." On the other hand, the notion of emotive has been criticized because it fails to adequately reflect the social situation in which the utterances are made, as well as for forcing the specificity of those utterances to speech acts over other forms of emotional behavior such as non-verbal expressions and bodily practice.[36] Nevertheless, concepts such as navigation of feelings, emotional suffering, emotional liberty, and emotional refuge seem appropriate tools to analyze the situation of women like Josefa, who appeared to have no option but to endure domestic violence or commit adultery. As we will see in the next chapter, several women who filed complaints for maltreatment and physical harm against their husbands navigated their feelings in other directions, attempting to find interstices of emotional liberty in which to alleviate the suffering. However, most of the time they only attained poor results, either because the police authorities disregarded their claims, or because the judges' sentences were too lenient. With the husband's return to the home, the dynamic of marital abuse was set in motion again. If finding refuge and freedom depended on the port which those navigators headed for, the available anchorages appeared not to have been the safest ones: reporting abuse to the police and filing a complaint in the court or abandonment of the marital home and adultery.

Josefa did not report the physical mistreatment Domingo inflicted on her, but rather she confined herself in silence, embarrassed by the marks he left on her body. Her first attempt to escape ended up plunging her into greater distress. The source covers neither the details of her runaway in Buenos Aires (who was the man with whom she escaped? Did the relationship continue after the police returned her to the marital home?) nor Josefa's fate after the judicial process—which was discontinued without a verdict, although there is no evidence that

Domingo dropped the charges. The opaque outlines of this story veil Josefa's reasons to refrain from reporting Domingo. Perhaps the shame she alluded to in her statement was the conjunction of her fear of a violent husband and her resignation to a failed marriage. However, her attitude might have also been a learned response, a result of the emotional education she received in Spain.[37] In those days, Spanish society was ruled by marital relationships of power and subordination that, as suggested by an observer of the period, forced women to seek "refuge in prayer, church, and tears."[38] Under the pervasive influence of Catholicism, women embraced emotional styles characterized by discretion, devotion, suffering, and obedience. Political conservatism and the cultural and institutional influence of the Catholic Church have been pointed out as the main explanatory factors of the subordinate position of Spanish women. However, Mary Nash has underscored the role played by biological essentialism—that regarded reproduction as the main feature of female identity—as the core feature in the construction of gender difference, representations, and discriminatory values aimed at legitimate female subordination.[39] Although by the end of the nineteenth century, the conventual life was no longer a valid model of femininity, women were assigned a sacred mission that led them to live a secluded life not in a religious convent but in the house. No longer as a devoted nun, but as the *ángel del hogar* (angel of the house), the Spanish woman was represented as a loving person who consoled the afflictions of the members of the family and suffered their faults, and whose virtues were patience and discretion.

As noted in the introduction, in the corpus of sources on which this book is based, Italian married couples far outnumber Spanish couples. This imbalance makes it difficult to compare the attitudes that both groups of women displayed towards the treachery, authoritarianism, and abuse of their husbands. However, Spanish women who, like Josefa, were sued for adultery, as well as those who, like Andresa, filed complaints against their bigamous husbands, tended to display a more submissive attitude than their Italian counterparts. Discretion, shyness, and shame—expressed in words, but also in gestures and physical signs—appear to have formed the core of their emotional style.[40]

## Compassion

That morning, on January 22, 1891, Teresa Salomone was alone in the room in the tenement house because her husband, an Italian peddler called Salvador Calabrese, had left at dawn for the countryside of Dolores, where he usually spent several days offering his goods in ranches and farms. A few hours later, she received a visit from her brother-in-law, José Rosciano, "who called himself José Rochart," the husband of one of her sisters, settled in Tres Arroyos, a town to the south of the province of Buenos Aires. José stayed in the room until the afternoon before Salvador's return, when he left "to run errands before taking the night train to Tres Arroyos."[41]

A few days later, a woman who lived in the same tenement house testified to the judge that:

> The long visit of Rochart to the room of the couple in the absence of Salvador aroused her suspicions in spite of knowing that they are relatives, that he [Rochart] usually sleeps and eats in the room, that Calabrese calls him compadre, and that Rochart uses the *tú* every time he addresses him.[42]

Salvador and Teresa had married in 1880 in Noepoli, a picturesque commune in the region of Basilicata, where she remained when three years after the wedding her husband emigrated to Buenos Aires. The separation lasted six years and, when that summer morning Rosciano visited her, it had been only eight months since Teresa had arrived from Italy. According to her testimony, when Calabrese called her, she left Italy expecting to have a better life in Argentina but "upon arrival, she soon realized that her husband's economic situation had not prospered at all."[43] Although the peddler had spent several years in the land of promise, he had not even been able to raise the money to pay for Teresa's fare. Then, when at the beginning of 1890, he learned that Rosciano was about to travel to Italy, Calabrese asked him to bring Teresa, promising to pay him back the fare as soon as he collected a sum that his clients owed him. But when Teresa arrived in Dolores, her husband argued that he had not yet been able to gather the money. This unpaid loan provided the perfect excuse for bringing Rosciano back to Dolores.

After spending three days in the countryside, Calabrese finally returned to the tenement house. As he found the door of the room ajar, he believed that Teresa would be in the courtyard. But upon entering he found:

> A great mess, he saw the daughter of the neighbor Lucía Palermo lying asleep in the matrimonial bed, the trunk where they kept the clothes was unlocked without the dresses of his wife and the handkerchief in which he hid four hundred and ninety *pesos* from savings that by hard labor and perseverance he had managed to gather was untied and empty.[44]

Bewildered, he went out into the courtyard where his neighbor, Lucía, told him that his wife had left. She was also from Noepoli, and ever since Teresa arrived at the tenement the two women had rekindled the friendship they previously had in Italy. Every time Salvador "was on the move selling his merchandise in the countryside," she sent one of her daughters to keep Teresa company. Lucía told Calabrese that the previous night "a murmur and movements in the courtyard" had awakened her and that the next morning, her daughter told her that "at around midnight, Teresa got up and slipped out of the room." When summoned to testify, the other residents of the tenement house said that they had seen Teresa leaving with all her baggage in the direction of the train station.[45] Two months later, the peddler learned that his wife had escaped with Rosciano and was living with him in Tres Arroyos, so he sued his compadre for abduction and his wife for adultery. In his statement asking the judge to order the capture of the lovers, Calabrese's attorney stated that his "client ignores the reasons for his wife's reproachable behavior, being public and notorious that the best harmony has always reigned in the home."[46]

The brief physical description of the criminals in the arrest warrant reflects a blurred image of their appearance. Teresa was 23-years-old, "brunette, short and chubby, with a scar on her cheek the size of an egg." Rosciano, almost twenty years older than her, had a "very pale, round face, with a blond beard, corpulent, and of regular stature." Almost a year had passed since they had run away when they were apprehended in Juárez (the same town in the province of Buenos Aires where Luis Aldaz, the bigamist whose story was narrated in Chapter I, remarried). In a missive to the investigating judge, the justice of the peace explained that such delay was caused by Rosciano's double identity "because calling himself José Rochart, he evaded the police, preventing his capture and that of his concubine."[47]

In her testimony before the justice of the peace, Teresa admitted—likely to mitigate the sentence of her lover—that hers had not been an abduction, but a voluntary abandonment of the marital home that she had proposed to Rosciano, with whom she maintained an "illicit relationship since before coming from Italy."[48] Like Felisa Lamar, Teresa defended herself by saying that after the migration of her husband she was forced to live in destitution because he never sent her any money, and that "when she complained about the hardships she was enduring, Calabrese wanted to do business with her,"[49] insinuating that her husband had tried to push her into prostitution.

For his part, Rosciano described the details of the "sad and miserable situation" in which he found Teresa upon returning to Noepoli. Although he did not refer to prostitution, he said that "to keep from starving" she had ended up cohabiting with a neighbor, with whom she had two children that "she had to leave in Italy to reunite with her husband in Argentina."[50] Was Rosciano telling the truth, or was he exaggerating Teresa's misfortune? Perhaps to portray the adulterous woman as a victim, he relied on the pervasive and powerful social representations available in the turn-of-the-century Italian press. When reporting about the political debates on the heavy price exacted by male migration, newspapers often conjured up images of neglected women sunk into poverty and sexual depravity.[51]

Rosciano's statement before the justice of the peace expressed compassion, the emotion that—as Martha Nussbaum points out—is most frequently viewed with approval and most frequently taken to provide a good foundation for rational deliberation and appropriate action in public as well as in private life.[52] When he was investigated in the court of Dolores, Rosciano insisted again on the misfortunes Teresa suffered in Noepoli after the departure of her husband, and remarked that her situation had not improved in Argentina either, because "she came forced by Calabrese to find here a life just as miserable as the one she had in Italy." In his visits to Dolores—the statement continues—he "witnessed that the situation was getting worse" and responding to Teresa's repeated request "and moved only by pity," he accepted to "take her with him, just as any honorable man would have done before a woman in such a desperate situation."[53]

Although it is understandable that both Rosciano and his defense lawyer avoided any allusion to the love affair he had with Teresa, it is striking that neither the prosecutor nor the judge investigated the defendant about the origin of this intimate bond that the adulteress herself had confessed to the justice peace of Juárez. This indifference prevented the justice officers from questioning her about the fruit of the "illicit love": Catalina, a baby girl who was baptized in the parish church of Juárez and registered as Teresa's "natural daughter" a few days before her mother was arrested.[54] Throughout the almost seventy folios of the court record, there is only one reference to the child. As Teresa became seriously ill while she was in prison, the judge wrote a letter to the director of the hospital saying that "not being possible in this jail to take care of Teresa Salomone and her daughter ... I request that they be transferred to the hospital of this town."[55] The file is a closed world in which only the evidence enters, the evidence on which the magistrate has to base his judgments. Although in this story of love, disaffection, and betrayal, Teresa's sister (who had been abandoned by her husband, Rosciano, and was herself the victim of his infidelity), and Catalina (the illegitimate child born from the adulterous relationship) were crucial characters—at least from the historian's perspective—in the theater of justice they did not even perform a supporting role, because no one asked about them.

Rosciano had to prove that he had not abducted Teresa, and she, in turn, had to justify her unfaithful behavior to obtain a mitigation of the sentence. In doing so, the woman resorted to an emotional style in which self-compassion and disdain prevailed. Perhaps it was the scorn she felt for her husband that led her to display such a disdain before the investigating judge. In her statement, Teresa seemed unconcerned about her precarious legal position: she was in jail accompanied by her two-month-old baby and had been charged with two crimes that could deprive her of freedom for several years. Nonetheless, when the judge asked her if she was aware that what she had done was punishable by law, she replied that she did not consider a crime "the fact of running away from a home where she suffered from abuse and misery." Furthermore, when asked about the theft of her husband's savings, Teresa answered that when she left, she had taken "only what she had on," because "Calabrese has nothing worth stealing . . . he has debts that he does not pay, and if he had saved the 400 pesos he refers to, he should have paid Rosciano what he owes him for her fare."[56] Although the allusion to helplessness and physical violence was common among women sued for adultery, Teresa's defiant emotional style was unusual. Unlike her, in court, the majority of adulteresses acted shyly and portrayed themselves as respectful and obedient wives who had been forced into adultery by neglect and deprivation.

Although the emotional experience that underlies the coarse stories of illiterate women whose voices were translated to the language of the law by the justice officials is not easy to access, in some cases the density of the defendants' statements sheds light—albeit tenuous—on the women's turmoil of inward feelings. To explore the diversity of emotions and bodily gestures entailed in these experiences, let's leave for a moment the outcome of Teresa's story to go into the case of Olinda Bértola, a 29-year-old Italian seamstress who arrived in Argentina with her husband, Mateo Bugni, in 1888. According to the public defender, when Olinda "reached the limit of what is tolerable" and ran away from the marital home to join her lover, Francisco Mélica, she had been married for twelve years.[57]

In the winter of 1894, Olinda told the judge a long story of suffering that had begun when, only two weeks after the marriage, her husband inflicted on her a horrible beating while yelling all sorts of obscenities. Ever since then, Mateo has taken advantage "of the fragility of his wife ... Oftentimes, she was unable to leave the house for several days because her body was black from the blows she received."[58] In the statement, Olinda expressed a variety of conflicting emotions: she said she felt fear, shame, and affection for Mateo. Why was she afraid? Because, given the difference in strength and Mateo's anger, she "believed he would end up killing her." What were the reasons for her shame? Here, the answer is more confusing, because despite having stated that her bruised body embarrassed her, it was "the sincere affection" she felt for Mateo that led her to conceal "the abuse and to suffer in silence and loneliness." But Olinda was also ashamed of her husband, a man who had ruined her marital life "with his debaucheries and bad business that induced him even to squander her dowry."[59]

Three years after the marriage, overwhelmed by debts, Mateo emigrated to Argentina. Olinda remained in Italy, but after a short while, responding to his call, she also traveled and joined him. However, she did it only to "fulfill the sacred vows of a wife" and because, by then, she already had two children from that "unfortunate union."[60] In her allegation, the public defender said that the prospect of the reunion "rekindled the love" she felt for her husband, "and revived the hope of better days, trusting that, away from bad companies, Bugni would change his behavior."[61]

But Olinda's illusions were shattered shortly after she arrived in Buenos Aires when her husband went back into debt and was reported for fraud. After a couple of months in prison, Mateo turned up "docile, promising in a thousand different ways that he would not disappoint her anymore," because he had gotten a job and housing in a small farm in Estación Alfalfa, a small rural settlement in the southwest of the province of Buenos Aires, "where they would start all over again." Even though Olinda did not trust him she had no choice but to leave Buenos Aires—where she had given birth to a girl a few months earlier—to follow her husband. In Italy she had relied emotionally and materially on her parents and siblings, who helped her in the misfortune but, far away from home and deprived of her kinship network, Olinda felt alone, defenseless, and fearful.

It was not long after the move to Estación Alfalfa that Mateo made her "a victim of all his strength again . . . and when his hands and feet were not enough, he resorted to sticks and pitchforks to attack her." When asked by the judge about the reason for the mistreatment, Olinda responded that she ignored the motives for her husband's brutality because she had "always fulfilled her obligations as wife and mother." She also made it clear that even though her affection for Mateo was over, she put up with that life "for the sake of her children."[62]

Despite the suffering and the hardships, Olinda did not try to abandon Mateo, and in the time between their move from Buenos Aires and the moment when her husband filed a complaint of adultery against her, she gave birth to another four children. According to the public defender, it was the husband who ran away "pressed by a new embezzlement . . . he left his wife with no means to live and seven mouths to feed." Her neighbor Francisco Melica, a 25-year-old Italian widower, "pitied" Olinda's miserable life, and "spontaneously offered to protect her and support her children, cruelly abandoned by a lousy father." In the words of the attorney, it was "neither for love nor for the weakness of the flesh that [Olinda] ended up living with Melica in concubinage, but out of gratitude for his generosity and noble heart."[63]

Two years had passed since the escape when Mateo returned to Estación Alfalfa and learned that his wife was having an illicit relationship with the neighbor and was in the fifth month of a new pregnancy. After a turbulent dispute, Mateo took the children with him and reported Olinda for adultery. She was immediately imprisoned. However, barely six months had passed after the beginning of the legal proceedings when Mateo sent a letter to the judge saying that he forgave his wife and pleading the magistrate to order Olinda "to come back home to care for the children, whom I am in no condition to look after."[64] The release order signed by the judge is the last folio of the file. As in other court records used in this book, this is also the point where I lost track of Olinda. Although I searched for her traces in other sources, I was not able to find out if she returned to the marital home or if she joined Melica, the father of her youngest child.

Unlike Teresa, who openly expressed the disaffection and the contempt she felt for Calabrese, Olinda—probably expecting to arouse the compassion of the magistrate—presented herself as an ashamed and shy woman who "out of love and respect" followed the erratic path of her husband until his runaway plunged her into hardships and despair. As noted in Chapter II, in a patriarchal society such as the one in which these stories unfolded, love and obedience were not incompatible terms. On the contrary, they were two inseparable components of the idea of marriage.[65] This conception was at the heart of the balance of power within marriage, but at the same time was a space for negotiation in the everyday functioning of the conjugal relationship. Patriarchy, as an ideological, cultural, and institutional framework, was not a static social structure of male domination and female subordination; it was also a system where notions of authority and obedience coexisted with a strong complementary and companionate ethos. In the day-to-day experience of wife and husband, the patriarchal system was flexible enough to be constantly negotiated. However, although "bargaining with patriarchy"—in Denize Kandiyoti's terms—involved agency and margins for maneuver, negotiation did not necessarily mean a "good purchase" for wives.[66] Rather, women lived in a "patriarchal equilibrium" in which their resistance achieved small victories that brought about short-term benefits, but that did not improve their status in the marital relationship.[67] Thus, although negotiation showed the instability of patriarchy it also ensured its continuity.[68]

Although in the cases analyzed in this chapter the relationships between men and women were antagonistic, we should not generalize the rivalry to the complete sequence of the married life of the protagonists of the stories of adultery and betrayal. The members of the patriarchal family were educated to believe that individual interest should not prevail over the interests of the family. This sense of the common good, which could obscure the exercise of male power, enabled harmonious interactions in pursuit of shared goals. Regarded as a family strategy, emigration illustrates both the sense of shared interest and the role of negotiation in the patriarchal marriage. In an ideal situation, the married couple would agree to a sequential movement in which the man migrated first and the woman was left behind—alone or with children—in the care of her in-laws. When the migrant husband achieved a certain stability abroad (a job and a place to live), he would call his wife, who in the interval between his departure and hers, received conjugal affection and material support in the form of letters and remittances. But these agreements, rooted in the conception that shared interest should prevail over individual desires, were not always the result of marital negotiations in which men and women worked together for the benefit of the family but rather of conjugal dynamics based on male authority and female subordination.

That is what happened to Olinda, who, despite being trapped in a violent bond before Mateo emigrated, when he called her, she answered out of obedience: "fulfilling her duties as a wife and mother" and "believing that in Argentina her children would have a better life. Upon departing, her husband left her under the supervision of her in-laws. Olinda, however, did not change residence and remained in the house of her parents, where she and Mateo had been living ever since their marriage. Then, one might assume that Mateo's migration was not an opportunity for her to gain autonomy from the hierarchies that ruled gender relations in the patriarchal family. If Olinda would have attempted to disobey her husband by refusing to join him in Argentina, perhaps not only her male relatives, but also her mother and mother-in-law, despite being aware of the abuse she suffered, would have disapproved of her insubordination. In fact, in what Kandiyoti refers to as "classic patriarchy," younger women are subordinated not only to men but also to the senior women, especially to their mother-in-law, whose control and authority—that eventually younger women will have over their own subservient daughters-in-law in the future—encourages a thorough internalization of patriarchy for the women themselves.[69]

Clearly, this is only a guess and that is why I cannot maintain that Olinda, unlike Teresa, believed that her husband's abuse and failure to meet his role of the male provider would excuse her for the crime of adultery. In fact, as noted above, one of the features that distinguishes the story of these two women is that while Olinda committed adultery because her husband ran away, Teresa initiated the love affair with her brother-in-law before leaving Italy and, in complicity with him, planned the escape to Tres Arroyos.

But let's return to compassion to take up again the story of Teresa and Salvador Calabrese. As Susan Bandes has pointed out, emotions are not monolithic, easily definable entities, therefore they need to be treated with a keen awareness of the role of a particular emotion in a specific context, since the same emotion takes different meanings according not only to who expresses it but also to the specific place and time in which it is expressed.[70] For example, the emotional style of defendants when making a statement at a police station or before a justice of the peace may not be identical to the ones they display in a first instance court— when they usually have legal counsel.

At the trial for Teresa's adultery, compassion adopted different meanings. In his declarations before the justice of the peace of Juárez and in the court of Dolores, Rosciano maintained the same compassionate tone. However, while in the first occasion he assumed the role of an observer and limited himself to describing Teresa's miserable situation and giving his opinion on the magnitude of her misfortune, in the courtroom he involved himself, expressing his own emotions. Pity and commiseration had allegedly moved him to become an accomplice in a crime at the request of a "desperate woman in need who is clearly innocent of the crime she is charged with." If there was anyone to blame, it was Calabrese, who had abandoned her in Italy with no means of sustenance.

According to Nussbaum, compassion is a painful emotion occasioned by the awareness of another person's undeserved misfortune. Like other emotions, compassion is concerned with value as it includes a judgment that the other person's distress is bad. However, as compassion takes up the onlooker's point of view, his judgment may differ from that of the person who suffers.[71] In fact, neither of Teresa's statements (before the justice of the peace and the investigation judge) referred to the desperate situation in which Rosciano depicted her. On the contrary, she appears determined to turn the tide of a miserable life. The migratory project, which perhaps originally had been a promise of well-being, imposed a long separation of the couple that ended up damaging the marital bond and brought her no material relief. What could Calabrese offer her when after six years in Argentina, he could not even afford the cost of a fare? In Teresa's view, a husband unable to support her could demand neither obedience nor love from her. Rosciano, instead, was the opposite of Calabrese: a prosperous small farmer who had gone to Italy for a visit, and who also afforded the cost of her travel to Buenos Aires. Was it a sexual attraction that drove her to enter an illicit relationship with her brother-in-law? Was it love? Or was it ambition? Most likely all these reasons converged. Perhaps even before departing from Naepoli, Teresa imagined a life that her husband would be unable to give her: a future safe from misfortune in the company of a man she could love and respect, who in turn could take care of her.

In nineteenth-century Italy, it was usual for adulteresses to defend themselves in judicial courts resorting to arguments identical to those of Teresa (and Felisa Lamar). The duty to provide sustenance to wife and children was constitutive of gender and family relationships. The husband's failure to fulfill it was legally enforceable and sufficient for the wife to obtain marital separation as well as an order of maintenance by her spouse. But with the reforms that followed the political unification of the peninsula and the adoption of a liberal legal system, the breach of that long-standing juridical and theological notion was perpetuated only in the civil courts, whereas in the criminal courts, an accusation of adultery was evaluated only as a sexual event. Nevertheless, cultural inertia meant that even at the end of the nineteenth century, many plaintiffs, and defendants, not aware of these changes, continued to rely on the legal language of the old regime system, which was temporal and spiritual at the same time. As Domenico Rizzo points out, until the adoption of the legal codes of the new state, the word "need," which denoted material and spiritual poverty, was sufficient to cause the convocation of the priest-judges of the *Tribunale del Vicario* in their concerns for pastoral care and the return of souls to sacramental practice. By confessing the truth of the accusation, and invoking "need" to justify the misconduct, women expected the adultery would be evaluated from a compassionate and comprehensive standpoint that took the overall situation of their marriage into account.[72]

Not surprisingly, the expectations of Teresa and Felisa were similar to those of the adulteresses Rizzo studies.[73] This might have been the reason why, although displaying different emotional styles, both women confessed having committed adultery. But what feelings did the accounts of their miserable lives provoke among the officers of the Argentine judicial system? It is not difficult to imagine how difficult it might have been for judges and prosecutors to feel compassion for these women. If they were to sympathize with anyone, it was not precisely with the adulteresses, but with their husbands, those betrayed figures who in their statements exaggerated the magnitude of the offenders' malice and claimed their lack of responsibility in the conjugal discord. Salvador Calabrese's lawyer requested a three-year prison sentence for Teresa, and the banishment for her accomplice, arguing that he had betrayed the trust and friendship of the plaintiff. The peddler acknowledged only a small portion of responsibility for what had happened: "having believed in the virtue and decency" of his wife, and "the honesty of his friend and brother-in-law . . . without his naiveté the crime would have not occurred." But the admission of the role played by his credulity did not prevent him from blaming Teresa, whom he described as "an ambitious and treacherous person," whose will to deceive him "became evident in the fact that she runaway at night," while he was in the countryside and those who could have "dissuaded her from committing the crime were asleep."[74]

Nussbaum noted that insofar as we feel compassion, it is either because we believe the person has come to grief without fault or because their suffering is out of proportion. However, if we believe that a person is in a painful situation due to his or her own fault, we will blame them rather than feeling compassion. As for the case of Teresa—and the other adulterous women—it must have been difficult, if not impossible, for the judge to sympathize with her. Social barriers of class, gender, and ethnic origin prove recalcitrant to the magistrate's imagination, and this recalcitrance prevented him from feeling compassion for the adulteress.[75] Hadn't Calabrese withdrawn the charges, in his sentence, the judge would have ended up—as usually occurred—blaming and punishing her anyway. Everything seemed to lead to that denouement as in Argentina, like in Liberal Italy, there was a clear separation between civil and criminal justice, and although the civil law also established the duty for the husband to maintain his wife, the failure to fulfill this liability had no defense value against the accusation of adultery. Such a case had to be treated by criminal court judges, who were limited to applying the law only to the sexual event since any other surrounding circumstance was outside of their legal competence. The representation of Calabrese as a double-betrayed husband, and the fact that Rosciano was married to one of the sisters of the adulteress, converged to make Teresa responsible for his sorrow.

Despite the peculiarities of each case, the judicial episodes in which Felisa, Josefa, Teresa, Olinda, and their husbands and lovers ended up involved, reveal the mutations that in the wake of the successive aftershocks of the small earthquake caused by emigration, female roles and representations of marriage and family life suffered. Adultery was one of the emerging features of these mutations. The affection that had once united the spouses—based on honor, the role of the men as providers, and the patriarchal value of obedience—was weakened when the husbands discontinued epistolary communication and eluded the commitment to send money. Then, out of compassion for the neglected wife, another man would offer her support, and in return, she would reward him with sexual gratification. The weakness of the flesh finally prevailed over the social norms of fidelity and decorum. Sometimes, the illicit relationship occurred in Europe, with a brother-in-law, a friend of the husband, a neighbor, or even with the parish priest.[76] But at other times, the adulteresses met their lovers after the couple's reunification.

Nonetheless, to estimate how extended this practice was on both sides of the ocean, and how much leniency adulterous women found in their moral communities is no easy task. As noted above, in southern Italy, detractors of emigration worried about the high social costs of the massive departure of men, insisted on an increase in the number of illegitimate children, concubinage, adultery, and women working as prostitutes.[77] Nevertheless, historians have proved that the unwanted effects of the departure of men on the behavior of women seem not to have been as deplorable as depicted by bourgeois critics (journalists, intellectuals, and politicians from northern Italy), who looked at the female peasants from the South of the country with moral disdain. Their gaze was biased by class privilege, misogyny, and ignorance of the logic that regulated work habits, gender, and family relations in peasant communities. In effect, illegitimate children, overcrowding, and lack of privacy were characteristic of the peasant life, not only in the South of Italy, but in several European regions long before the migratory fever spread over the continent.[78] An additional factor to bear in mind is that the departure of young men altered the balance of the sexes and therefore the number of available candidates for illicit relationships decreased. As young males departed, in the new social landscape children and women, both single ones and "widows of the living," abounded. Then, the opportunities of committing adultery were decreasing not only by moral norms but also by the weight of the new demographic reality.

The reunion of the spouses in Argentina did not always mean the continuation of the marital communion interrupted by distance, or the consummation of a shared project, since the promise of prosperity often vanished in the middle of hardships, overcrowded *conventillos*, and unfulfilled expectations of upward mobility. The outcome of such an onerous material and emotional venture looked even more disappointing when the woman joined her husband not out of desire but out of obedience and resignation. When the disparity in expectations provoked in one of the spouses the sensation that life in Buenos Aires was just the replica of a miserable past, the reproach, the insults, and the mistreatment ended up colonizing the marital relationship. In some cases, this violent magma migrated along with the married couple—as we will see in the next chapter—but in other occasions, love was transfigured into indifference, contempt, disaffection, and rancor, feelings that also arose from disillusionment. Rooted in a deep sense of frustration, men's anger was channeled through domestic violence, and when the situation reached "the limit of which [was] tolerable"—in terms of Olinda's defender—some women abandoned the marital home and committed adultery, in a society whose moral standards, and legal and religious prescriptions, were not much different from those that ruled in their places of origin.[79] Behind the notion that marriage protected women lay a gender and power asymmetry which, as Mark Seymour notes, gave the husband distinct privileges and helped to construct masculine identity.[80] In the religious sphere, marriage was a sacrament, and in the civil area it was a contract. Dominant values upheld the indissolubility of the bond in both domains, since the husband's superiority and honor were based on his wife's submission, fidelity, and domesticity.[81]

In Argentina, where cohabitation, illegitimate births, and female abandonment of the marital home were long-standing practices,[82] immigrant women had more chances of finding refuge in another man's arms. Unlike the case of the emigrant villages from where many of the women hailed, here demography played into immigrant women's hands. A fluid universe where more than half of the population was made up of young foreign men, turn-of-the-century Buenos Aires was a promise of anonymity, secrecy, and new love. Therefore, running away in the company of another man seemed easier and less daring than in the small close-knit communities where those women came from. When the escape occurred in the interior of the province, the sparsely populated territory of the Pampa, where police and justice exerted an uneven control, would mitigate the fear the determination to break the sacred vow of fidelity entailed.

# 4

# The Anatomy of Everyday Hatred

Mistreatment and psychological abuse were part of the family dynamics of both the places of origin of the immigrants and the society of destination. Although violence was not a structural feature in either context, both were social worlds in which attitudes to it oscillated between condemnation and indulgence.[1] In-turn-of-the-century Argentina, violence was a way to solve daily conflicts not only within the domestic sphere but also in public life. The household, the tenement courtyard, and the street often turned into the scenes of abuse and fights among neighbors, acquaintances, workmates, or bar patrons which usually resulted in physical harm. In the private domain, corporal punishment of wives and children was used to discipline, whereas in the public sphere, blows and fights with knives or firearms would be socially accepted as a redress against *injurias*, inflammatory words, or actions that harmed the reputation of an individual.[2] Although lawsuits over *injurias* were quite common in Argentina at that time, for many people violence seemed to be a more practical and effective remedy. Police reports and court records contain numerous complaints against individuals who resorted to physical force or weapons to solve a variety of situations: suspicions of infidelity, quarrels caused by daily trivialities, marital disputes over money, insults that harmed honor, and disagreements over the use of common areas in the tenement houses. However, this does not mean that violence organized social relationships, but rather that individuals regarded it as a legitimate means (among others) of defending their reputation and male authority, punishing deviant behavior, or solving domestic family tensions and everyday conflicts occurring beyond the boundaries of the home.

The Argentine press of the late nineteenth and early twentieth centuries portrayed daily violence in a myriad of scenes that, unlike the court record with whose information it is possible to trace a path and tell a story, narrate ephemeral episodes, which vanish from one day to the next. However, regarded as a whole, the police news section configures a catalog of events organized according to a kind of hierarchy of victims and aggressive behavior that sheds light on the gradations of tolerance or reproval of physical aggression. Approached from this angle, the press reveals a social macrocosm in which it is possible to frame and give meaning to judicial proceedings. To this end, I explored the police news from three newspapers published in late nineteenth- and early twentieth-century Buenos Aires: the Italian-Argentine *La Patria degli Italiani*, the Spanish-Argentine *El Correo Español*, and the Argentine *La Prensa*. Both the ethnic and the local press reported multiple news concerning domestic violence, but whereas the first one always revealed the identities of the individuals involved in the cases, *La Prensa* usually kept them anonymous, except when it came to homicide or child maltreatment. By contrast, *El Correo Español* devoted less space to crime news, did not seem interested in domestic violence, and usually described the episodes in a sober and discreet style, unlike the sensationalism used by its Argentine and Italian counterparts. In effect, on several occasions, the editor of *Correo Español* criticized the journalism that disclosed gory details and intimate information which, in his view, should remain confidential. For example, when the Spanish tailor Joaquín Turero y Miga killed his wife by cutting her throat because he suspected her of infidelity,[3] *La Prensa* published a long report laying bare the private life of the married couple and uncovering the most gruesome details of the murder. This "morbid interest" was condemned by *El Correo Español*, which briefly reported the uxoricide in a circumspect tone.[4]

Far from moderation, like a prying neighbor, *La Patria degli Italiani* published with the same degree of indiscretion both trivial brawls and horrible homicides, disclosing the names and even the addresses of the individuals involved. In an equidistant position, *La Prensa* covered a wider range of acts of violence than its Italian counterpart, which naturally privileged the events that occurred within the ethnic community. But regardless of the nuances, both papers abounded on the news about women injured by their husbands, children brutally punished by their fathers, and wives who, overwhelmed by mistreatment, grabbed a weapon to defend themselves from their abusive spouses. Although resorting to the evidence assembled from the newspapers it is not possible to assess either the intensity or the scope of domestic violence, the journalistic account gives access to the representations of violence circulating in the society of the time. These ideas, values, and meanings were based on (and, at the same time, sustained) the standards of the different emotional and moral communities that co-existed in Argentina in the late nineteenth and early twentieth centuries.[5]

Newspapers outlined scenes of marital life in which violence erupted and escalated, such as that of a husband who, in the middle of a quarrel, threw a plate over his wife's head, causing her a minor wound; or that of a laborer who came home from work to catch his wife *in flagrante* with another man and, dominated by fury, dragged her by the hair out into the tenement house courtyard to humiliate her in front of their neighbors, while the cowardly lover ran away half-naked. The newspaper headlines, as well as the preeminence of rhetorical devices such as sarcasm and hyperbole, reveal that in the face of domestic violence the press moved easily from tolerance to moral condemnation. In between stretched the vast territory of indifference, a sort of inertial attitude which resulted in dispassionate transcriptions of the reports that journalists picked up from police stations. Suicides, infanticides, thefts, street fights, and homicides constituted just another component of social life. Uninspiring titles like *Tra moglie e marito* (Between Wife and Husband), *Vita di famiglia* (Family Life), *Mujer herida* (Wounded Wife), or *Cansada de Denunciarlo* (Tired of Denouncing Him) were used time after time to report almost identical episodes in which only the names of the protagonists changed. Those brief accounts talked about wives who, after a marital quarrel, ended up hospitalized with bodily injuries of different gravity; about women who, despite the indifference of the police, insisted on reporting their abusive husbands; and about fathers who resorted to cruelty to educate their children.

Some news stories had sarcastic titles: *Carezze de marito* (Husband Caresses), *Le delizie della vitta conjugale* (Delights of Marital Life), or *Un marito modello* (A Model Husband), which introduced accounts of domestic quarrels caused by trivial matters, like the argument between Giovanni Nicoletta and María Cosentino over how to season cod. As the woman disregarded her husband's indications, he, "desperate to persuade her that she was using a wrong recipe," threw a plate at her head.[6] A similar situation occurred with a married couple lodged in a tenement house on Maipú Street in downtown Buenos Aires. Although *La Prensa* reported that they were Spanish immigrants, it did not reveal the names of the abuser or his victim "who has minor injuries in her face and her left arm." The newspaper reported that as the food was not "to the taste of the husband," he got angry and threw a saucepan at her.[7]

But among a myriad of small, everyday battles, the newspapers used to describe the stories of women brutally beaten or wounded with knives and guns by their husbands. On those occasions, when the victims were put on the verge of death, the newspapers expressed a moral sanction. *La Prensa* and *La Patria degli Italiani* sympathized with these women, pointing out the calvary of physical and spiritual abuse they had gone through until the "irascible behavior" of their husbands turned into physical aggression. The reporters used to condemn the abusers' brutality, degrading them to the inhuman condition of the beasts, and showed compassion for the mistreated women by using expressions such as: "the wretched woman," "the unfortunate wife," and "a miserable woman with an unbearable life." At the same time, however, the newspapers resorted to prescriptive scripts about family, female submission, and male authority, particularly when the victim was suspected of infidelity. In tight prose, the news spoke of wives who, after suffering fierce aggressions, were abandoned by their husbands and without medical assistance, bled out, suffering the piercing pain of a broken limb or a belly kicked and punched. On the verge of death, lying in bed or a pool of blood on the floor of a dark tenement room, many of them had their lives saved because neighbors called the public assistance and the police, or stood in the way of the aggressor, using force to curb his merciless rage.

Although it was more unusual, women's violence against their spouses also existed and was reported. To defend themselves from an attack or to prevent a beating announced by the increasingly exalted tone of an argument, wives wielded weapons or used blunt objects to defend themselves. That was what Catalina Garozzi did when, in the middle of a brawl, her husband threatened to kill her. She knew it was not a simple rhetorical declamation arising from the heat of a verbal contest, because in a kitchen cabinet the man kept a Bulldog revolver, which he had displayed in previous quarrels. But this time, Catalina went ahead of him, took the gun, and shot him five times in the legs. *La Patria degli Italiani* titled the news as *Furia di Una Moglie* (A Wife's Fury) and, at the end of the brief chronicle, pointed out that the "irascible lady" had been arrested.[8] Underlying the irony of the title and the characterization of the aggressor is a cultural script that weighs up anger from a gender perspective. Because of its inherent fragility and weak will, female anger was regarded as a challenge to male authority. While in a man a fit of rage was justified, in a woman it was considered a serious and dangerous character flaw because women's rage transgressed the notion of civilized female conduct. Self-control and restraint were crucial among the bourgeois list of women's virtues, and those who could not control their emotions were marginalized not only because they lost their femininity but also because anger was regarded as a "male" emotion. According to the standards of conduct and the display rules that regulated the expression of feelings, women should refrain from showing anger. When they did show it— transforming weakness and passivity into strength—that improper behavior was thought to be harmful and dangerous.[9]

Day by day, readers accessed these intimate worlds torn by conflict, moved by rancor, fear, and boredom, and immersed in suffering. Scenarios, protagonists, and details changed after a day, but the substance persisted. And although domestic violence was not the norm, it was present in many homes. In the case of immigrants, it is difficult to know if the easy insult and physical abuse was part of a dynamic of the marital relationship before migration or if, on the contrary, it was part of the emotional cost of a complex migratory process that entailed waiting, expectations, anxiety, and the mutation of the spouse's subjectivities. Although it is impossible to give a complete answer to this question, the legal proceedings for bodily harm that I analyze in the following pages allow us to look simultaneously at the individual (the microcosms enclosed in a file) and the collective (the broader social macrocosm); a connection about which, however, I will only dare to conjecture.

## The poverty and the rage

Running away from the fury of her husband, who had hit her head with an ax, Elvira Venezia slipped and fell on the floor. Warned by the screams, insults, and moans of pain, the neighbors crowded into the courtyard and, seeing what had happened, called the police. Elvira ended up in the hospital and her aggressor, Francisco Debenedetti, was arrested.[10]

Responding to the call of her husband, a 36-year-old Italian, the victim had arrived in Argentina in 1903. Francisco worked as a longshoreman in the port of Buenos Aires, was 38 years old, and had emigrated in 1896, leaving behind his wife and a small son with the vague promise of family reunification. Although seven years after his departure, he still had not managed to improve his economic position, Francisco managed to save enough money to pay for the tickets and called his family, because he believed that in Buenos Aires the prospects were more promising than in the small Neapolitan village he was from. However, according to Elvira's statements, almost three years after he had "forced her to travel to Argentina, the situation [of the family] was as bad as in Italy, and since the money was not enough, Debenedetti would press her to engage in prostitution."[11]

Elvira was still in the hospital when she testified about the brawl. She stated that it was not the first time that Francisco had injured her, and that night:

It was about 8:30 p.m. and she was in the room with her husband who was undressing to get into bed when she had a small altercation provoked by him, as a result of previous discussions . . . Debenedetti tells lies and is always quarreling just to elude the truth, which is that he does not bring any money because he has the same miserable job since he arrived in this country where supposedly he would become rich.[12]

However, when they were summoned to testify, the neighbors exposed a slightly different version, assuring that "the fights are frequent in the room … amid mutual insults and blows, Debenedetti always accuses Venezia of being unfaithful to him."[13] In line with the statements of the tenement house dwellers, Francisco claimed that the reason for the marital fight was that Elvira had cheated on him with an Italian called Silvio. He said that some months earlier, his wife had escaped from the marital home and after two days' search, he had found her "naked in bed in her lover's room." The scene "exasperated him, and so he threatened to kill Silvio, who reported him to the police."[14] Accused of public disorder and bodily harm, the Italian longshoreman spent six days in detention at the police station. When he was released, "the crime of adultery being ostensibly," he went to Silvio's home accompanied by a police officer and forced Elvira to return "to the marital home, where she has to live."[15]

In his statement before the judge, Francisco confessed that he had assaulted Elvira and that, "amidst the insults" she was uttering, he threatened to kill her lover. His testimony recreates the climate of tension in which the family lived. Anger was the emotion alluded to by both him and his lawyer to justify the beating and to request an exemption from prison. The accused argued that his wife's insults during the discussion "blinded him with anger" to the point that he could not remember how he went from screaming to hitting her, nor could he specify what object he used to attack her: "it could have been an ax or a shovel," he said. According to Francisco, the fury had also prevented him from noticing that Elvira was lying bleeding in the corridor of the *conventillo*. The witnesses confirmed that the aggressor had remained in the room, indifferent to Elvira's suffering, although they maintained that the reason for her brutal behavior had not been the blindness of anger but rancor and desire for revenge, although none of these emotions were mentioned again—neither by the aggressor nor by his defender—throughout the trial.

In turn, the public attorney pointed out that Elvira's statement was riddled with slander and exaggeration, that the beatings had not been of the magnitude "that [she] attributes to them," and that it was an "infamous lie that [her husband] had forced her into prostitution."[16] He argued that to judge Francisco's conduct, it was necessary to know the history of humiliation and dishonor to which his wife had subjected him, "a situation that could only lead to what finally happened." According to the lawyer, Elvira insulted her husband in private and in public, and every time he reprimanded her, she "showed him contempt." These attitudes, added to the repeated escapes from the marital home, had ended up filling Francisco with "an angry passion that weakened his nerves."[17]

As the public attorney alleged that the injuries inflicted by Francisco on his wife's body were mild, the judge ordered Elvira to be examined by the forensic doctors. The examination was carried out in the tenement house—where Francisco had forced her to return—four months after the incident. The medical report concluded that none of the injuries had been serious; that "they only took between fifteen and twenty days to heal;" that they were scarred at the time of the examination; and that they had not caused "physical defect, functional disorder, or incapacity to work."[18] Although Francisco was sentenced to nine months in prison, in his verdict the judge noted that the act had been "provoked by the offended party because of her constant insults, her serious misconduct, her expressions of contempt and disobedience to her husband and her repeated and public illicit behavior."[19] Unlike the defender, the judge did not allude to the blinding effects of rage and passion; however, by focusing on the victim's improper and irreverent behavior, the magistrate circumvented Francisco's responsibility, at least at the discursive level.

In this court proceeding, anger was used as an argument by both the defendant and the lawyer to mitigate the punishment, while the judge considered that the humiliation to which Elvira had submitted her husband, running away on several opportunities with Silvio, explained the bloody outcome of the fight. The woman's body, a map furrowed with scars that delimited the territory of a turbulent relationship, was explored by the public authorities to assess the sharpness and depth of the traces left by Francisco's virulent incursion. The doctors' diagnosis was one of the main inputs to the judge's verdict, which, however, also made use of a moral appreciation of the victim's conduct, which he described as "illicit" and "improper," in a clear allusion to adultery.

Although this sentence still rested on the notions of classic law, the influence of the positivist criminology—that was gaining ground in the Argentine criminal justice in the late nineteenth century—is hinted at in the biological notion of "responsibility" introduced by the public attorney when arguing that the aggressor's anger was a passion rooted in the nervous system.[20] Furthermore, the trial not only reveals an eclectic intermingling of moral condemnation and the criteria of positivist criminology, but also the existence of a point where the conception of the accused and of justice converged on the social relevance of male honor, and of female decorum and obedience. Embedded in a web of common meanings, the differences of class, power, and origin between a poor immigrant, an official defender, and a judge were blurred—at least rhetorically—when the responsibility of the aggressor was weighed in the light of the feminine conduct that was deviated from the standards and norms of the patriarchal family.

By contrast, when in February 1908 Teresa Brasca reported her husband, Mariano Darbano, it was she who evoked the "angry passion" to explain the brutal attack she had been the victim of. The woman, a 34-year-old Italian, told that on the morning of the event she was denouncing, "her husband had placed a piece of zinc sheet in the kitchen to improvise a door, and as she thought it was dangerous to leave it there," she decided to remove it. When he noticed what his wife was doing, Mariano got upset and started insulting her, but as she replied, the man pulled her hair and started punching and kicking her until Teresa fell to the floor. The husband then placed one of his knees firmly on the woman's belly and continued to beat her. Her screams caught the attention of the neighbors of the house next door, who ran to her aid. In between struggles, they tried to get the angry husband to stop punishing Teresa, but the man did not back down and, although he freed the woman from his grip, he threatened to kill her while he sought "some blunt object that could serve as a weapon." However, according to Elvira's testimony at the police station, "he did not find anything suitable to kill her because of the obfuscation and the angry passion that seized him." When the neighbors let their guard down and left the house believing that the aggressor had finally calmed down, Mariano bit Teresa on the arm, causing her a wound. It was not the first time he had had such an extreme reaction, as he had already marked her body with his bites on several occasions.[21]

Francisco Debenedetti ended up at the police station because his neighbors reported him. By contrast, and despite their intervention, the neighbors of Darbano did not report him to the police, perhaps because they were afraid of the Italian's brutality or most likely because they were used to those furious explosions in which, after showing his wild side, Mariano would cool down. Then, the neighborhood recovered its calm and in that tense silence, Teresa's injured body began to heal. Unlike Elvira and so many other women who ended up unconscious, lying on the floor, bloody, and with broken bones, Teresa was able to stand up. But once the neighbors left the scene, her husband locked her in a room and, indifferent to the pain and severity of her injuries, placed a chair in the doorway and sat there insulting her. When he finally fell asleep, Teresa slipped out of the house and reported him at the police station.

A few hours later, the aggressor was arrested by the police and, in his statement, he admitted to having physically and verbally assaulted his wife. He argued that he had been "forced to do so to prevent his wife from behaving like the head of the home." The 46-year-old illiterate Italian day laborer told the story with detachment and conviction. He explained that he had placed a piece of zinc sheet on the floor of his house to prevent water from entering on rainy days and that his wife, whom Mariano described as grumbling and unhappy, "protesting that it was dangerous, removed it."[22] Mariano further declared that he placed the piece of zinc again warning her that if she were to remove it, he "would slap her." Teresa "replied in a bad way" and that unleashed a fight that soon went from insult to physical aggression. Allegedly, the woman scratched his face, and "to defend himself," Mariano began to punch her, but "the curses and insults did not stop, and he was forced to bite her." He finished his statement by asserting that "Brasca is not a bad person, but she is very nervous, and her irritability causes permanent fights in the marriage."[23]

When the forensic examination confirmed the injuries on Teresa's body, Darbano was brought to justice and the judge ordered his pretrial detention. But the day he was to be transferred to the penitentiary, Teresa appeared at the police station pleading for his release. She explained that it was not her intention that her husband should end up in jail for a simple marital dispute, and tried to withdraw the complaint by arguing that she was forgiving Mariano because "in no way can she allow her husband to be put in prison . . . since her livelihood and that of her minor children depends entirely on the resources that Darbano brings home and if he is imprisoned, the whole family will be left in destitution."[24]

However, the woman's clamor could not interrupt the course of the process which, eight months later, ended with a sentence of one and a half years of effective imprisonment. After denouncing her husband, Teresa's existence entered a gorge flanked on one side by the fear of Mariano's physical aggression and the other by fear of misery. She had turned to the police out of a combination of impulse and ignorance. She was probably unaware of the procedures that a complaint of abuse would trigger. Although the popular classes made intense use of the judicial system (both the justice of the peace and the legal system), which suggests that they possessed a body of legal knowledge—what Lila Caimari has called *la ley de los profanos* (the law of the profane)[25]—it is also true that they perceived the police as an extra-judicial actor, as an institution that embodied the law and was capable of resolving domestic disputes—whatever their gravity and nature—within the police station. This was not a conventional notion of the law, but rather an imprecise version that was born in the popular imagination, which ignored the categories of codification and the existence of procedures that guided a path of which the police were only the first step. Perhaps it was this mistaken perception that led Teresa to suppose that reporting her husband to the police would have no more consequence than a few days of arrest. What she did not know was that bodily harm was considered a crime under the Penal Code and that a complaint like hers would end up being the first folio of a court record. When that happened, the medical examiners, prosecutors, and lawyers came on the scene, and the arrest through which Teresa had tried to teach her husband a lesson became a pretrial detention. She realized then that her chances were so slim that she was not even allowed to choose between a violent but providing husband or misery.

In the cases of Debenedetti and Darbano, the allusions to anger (sometimes referred to as rage or passion) and nerves were part of the narrative of defendants, litigants, defense attorneys, and judges. However, those words which expressed both an emotion and its pathological manifestation had different meanings and uses in each of the trials. In the first one, Francisco Debenedetti and his defender resorted to anger to avoid punishment. Although the attorney appealed to expert knowledge talking about excitability and weakening of nerves, and the defendant related his emotions in a more "profane" way, both interventions converged in the intention to represent Francisco as a victim of his own feelings. On his part, Mariano Darbano, far from hiding behind the rage that according to Teresa had dominated him during the quarrel, justified his criminal behavior by claiming the right to exert his authority over his wife. He described the facts unmoved, trying to present arguments that would sound reasonable in a patriarchal society where women owed obedience to their husbands. But in addition to portraying Teresa as insubordinate, he stated that his wife was "irritable and nervous," two traits of character that aggravated her deviant behavior and justified his resorting to mistreatment to correct her.

## The women's money

As we saw in the previous chapter, overwhelmed by domestic violence, women used to find emotional refuge in infidelity and abandonment of the home. Escape and adultery (which did not always go hand in hand) were the final chapter of stories of marital disagreement punctuated by cross-insults, abuse, and humiliation. These stories often repeated a pattern: after a beating, the woman was either expelled from the home by the husband or she ran away, seeking the protection of relatives, friends, or neighbors. When the anger ceased, the husband would try to get her back and she would usually agree to return home, even if she did so not out of love but out of necessity, to ensure her subsistence. This fragile equilibrium was broken again and again until, if another man crossed her path, adultery, and runaway—although these were risky options—became the promise of a better life. However, that was not the only way out of abuse. For some women, a de facto separation was also a way to escape authoritarianism and domestic violence. But going down this road required minimal conditions: a job, money, and a place to live.

Each in their own way, María Schiavo and Emilia Vigo tried to turn the tide of their miserable existences by freeing themselves from emotional landscapes pervaded by disaffection, contempt, resentment, and fear. But in a society that severely punished adultery and whose civil legislation obliged the wife to live with her husband "wherever he fixes residence,"[26] and established her obligatory subordination to the man's legal representation, this freedom could be ephemeral, because it placed these women on the margins of the law.

Ángel Marinelli made use of this situation of legal vulnerability when, in 1891, he denounced his wife, María Schiavo, because she was living "in scandalous concubinage with Eustaquio Ardil, a married man with a family, with whom she had a child."[27] The husband claimed that his wife had run away from home in late 1889, leaving him in charge of two small daughters and stealing money from him. A few days later, María was arrested. At the police station, the adulteress declared that she had married Ángel in August 1884 and that two months later he, "a man inclined to drink and very lazy," began to subject her "to all kinds of punishment."[28] However, while they still lived in Italy, surrounded by relatives and neighbors, Marinelli would restrain from showing "his beastly character" because María "had once denounced him before her father and brothers, who had severely admonished him."

When María and Ángel emigrated to Buenos Aires, freed from María's family vigilance, he continued to beat her "more and more brutally and after each fight, he would throw her out, forcing her on one occasion to go out naked in the street." However, when the rage subsided, Ángel would go to a friend's house, where María would take refuge, begging her to return home, and she would agree, "not out of love or obedience, but out of necessity."[29] María's situation changed in the fall of 1889, with the arrival of Eustaquio Ardil's at the *conventillo*, which offered her an emotional refuge. Ardil, whose room was next to that of Ángel and María, a location that made him an involuntary witness to the couple's fights, ended up becoming María's lover. For a while, they kept the relationship underground until, tired of her husband's abuse, María, who had just turned 22, decided to run away with Ardil, with whom she lived for two years, until he committed suicide. A few months had passed since that misfortune when a police officer knocked on her door. Ángel had reported her for adultery and theft.

However, during the trial, the woman's unfaithful behavior shifted to the margins of judgment. Ángel's only interest was to recover the money that his wife had allegedly stolen from him. According to María's testimony before the investigating judge, she had deposited the money in a bank account using a false identity and marital status: "Mercedes de Ardil, widow," and had given the passbook to her friend, the one who would help her every time Ángel threw her out of the house.[30] However, during the investigation, María defended herself saying that the real motive behind the accusation of adultery was that Eustaquio had "donated her some *pesos* of which her husband wanted to appropriate, as well as of four chairs and some chickens which also belong to her."[31]

While his wife was detained, Ángel requested authorization to dispose of the deposit and provided the court with information obtained from his own investigation: the name and address of the bank and the identity and whereabouts of the woman who had the savings book in custody. According to María's public defender, behind such a thorough research hid "Marinelli's true intentions: revenge, greed and malice." The attorney affirmed that Ángel was not only aware that María cohabited with another man, but that he "consented to it."[32] Nevertheless, Marinelli's attitude changed because of greed:

> After the sad event of the suicide, when he learned of the existence of the deposit which is the inheritance that Ardil left to Schiavo shortly before making his fatal decision, it only then occurred to him to accuse her! ... Under the cover of adultery, he wants to take possession of that money and other property.[33]

Ángel tried to prove the fallacy of the defender and the adulteress, in a letter addressed to the judge where he asked him to summon twelve witnesses to testify that "in his condition of an honorable man he never approved of Schiavo's illicit relationship." He alleged that although he had tried to get her back by denouncing the escape, "it was not possible to find her whereabouts because my wife and her beloved were moving permanently." In the letter, Ángel remarked that while they were married, María "was never treated cruelly ... she enjoyed freedom and had all the money that [he] obtained by working as a bricklayer."[34] To complicate the woman's situation, he further asserted that she was aware that her accomplice was married. According to Ángel, Eustaquio had left Italy, promising to call his wife and his two children to Buenos Aires, but when he met María he broke the promise and abandoned them to live with her in concubinage.

The witnesses corroborated Ángel's testimony, his wife was sentenced to two years in prison, and the judge authorized him to dispose of the bank deposit. The defense appealed the sentence alleging that the husband and the lover were co-responsible for having pushed "this unfortunate woman into adultery, Marinelli by subjecting her to suffering, and Ardil by awakening in her the passion."[35] But this argument did not convince the judges of the Chamber of Appeals and María had to serve her sentence in jail.

Marital abuse also drove Emilia Vigo to separate from Guillermo Guardamagna after two decades of marriage. Emilia had come from Italy in 1886 to reunite with her husband, who had been living in Buenos Aires since late 1884. The new century found them still living in a *conventillo* and subsisting on temporary jobs, he as a bricklayer and she as a laundress. The lack of money was the cause of recurring verbal disputes, threats, and abuse. Unable to escape her husband's authoritarianism, Emilia sunk into bitterness and resignation, until a job as a cook in the Gowland residence, the home of an upper-class Buenos Aires family, and a tiny service room opened a window through which she could escape her suffering.[36] In the fall of 1902, at the age of 52, Emilia abandoned her husband and her job turned into her emotional refuge.

Only six months had passed when Guillermo appeared at Emilia's workplace asking her for money to travel to the countryside to look for work. But she refused, even though he insisted that as he was her husband, he had the right to dispose of what she earned. Then the couple was caught in a tide of crossed insults and reproaches amidst of which Guillermo, "full of anger and malice," attacked Emilia with a knife that he had hidden in his clothes. He inflicted upon her nine stab wounds that brought her to the brink of death.[37]

Although in court Guillermo confessed to the crime and expressed his repentance, he subsequently portrayed his wife in an unfavorable manner:

> Emilia Vigo has always been a woman with a bad temper, but in recent years her temper has worsened because she turned sour and grumpy and very prone to insults and recrimination. This bad behavior has filled the defendant with unhappiness, even taking away his work habits.[38]

He also told that shortly after he and his wife settled in Buenos Aires, he had been arrested for a month for threatening Emilia with a gun, although when he regained his freedom, she forgave him, and they resumed marital life. According to a niece of the defendant, after that episode, her uncle's behavior continued to be "just as aggressive and brutal as always," and her aunt's marriage was dominated by rancor, and constant brawls and fights over money, because:

> Although [Emilia] received clothes to wash and iron at home for many years, the
> family income was always low because Guardamagna worked little and spent a
> lot drinking in *boliches* [small bars] without making any contribution to the
> sustenance of the household.[39]

The witness described Emilia as a "perpetual victim of her husband" and told the
story of "beastly treatment, beatings, wounds and threats" that her aunt had
suffered "for years because of the lack of money." His words convinced the
prosecutor that Guillermo was "an extreme type of human beast" capable of
murdering his "miserable, old wife, whom the law and religion oblige to love and
protect for the sole purpose to appropriate her savings to satisfy selfish instincts."[40]

Instead, the defense attorney, appealing to the usual recourse to anger to
justify the conduct of the accused, alleged that:

> It was Emilia's refusal to give her husband the money that also belongs to him
> because they are legally married . . . her recriminations, insults and screams what
> prompted Guillermo Guardamagna into a fury that blinded him to the point of
> drawing a knife that he always carried with him and unwittingly wounding his
> spouse.[41]

Although one of the stabs may have caused Emilia's death, the defense attorney
argued that neither the attempted murder nor the premeditation was proven.
Therefore, Ángel should be tried for "only the crime of injury."[42] The judge agreed
with the attorney that the evidence was not enough to determine the existence
of the intention to kill; however, he maintained the charges and sentenced
Guillermo to three years in prison.

At different stages of their lives, María and Emilia walked through divergent
paths to escape their husbands' cruelty. Their stories, however, converge at the
same point: money. In the cases of Marinelli and Guardamagna, money was the
cause of repeated marital disputes which resulted in physical and emotional
abuse. Money played a central role in the family migratory project and its
prominence—not only in these cases, but in the rest of the stories told in this
chapter—reveals the complex dynamics of marital relationships marked by the
expectations that migration awoke in those women who had no other choice but
uprooting to obey the call of their husbands.

When Ángel and Guillermo migrated, they left their wives in Italy to take care
of the children and the management of the family's scarce resources (possibly
including remittances). In Chapter II, I noted that the work of waiting understood
as "an active attempt to realize a collectively imagined future" was an integral part
of the migration strategy.[43] As several studies that explored the intersection of

gender and migration have demonstrated, the departure of the husbands transformed women's lives and social roles, as they were crucial for the realization of the migratory project by looking for the interest of the family, and carving new economic opportunities with the remittances their husbands sent from abroad. Performing their new roles, while their husbands were toiling far from home, women crossed the borders of the domestic and community life to participate in the consumer economy, made financial and real estate transactions, and went to post offices, banks, and civil registers. Nevertheless, all those activities remained supervised at a distance by the absent husbands.[44] Migrants' letters reveal how husbands intended to exert control over the use of the money in a language that reinforced both the notions of marital and parental responsibility, as well as the idea that migration was a common family endeavor.[45] But when remittances were insufficient (like those few pesetas that Luis Aldaz sent to his wife so that she would buy a floral dress for their little daughter);[46] or when the money never arrived, women provided for the subsistence needs of the family through their own income, and their dreams of upward social mobility were deferred until they received their husbands' call to join them in the "land of prosperity."

Abundant or meager, money was the core of the migratory strategy and affected the bond between wives and husbands separated by the ocean and united by remittances. With its dramatic intervention in marital relationships, money caused anxiety and uncertainty. Perhaps for those women who endured abuse, more than the promise of material prosperity, migration represented a chance for achieving conjugal harmony. Getting out of poverty would help them to break the vicious circle of marital disputes over money, which inexorably ended up in domestic violence. As noted by Kwon, present and future were not stable temporalities for couples engaged in a migratory project, but rather a set of "malleable possibilities" that partners actively manipulated to overcome uncertainty and despair.[47] Nevertheless, when after the reunification of the spouses, long stays of the family in crowded tenement houses, job shortages, and low family income dissolved the expectations of having a house of their own, attaining upward social mobility, and enjoying some kind of marital harmony, violence would take over the daily life of the couple again. The shadow of the past used to pervade the present, taking the shape of the scene masterfully narrated by Cesare Pavese in *The Moon and the Bonfires*. When the old Valino took off his belt and beat his wife as a beast, one could hear her shrieking from the valley of the Belbo. People said Valino used to do it when he was drunk, "but it was not wine, they did not have as much as that, it was the utter misery and his rage at his life which never gave him a break."[48]

As pointed out above, to break free from marital abuse women needed economic resources and a place to live. María Schiavo secured her livelihood and shelter by becoming the concubine of Eustaquio Ardil. Shortly before her partner committed suicide, she began to manage money that, according to her understanding, belonged to her. Emilia, instead, escaped a long history of submission and abuse by separating from Guillermo when she got job as a domestic and the possibility of a room in her employers' home. Until then, she had earned an income working at home as a laundress. In Guillermo's perspective, that money was not hers, but rather constituted a contribution to the family budget, of which he could dispose at will (let us remember that, in a moral allusion to the use of money, one of the witnesses pointed out that what Emilia earned with effort, her husband spent on alcoholic beverages). That perception—apparently oblivious to any moral tension between collective management and individual spending—did not change much with the separation.[49] The fact that Emilia did not live in the marital home did not mean that the money she earned no longer belonged to the marriage. This is revealed by the conviction with which Guillermo declared at the trial that it was "his right to have it available to pay for a trip to the countryside."[50]

However, when his wife refused to give him the amount he was asking for, Guillermo understood that a new logic was beginning to regulate the power relationship in his marriage. Emilia's refusal not only affected him in that situation of shortage (he had no job and no means to get one) but also reverted the asymmetrical relationship he had maintained with his wife for almost twenty years. Guillermo sought to solve this asymmetry by using physical strength—a resource he had resorted to since the time they were still living together, and Emilia behaved as a submissive wife in the attempt to recover material and symbolic power. Let us recall that in his statement, he insisted that it was his wife's insults rather than her refusal to give him money that provoked the fury that drove him to wound her. As in other bloody incidents, in this case the violent action was rooted in old and recurrent marital conflict over the use of money. But given its expressive effectiveness, the physical aggression suffered by Emilia exceeds its instrumental meaning. That effectiveness reveals its eminently relational and intersubjective aspect, since the violent act always refers to others and, particularly, to one's place in front of others. As Myriam Jimeno maintains, the expressive efficacy and the coercive capacity of the act of violence may be regarded as a means of reaffirming the person in the world and a form of negotiation with the other.[51]

Despite the differences, in these two episodes, money was conceived as a moral account unit rather than as a unit of payment or exchange.[52] Regarded from this perspective, the value of a piece of money shows how people create and recreate the family social order in the monetary sphere, which involves both mutual assistance and conflicts, helping complete the family projects or tearing them apart. Emilia's money had not only been "earned," but it had been also "safeguarded" by the frugality and careful administration.[53] According to the prosecutor, it was "the product of the work, sacrifice, and savings of a poor woman subjected to mistreatment by a husband who never did anything with perseverance, apart from spending the fruit of his wife's effort on drinking."[54]

During the years when Emilia lived with Guillermo, her effort to safeguard their household economically by increasing, administering, and sharing the family income failed over and over again due to the selfishness of her husband. On the other hand, in the case of María, money in its moral sense turned out to be inseparable from adultery. In the trial, it was never quite clear whether it was "ill-gotten" or "donated" money, because even assuming that it was a bequest from her lover, the idea that it might have been a payment for sexual favors pervaded the arguments in the trial. When the public attorney appealed the sentence in the first instance, he emphasized that the defendant had "fallen into adultery and cohabitation, overwhelmed by suffering and weakened by the passion that Eustaquio Ardil had aroused in her." But this did not "turn her into a prostitute, as shown by her irreproachable conduct after the suicide of her lover."[55]

The female protagonists of the four stories narrated in this chapter ran away— by different means—from their abusive husbands. In a context that replicated the miserable living conditions in their places of origin in Europe, loud arguments, insults, threats, and physical aggression were not new to the dynamics of the conjugal life. On the contrary, violence was ingrained in these marital relationships. The statements of María Schiavo, who recounted how her husband beat her in Italy and how migration had made the aggressions even more intense, or Teresa Brasca's call for the release of a man who was trying to subordinate her by beating and biting her reveal that beyond the uniqueness of each case, domestic violence also migrated. Furthermore, when the expectations awakened by the "land of promise" were not met, marital conflict and maltreatment tore the marriage apart, and even more dire, put women on the verge of death.

As Katie Barclay argues, in the patriarchal system, obedience and love were not incompatible terms.[56] However, it is also true that an emotional education based on submission of women to their husbands' authority legitimized the exercise of male power through force and abuse. And even if it was a symbolic legitimization—because the law provided a penalty for anyone who caused injury to another's body—obedience as a social habitus tolerated the female's body abuse. Mariano Darbano justified his violent conduct in Teresa's insubordination and she, faced with the dilemma of misery or beatings, resigned herself to violence. This resignation was probably also what plunged Emilia Vigo into the condition of "perpetual victim" of her husband, until she finally dared to abandon him, when she had already crossed the threshold of 50 years old. In the sentence that condemned Francisco Debenedetti, the judge showed his attachment to the prescriptive conception of marriage as a system of power when he reproached Elvira for her insulting and disobedient behavior. This attitude reveals a convergence of the cultural scripts of the defendants (who represented themselves as victims of unfaithful and insubordinate wives and of passions that blinded their reason) and of those who should judge their crimes. Dominant patriarchal values created a common ground for these men to share a similar perspective that crossed over sociocultural and national divides. The same background appears to have sustained a common vision about the role of women in marriage, power relationships between spouses, and female obedience, regardless of whether they were defendants, defense attorneys, prosecutors, judges, Argentinians, or foreigners.

# 5

# The Passion of Jealousy

Misery, male alcoholism, disobedience, and infidelity—real or presumed—were the reasons alleged by women and men involved in domestic violence court cases. When summoned to testify, witnesses often revealed that the event reported was not exceptional, but part of a chain of boisterous marital brawls crossed by insults and abuse. But when, in addition to the blows, the aggressors resorted to threats and wielded a weapon—even if it was only for showing off power—the dispute pushed the victims to the edge of life.

In the uxoricides (wife killings) committed by Ángel Fiorda and Joaquín Turero y Miga, which I analyze in this chapter, death was the dramatic ending of a multiform domestic conflict.[1] The relevance that adultery, jealousy, and insanity took on in both trials blurs the full picture of the marital dispute, and although in each case the witnesses alluded to it, the underlying causes (besides adultery itself) are barely described. In their testimonies, the witnesses strove to describe the fateful hour, when the victims' cries for help led them to the bloody scene. And although they all evoked the powerful echo of the marital fights that from the time before the crime, day after day, flooded the courtyard of the *conventillo*, they do not speak of the reasons—likely for they ignored them. However, intertwined in the ambiguous declarations in which the killers blamed the victims to justify their murderous acts, the first blows of the stormy winds that were to turn the marriage into a hurricane were insinuated.

Both ethnic and Argentine newspapers covered extensively these uxoricides, describing them in a bombastic rhetoric that departed from the more subdued judicial semantics, in which phrases common in journalistic chronicle were rarely used. One of them was the word *amor* (love), to which the newspapers resorted to address the turbulent intimacy of marital relationships caught in a spiral of violence. Although without avoiding the moral sanction against the murderers, the journalists found in love the reason for the murderous behavior. Considered as a two-faced emotion, love is a source of happiness and pleasure, and at the same time, a sick passion that causes jealousy and insanity. Journalists relied on these notions in their attempt to elucidate the reasons that drove a husband to kill his wife. However, in their chronicles, these two notions of love usually provoked tension between admonishment and sympathy for the perpetrator. For example, in the fall of 1902, *La Patria degli Italiani* reported the tragedy that adultery and betrayal had caused to the marriage of Giuseppe de Simone and Rosa Pastori. The husband had killed his wife by hitting her several times with a hammer on the head because he caught her *in flagrante*, lying in bed with his own brother, whom Giuseppe had hosted upon his arrival from Italy a few weeks before the tragedy. Although the newspaper described the crime as "brutal and horrific," it also expressed pity for "the poor Simone, who was deeply in love with his wife, and upset by the collapse of his happy marriage, ended up killing her."[2]

The press often portrayed the victims as "ardent and sensual" women "of loose morals" and presented their murderers as individuals tormented by a sick love that turned them into "myopic and maniac men" capable of forgiving their misguided wives again and again until, subdued by jealousy, they ended up committing a crime. Seized "by the ungovernable passion," the husbands, who not only felt love for their wives but also "professed it,"[3] crossed the blurred line that separates physical abuse from uxoricide, and instead of resorting to justice, they punished the adulterous wives, imposing sentences according to their own discretion within the four walls of a tenement room. In contrast to the newspapers, the law maintained the illusion of impartiality and aloofness by representing itself—mainly through the figure of the judges—as an emotionally neutral territory.[4] However, although more restrained than that of the press, the language of the court records also was permeated by emotions and often referred to "the passion of jealousy" both as a temporally mental disturbance and as a catalyst for the violence caused by female infidelity.

## While Virginia was sleeping

It was seven in the afternoon of August 5, 1893. The sun had already set. Gerónima Lauría, a young Italian woman who lived in a tenement house on Azcuénaga Street in downtown Buenos Aires, was alone in her room when she heard screams coming from the back of the building. Believing that it was just another one of the usual quarrels between Filomena Mastrostefano and her husband, Ángel Fiorda, the young woman continued with her chores and did not even come out to look. Other neighbors also heard the noise, but nobody paid attention, perhaps because, within the emotional repertoire of the dwellers of the *conventillo*—inhabited mostly by Italian immigrants—a marital brawl was a common occurrence. But when Filomena's cries for help revealed that it was more than just a quarrel, Gerómina called the street police officer and they both discovered the Fiordas' room had become a scene of horror. Filomena was lying on the floor in the middle of a pool of blood, while her daughter, Virginia, a 5-year-old girl, was sleeping at the foot of her parents' bed.[5] When the police station chief and the doctor arrived in the tenement, Filomena's cries had turned into weak moans. But before being transferred to hospital, where she died some few hours later, she managed to point to her husband as the aggressor. When the police captured Ángel, who was trying to run away after throwing the weapon into the courtyard of the adjoining house, he not only confessed to stabbing Filomena, but "raising his arms, said he did not care a bit if the police put him in jail for he had done to his wife just what she deserved because she had a *macho*."[6]

The intricate storyline of the relationship of Ángel and Filomena (detailed in the following pages) reveals several aspects of the dynamic of male authority and how it was emotionally expressed. Likewise, the case shows that marital conflict usually went through successive instances of resolution, which involved conflicting emotions and did not respect a unidirectional trace. In other words, these conflicts did not necessarily go from the intimate to the public domain, but rather their path alternated between one sphere and the other, configuring a complex transition that involved different emotions articulated in a *crescendo* of violence in which shame, indignation, and jealousy usually turned into rancor, hatred, and contempt.

Before the tragic ending that changed the destiny of his family forever, Ángel's emotional journey adopted a circular shape. When he discovered his wife's infidelity, he sought a resolution to his marital conflict in the private domain, but later he turned twice to the police. On the first occasion, he had an agent accompany him to recover his wife, who had escaped with her lover. On the second, he reported Filomena for adultery and had her arrested. But on the eve of the murder, he withdrew his complaint and brought the conflict back into the home, where he tried to mend the bond—or pretended that this was his intention—in the same intimate domain in which it had been broken.

In an idyllic, albeit not innocent, tone *La Prensa* reported the crime, choosing a chronology of the story that allowed both to depict the gradual deterioration of the marital bond, and to reinforce the patriarchal ideology. Dating back to 1886, the newspaper began the chronicle of the crime by evoking the arrival of Ángel and his brand-new wife in Buenos Aires. Two years later, Filomena gave birth to a girl. Then, while her husband worked as a bricklayer, she took care of the household chores and the baby girl. According to *La Prensa*, "the happiness of that modest home was complete," until Francisco Cocucci, a neighbor of the Fiordas, "decided to ruin the peace and harmony that reigned in the young couple." In Ángel's absence, Francisco visited Filomena and began to "paint with vivid colors the love she had inspired in him." Little by little, she was lured by his advances, until she finally succumbed to "an intense passion for the seducer that made her feel uncomfortable every sunset when her husband returned from work." At this point—the journalistic chronicle continues—the lovers "needed complete freedom to live the passion, therefore, they decided to run away, taking the child with them, along with Fiorda's savings, the fruit of long-time thrift and deprivation."[7]

According to *La Prensa*, "after discovering that Filomena had deceived him and not knowing her whereabouts, [Fiorda] did nothing but weep." But when he finally learned that Filomena and her lover were in Rosario, a city in the province of Santa Fe, "he was determined to get his wife and little daughter back."[8] Then, he abandoned his job and traveled almost 300 kilometers to force Filomena to return, which he accomplished with the help of a police officer. However, despite his efforts, the bricklayer did not manage to break the bond between his wife and her lover. A few weeks after the couple resumed marital life, Ángel learned that Francisco Cocucci had returned to Buenos Aires. He decided then to move his family to the tenement house on Azcuénaga Street, where soon afterward he would take the life of his wife.

In court, Ángel declared that the afternoon before the murder, upon returning from work, he caught Cocucci "kissing and fondling his wife." Moved with indignation, he called the street police officer to take them to the police station, where he filed a complaint for adultery, which resulted in the arrest of Filomena and her accomplice. The happiness to which the chronicle of *La Prensa* alluded does not seem to have been what troubled Ángel, but the sense of marital authority that his wife had broken for the second time, and the way in which his wife's behavior affected the dynamics of power distribution in the marriage. Ángel transferred the conflict from the private domain to the public one so that the police would mend a relationship that he could no longer control. However, the day after the complaint was filed, he appeared at the police station and, arguing that he had forgiven Filomena, he requested that she be released.

As noted above, it was not an uncommon practice for husbands to forgive adulterous women. To some extent, the duration and intensity of the punishment depended on the will of the offended party, since the Penal Code gave him the right to "remit the punishment of his spouse at any time."[9] In the late nineteenth and early twentieth centuries, several Argentine jurists proposed that adultery should no longer be considered a crime because, in practice, the unfaithful spouse was never convicted.[10] In 1903, one of the members of the commission in charge of the reform of the Penal Code, Deputy Juan Antonio Argerich, presented evidence of 100 trials for adultery of which only three had ended with a sentence, although the penalty was not effective "because the husband had forgiven the convicted woman to resume conjugal life with her."[11] In line with these assessments, the adulteries analyzed in Chapter III reveal that, in most cases, the charges were dropped at the close of the investigation and only a minority of the litigants did so after the conviction.[12] The length of pre-trial detention and the suffering of women in prison were the unit of measurement for the resentment and anger that adulterous women caused in the betrayed husbands. Let us recall the case of Pedro Lamar, who did not hesitate to send his wife to prison knowing that she was pregnant, nor was he moved when he learned that her delicate state of health had forced the authorities at the Dolores prison to transfer her to the hospital. Pedro waited for his wife to give birth in prison and only then requested her release.

Filing the adultery claim and speculating on the extent of the imprisonment and the amount of the adulterer's suffering involved cumbersome bureaucratic procedures, time, and money, but it also required emotional organization. Although I do not have sufficient evidence, it is possible to hypothesize that those who went through the whole process—that is, the husbands who, upon discovering the infidelity, had their wives arrested at a police station, filed a lawsuit, went through the legal proceedings and, when they felt that the offense had been redressed, withdrew the charges—had an ability to manage their emotions that Ángel Fiorda did not possess.[13]

The murderer's last movements mirror his inner turmoil. In the evening, Ángel had denounced his wife and managed to have her arrested after she had stated unequivocally before the chief of the police station that she "no longer loved her husband, but she did love Cocucci."[14] However, the next morning, he requested her release and returned with her to the *conventillo* where, according to Gerónima Lauría, he put on a public demonstration of his affection for his wife in front of several neighbors (who had witnessed the couple's heated argument the previous day), "effusively caressing [his wife's] hair while he hugged her."[15] Filomena, however, was annoyed and after a while unmasked her husband's performance, saying "in front of anyone who wanted to hear it, that [Fiorda] had made her spend a night in prison, but he would spend the rest of his life in

Palermo."[16] In his sentence, the judge relied on Lauría's testimony to argue that Filomena was aware that, despite Ángel's solicitous gestures, "indignation was growing in her husband's heart, however, she did not hesitate to challenge him." Furthermore, the magistrate posthumously admonished her for not having restrained the expression of her emotions when it was evident that "jealousy completely disturbed Fiorda's mental faculties."[17] This argument must have not sounded unfamiliar to the accused, since in Italy the overpowering emotions and *l'impeto d'ira* (fit of rage) lay at the heart of the discussion regarding adultery and the *delitto d'onore* (honor killing). This resulted—as Hughes has recently demonstrated—in large part from the power of emotional empathy that characterized the discussion of the issue. Both Italy's legislators and judges could vividly imagine the shock, dismay, and revulsion that would attend such a discovery, and references to pity, sadness, and pain punctuated their discourse, just as it would appear in the arguments of defense lawyers.[18]

To recreate the details of what happened in the time that elapsed between Fiorda's display of affection in the courtyard of the tenement house and the homicide, I only have the version of the murderer who, before the judge, declared that after dinner he was in bed with his wife and his daughter, and they were chatting as they usually did when, unexpectedly, Filomena told him that "she was going to kill him that very night." Then he noticed that she had a knife under the pillow, which made him "lose his patience, took the knife and began to stab her, first on the neck and then on other parts of her body." In the middle of the attack, the victim got up from the bed, intending to escape, but "immediately fell on the floor, where he continued to stab her."[19]

What drove Fiorda to commit the murder? The defense of honor? Shame? Jealousy? Resentment? Love? Insanity? All of these reasons were evoked at different points of the judicial process: in the accused's statement, in the allegation of the public defender, in the indictment of the prosecutor, and the verdict of the judge. On the other hand, the newspapers, more concerned about morals than on the motive for the crime, did not venture a hypothesis on the reasons for the uxoricide. The emphasis on happiness and harmony that reigned in the home until Cocucci broke into the life of the couple reveals the newspaper's intention to amplify a prescriptive representation of family and marital life. At the same time, by connecting Filomena's unfortunate fate with her capitulation to "flirtation and sensuality," *La Prensa* reproved the victim's behavior and obliquely urged women to decency and virtue.[20]

Although expressed in a different register, that was also the premise of the judge, who held that the victim's irregular conduct had offended her husband's honor because "[Filomena] performed acts that caused shame, indignation, and anger [in Ángel] and completely disturbed his faculties."[21] The judge alluded to the loving gestures of the accused who, abandoning his job and traveling to Rosario to recover his wife and asking for the adulteress' freedom at the police station, showed "the affection he had for her ... that he further expressed by caressing her hair in the house where they lived, in the presence of neighbors."[22] But in spite of the evocation of those loving actions, Ángel was sentenced to life imprisonment. His lawyer contested the court's decision, arguing that on the night of the murder, Filomena had threatened her husband "challenging him to a duel and insinuating that she and her lover would take his life."[23]

In the statement attached to the submission of the case to the Court of Appeals, the prosecutor resorted to the same arguments he had raised during the proceedings in the first instance. He maintained that Filomena's uxoricide was motivated by "the very understandable jealousy of the murderer, whose love had been rewarded with repeated and evident infidelities."[24] It seems worth noticing that the word *love* is rarely found in an indictment of the prosecution, unlike what happened in the defense attorney's statements. In the courtroom's emotional regime—and the legal culture in general—the issues concerning the ethics of objectivity are a common subject for all the legal professions. However, lawyers had a broader set of rhetorical tools at their disposal, and their emotional performative scripts appeared to be less rigid than those of a judge or a prosecutor, whose role traditionally embodied the principles of rational and dispassionate justice.[25]

The magistrates of the Court of Appeals ratified the sentence of the first instance; however, they argued that neither the jealousy of the husband nor "the improper behavior of the wife" explained the uxoricide, since Fiorda had forgiven Filomena, "as it was proved by the fact that a few moments before the murder he was with her in the same bed." They argued that the key to understanding Fiorda's criminal conduct was "an irresistible fit of rage" and the murderer's nervous excitement aggravated by Filomena's expressions of disaffection, emotional closeness to Cocucci, and death threats. As noted in Chapter IV, a "nervous excitement" caused by the provocative and the injurious public behavior of a wife was often invoked in the courts not only by the defense attorneys but also by the judges. The male prerogative embedded into the legal system mitigated the gravity of the offense and attenuated the punishment because, as noted by Hyland in his analysis of the uxoricide committed by the Syrian immigrant Salomon Matti in front of his two sons in the city of Tucumán in 1914, the honor of a cuckolded husband continued to carry important consideration in this type of crime. Usually, the courts and the Superior Tribunals sympathized with the accused, although the justices were compelled to enforce the law and condemned them according to the punishment provided by the Penal Code.[26]

Filomena could not speak, but everyone spoke for her. Ángel said that she had threatened him with death; Gerónima Lauría asserted that the woman had defied her husband in front of the neighbors; the other dwellers of the *conventillo* confirmed that she had a *macho*; and Cocucci declared that Filomena had "dispensed her favors by having sexual intercourse with him many times" and that, when he told her he was moving to Rosario, "without hesitation she abandoned her husband to follow him."[27] What would the victim have said in the face of all these assertions? The only answer was in her body, which spoke through the autopsy. The agonizing pain that marked her transition to death underlies the technical language of the forensic doctor. In each wound he reports, the victim's cries become audible.[28] In the nine folios containing Filomena's autopsy, the coroner counted more than thirty stab wounds. With them, he traced a map that oriented the route of the homicidal excursion with which Ángel had put an end to the story of "a happy family." Most of the cuts were superficial and the killer had executed them as his wife was lying on the floor. Only one of them, located in the intestine, was deep. That was the one that, after several hours of suffering, caused her death. Although the medical report was not enough to determine the possible premeditation of the crime, it exposed what the justices of the Court of Appeals characterized as "an extraordinary cruelty from which Filomena Mastrostéfano was unable to defend herself."[29] Nevertheless, adultery continued to influence the magistrates' decision of exempting the accused from the death penalty.[30]

The defense attorney, the prosecutor, and the judges and justices placed the murder at the intersection of infidelity, jealousy, and love. However, what played a crucial role in the mitigation of the punishment seems to have been the gender script of the patriarchal family. The social, cultural, and legal enablement of the husband to exert power on his spouse was at the core of the marital relationship and influenced the interpretation the judicial system made of the uxoricide. Female adultery was considered not only a grave offense to male honor but also a challenge to a man's authority. The court record reveals that Filomena resisted obeying Ángel on various occasions and in different manners. Her insubordination and the contempt she felt for her husband only resulted in recurrent episodes of mutual verbal and physical violence, which increased "Fiorda's exasperation."[31]

In her testimony, Francisco Cocucci said that Filomena did not want to live with her husband anymore because "she was tired of the disagreements [. . .] that Fiorda always scolded her and that every time she replied, [he] beat her and [she] had to defend herself by hitting him back as much as she could."[32] That was the emotional atmosphere in which Filomena was immersed when she decided to follow her lover to Rosario. More than a search for freedom to live out "the vehement passion" she felt for Cocucci, as held by *La Prensa*, Filomena seemed to have challenged the prescriptive conception that linked conjugal love to the wife's obedience to her husband. Shortly before the crime, she had admitted openly that she felt love for Cocucci. From his profane perspective, the extinction of love dissolved the marriage bond that the religious and civil legislations of Argentina and Italy considered to be indissoluble.

The tenants of the two *conventillos* where the Fiordas had lived, and their respective landlords, were summoned to testify at the trial. Their testimonies outlined the portrait of the adulterous woman. On a few occasions, discretion led the witnesses to answer negatively to the question of whether they were aware that Filomena was unfaithful. A laconic "not aware" left a gap in the questionnaire, casting a shadow of doubt over the victim's conduct. Perhaps the habit of not speaking ill of the dead motivated this reaction. However, most of them said they had heard the rumor that Filomena was unfaithful and admitted to knowing the details of the adultery and the escape. One of the neighbors of the house where Francisco Cocucci lived (from which the Fiordas had moved shortly before the crime), referred to an altercation between Filomena's accomplice and his mother. After Ángel made Cocucci spend a day in detention at the police station, Francisco returned to the *conventillo*, and when he was washing his face in the basin of the courtyard:

> In the presence of the witness and several other neighbors, his mother admonished him for his improper behavior with Fiorda and his wife and asked him to stay away from those people and stop causing trouble ... warning him against the relationship with a woman that would only cause trouble to the extent that he had ended up arrested at a police station for having an affair with a woman who was just a slut.[33]

Just like in Italy, in the emotional community of Italian immigrants in Argentina, marriage was conceived as an indissoluble union. That notion, enshrined by law and the Catholic religion in their home country, was reinforced by the cultural, emotional, and legal prescriptions of the host society. As noted above, in its description of the family life that Filomena, Ángel, and Virginia enjoyed before the tragic occurrence, *La Prensa* resorted to the representation of the hard-working immigrant and the devoted "mother and housewife" spouse, a bread-winner model of the household organization that not only ensured "happiness" in the private domain but also social harmony. This rhetoric evokes the arguments raised in Italy during the heated debates on the divorce law which emerged at different moments between the unification and the 1920s. The most frequent anti-divorce allegation was that the indissolubility of marriage protected the woman, the family, and the "natural" order of gender, from the corrupted tendencies of modernity. But, as Mark Seymour notes, it was a nature full of asymmetries since the civil law gave the husband distinct privileges, such as the complete control over the financial and personal affairs of his wife, and established a double standard of adultery, making it much easier for a husband to prosecute his wife than the other way around.[34]

Custom and legislation shaped the way men and women conceived marriage, and how they negotiated notions of authority and obedience and reconcile the hierarchical relationships of a patriarchal society with affection within the conjugal unit. However, although female submission to the husband's authority was not at odds with love when the balance of power within the marriage was broken, love vanished, and contempt, resentment, and hatred took their place in the conjugal relationship. Filomena twice broke the scheme of authority that regulated married life. She escaped to a large city in another province, perhaps believing that distance would keep her off her husband's radar. And when she was forced to return to the marital home, she again challenged Fiorda with gestures and words: she took her lover to her new home and at the police station she did not shy from herself confessing that she had stopped loving Ángel. In her testimony, Cocucci portrayed her as an ardent and resolute female who, moved by her feelings, did not hesitate to run away from the marital home even knowing that she was committing a crime.

When the judge ordered an inventory of the Fiordas' belongings, the officer in charge of the task recorded "a photograph cut in half," clothes of a woman and a man, a girl's dress, kitchen utensils, loose pieces of ordinary crockery, two chairs, a table, and a bed with an iron back, the one in which Virginia slept when Gerónima Lauría and the street police officer discovered Filomena's body lying in a pool of blood. The objects were handed over to the landlord of the *conventillo*, although the justice withheld the photograph (which now illustrates the cover of this book). Filomena appears in it on her wedding day in Italy. But someone cut out the image (did she do it herself? or was it her husband?). Ángel's right arm is barely visible, and his hand is intertwined with his wife's. Although it is not possible to know under what circumstances or for what reason the photograph was cut out, what can be seen in this severed image is a metaphor for the breaking of the marriage bond that makes sense in the context of a process in which, except for the agent who made the inventory, no one refers to it. Someone attached the photo to the court record; however, I was not able to figure out who and why. But it is there, labeled folio "70," putting a face to the body furrowed with wounds described in the autopsy and exposing the hand that wounded it to death.

According to the judge of the first instance, jealousy, honor offense, and challenge to marital authority explained Fiorda's murderous behavior. To the justices of the Court of Appeals, however, those were just secondary factors that only accelerated the "violent reaction" that led the accused to kill his wife. Was the influence of an emotional imbalance what drove Fiorda to commit the crime? Were his mental faculties altered?

The trial ended in the first days of October 1894. Ángel Fiorda, who was then 36 years old, became "convict number 12" and started to serve a sentence that bore a strong resemblance to death. Unlike most other proceedings that usually conclude at this point, four folios containing a medical report were added to the record during Christmas week of 1897. According to the doctors, Fiorda suffered from general paralysis of the insane, "a condition of inevitable fatal progress which demands his immediate transfer to the *Hospicio de las Mercedes*."[35] That was probably the last time he went through the city of Buenos Aires: from the penitentiary to the mental asylum where he would continue to serve the sentence.

It is not clear what the diagnosis exactly meant, because even when in the nineteenth century, the French alienists had already associated the general paralysis of the insane with syphilis, its syphilitic origin was not confirmed until the early twentieth century. Before that time, paralytic dementia had a broad meaning that included several degenerative illnesses of the brain and had become the paradigmatic model of insanity. The interest in the illness was not exclusive to medicine; it was also relevant to the legal field, because it was believed that this dementia predisposed individuals to criminal behavior.[36]

No one had ever mentioned insanity throughout the entire proceedings. It is likely that the murderer still did not show signs of the illness, and for that reason, the whole trial relied on the emotional script of the jealous husband seized by a passion that blinded his senses. Only the justices of the Court of Appeals alluded to mental disorder. In their verdict, they wrote that the only valuable fragment of the murderer's account of the night of the crime was the confession of authorship, which they considered "perfectly divisible from the irrational and the absurd content of most of the statement."[37]

## The tailor's nervous temperament

A few years before Fiordas' tragedy, insanity had been the central argument in the trial of another immigrant, the Spanish tailor Joaquín Turero y Miga, who attempted to commit suicide after cutting the throat of his wife, Paula Lamas, in November 1889, only nine months after they arrived in Argentina.[38] In their early days in Buenos Aires, they settled in a tenement house in the neighborhood of San Telmo, where, according to one of the witnesses, the couple seemed to live together "in full harmony." Three months later, at the suggestion of a countryman, Joaquín and Paula moved to San Nicolás, a town in the province of Buenos Aires, where the tailor began to suspect his wife of cheating on him. One day, while they were having lunch at a tavern, "Mr. Sánchez approached to greet them, and she blushed very much, as it happens every single time that she does something inappropriate," declared the murderer.[39] Shortly after, and settled back in Buenos Aires, Turero y Miga's suspicions grew, since when he came home from work he found cigar butts in the room, "which was a clear sign that in his absence she received another man." According to his statement, his wife's character changed with migration. In Spain, she was "very affectionate and cheerful, but here in Argentina she became cold, she barely spoke, scolded much, and stared into the distance and wept while murmuring: 'God, what a torment!'"[40] The tailor attributed the change in Paula's behavior not only to the fact that she did not love him anymore, but also to having chosen "the path of sensuality, driven by the greed for luxuries that he was not in a position to offer her."

The court record is sparing of details of the couple's daily relationship, but the chronicle published in *La Prensa* the day after the crime revealed that, in the month preceding the murder, the neighbors witnessed heated arguments between Paula and Joaquín, caused by his "little dedication to work." According to the newspaper, she reproached her husband for the lack of money and expressed her anguish because "the means of subsistence they had brought from Spain were running out. Since Joaquín was not able to prosper in San Nicolás, they returned to Buenos Aires, where he got a job in a tailor's shop near the *conventillo*. However, a few weeks later he resigned because "his sickly imagination led him to suppose that his wife intended to take him away from home to freely attend to the loving requests of an honest, married shoemaker who lives in the same tenement house." *La Prensa* portrayed Paula as a victim of a husband whose "exuberant imagination and obsessive jealousy made happiness impossible."[41]

Unlike Fiorda's case, in which almost twenty witnesses were summoned to court, only four people testified in this case. Two of them, the closest to the family, declared that after returning from San Nicolás, they noticed that Joaquín "looked mentally upset," and that Paula believed that "her husband might suffer from some mental disorder because he was obsessed with the idea that she had the intention to poison him."[42] The shoemaker—allegedly Paula's lover—said that the night before the murder, the couple had a noisy altercation, and he had to intervene to calm the tailor down, "because he was enraged by jealousy." The next morning, the testimony continues, Paula told him that "as Joaquín had something wrong in his head they had gone to see a doctor, who prescribed him some medicines . . . which he refused to take."[43]

In the second half of the proceedings, the focus shifted from the crime to the insanity of the tailor. Certifying that the accused suffered from a mental illness was crucial to convict him or rule the exemption of punishment.[44] So the doctors became key figures in the trial, and their technical language pervaded the court record, causing a shift in the register. Nevertheless, the diagnoses were not immune to the emotional and gender scripts prevailing at that time.

During the trial, two medical reports were elaborated. The first one was requested by the prosecutor, who stated that he found it an enigma that "insignificant motives had led the accused to commit such a brutal murder."[45] The result of this examination confirmed that jealousy was what drove Joaquín to kill his wife. According to the medical expert, the criminal act was "the result of an emotional outburst" that did not have a "pathological origin." The doctor noted that the accused "has an extremely nervous temperament that dominates him . . . without the slightest hint of delusion or extravagance which might suggest a mental disorder."[46]

The expert's report underlined that Joaquín's nervousness had no physiological or genetic explanation, because, "although the inmate is not aware of the cause of his father's death (who passed away when he was very young), he said that his mother had died of gall bladder disease, and his only sister of measles."[47] Resorting to the cultural script of a jealous husband who, seized by rage, kills his unfaithful wife, the doctor concluded that "rather than a pathology the cause of the crime was the exaltation of the passion of jealousy awakened in a completely nervous individual."[48] The defense contested the report and asked for a new one because the medical expert had sidestepped the fact that the accused not only was nervous but also suffered from a mental illness.[49]

As imprecise as the previous one, the second report nevertheless added some considerations that would support the hypothesis of Joaquín's insanity. Just like his colleague six months earlier, the new physician underscored the "complete absence of hallucinations and delirium."[50] He dismissed the relevance of the obsessive jealousy (which the prosecutor had considered the only mitigating factor) and held that the crime had occurred because of the nervous temperament of the accused, whom he described as "a victim of the weakness of his mental and affective faculties and [with] a predisposition to violence." However, besides the clinical diagnosis, the doctor ended his report with a sympathetic assertion that would end up being crucial in the sentence: "the accused is *completely* remorseful."[51]

The medical expert's assessment was based on the prolonged observation of Joaquín's routine and its effect on his emotional condition. The doctor said that the only thing that kept the accused from worrying was his work in the prison tailor's shop. However, in moments of leisure, he sank into oppressive pain, and "he seats speechless with his head bowed like a man who has allowed himself to be defeated." Sometimes, the murderer became dominated by sorrow at the evocation of the murder. Haunted by memories of the past, the report further added that "he gets deeply moved and breaks down in tears when he evokes his wife, for whom he still feels a profound love. He blamed himself for having made her his victim on that fateful day."[52] At this point in the proceedings, the victim had lost prominence and was only invoked to outline the psychological profile of her murderer. In the medical report, Joaquín's "sorrow" and "pain" were emotions typical of the script of the jealous husband and the adulterous wife, which portrayed the perpetrator as a victim and justified the crime by alluding to the unfaithful conduct of the woman, whom, according to the doctor, the tailor had forgiven "for the affairs she might have had."[53]

The doctor's emotional language—more than his professional assessment and the technicalities he used—was crucial for the court to determine Joaquin's criminal responsibility and to consider mental infirmity a mitigation factor. The judge maintained that the nervous temperament of the accused was a fertile field for "passion [referring to jealousy] to cause in him the fit of rage and the impulsive aggression."[54] Nevertheless, rather than relying on the insanity plea made by the public attorney, the main reason for granting an acquittal was Joaquin's remorseful attitude. Although the medical expert referred to the accused's emotional suffering as the evidence of his remorse, according to the judge, its most telling sign was his attempt to commit suicide immediately after murdering Paula.

Remorse is the point where the cases of Ángel Fiorda and Joaquín Turero y Miga diverge. While the Spanish tailor showed sorrow and said he felt love for Paula, the Italian murderer never expressed regret. The language in which he referred to his wife revealed resentment and contempt, and his emotional practices—the bodily gestures as well as the verbal expressions—were contrary to compunction.[55] Upon being arrested, "raising his arms and in a gesture of satisfaction" Fiorda confessed he had stabbed Filomena "because she had a *macho*."[56] Some days later, in court, "clenching his fist as if to punch," he recreated his gestures at the moments before the murder, when he hit her wife in the face "because she was a slut."[57] Unlike the Italian murderer, Turero y Miga attempted suicide, an act that although the judge interpreted as remorse, could also be read as a way of evading criminal responsibility.

The decision for one or the other interpretation depends on how the accused communicates remorse and how the expression of his/her feelings is perceived by others. Remorse is an emotion that is shown more than spoken; it is communicated through gestures rather than only through words. Thus, feeling norms play a crucial role in the display of remorse since they prescribe when it is appropriate to experience a feeling, and how it should be expressed to be credible.[58] In his examination of the concept of remorse Weisman notes that while offering an apology may refer to the anguish and pain that the offender feels at having contravened the norms of the community, the remorseful individual demonstrates the pain by making the suffering visible. By showing remorse the offender takes responsibility for the crime and presents him/herself as deserving the social reprobation and the punishment imposed. Although words are relevant, the consistency between what the person utters about remorse and what he/she shows is crucial for the court to confirm it does not deal with a defense strategy, but with a genuine act of contrition before a moral community that establishes for which acts a show of remorse is expected. In the process of showing remorse, what is revealed is that the private self as well as the public self has been touched by the values of the moral community that punishes the crime.[59]

While Fiorda appears as a remorseless person who did not even utter a word of apology and rather reinforced with gestures and words the resentment he felt for his victim, Joaquín's bodily and verbal languages were regarded as an expression of genuine remorse. The second doctor, who examined him over several months, ended up convinced not only by speech but in particular by paralinguistic cues (tears, bowed head, his work in the jail's workshop) that the Spanish tailor was truly remorseful. His expression of remorse did not even lose communicative effectiveness when translated by the medical expert in the forensic report, as is proved by the fact that by reading it the judge considered that Joaquin's painful inward feelings were spontaneous and sincere.

However, although remorse is the feeling in which the two cases diverge, they seem to share a common emotional ground. What kind of homicides were these?

Were these crimes of hatred or crimes of passion? These are difficult questions to answer, because while the term passion is repeated in the arguments of doctors, attorneys, prosecutors and judges, hatred did not form part of the lexical-semantic repertoire of the proceedings. However, a reading of the records focused more on what they silence than on what they mention allows us to hypothesize on the place of hatred in the emotional landscape of these homicides.

Hatred has effects on the bodies of those who become its object. It establishes a negative link with the other, whom the hater wishes to remove from his/her bodily and social closeness.[60] Whereas it is possible to feel hatred for an entire kind of people, rage (an emotion with a widespread presence in the trials for adultery addressed in Chapter III and invoked also by the judge in the first instance in Fiorda's case) is felt towards specific individuals. According to Sara Ahmed, in crimes motivated by hatred, "againstness" is felt towards whole classes of people, because even when hate may respond to the particular, it tends to align the particular with the general.[61] Thus, one of the central features of hate crimes is the perception of a hated group in the body of a person: the victim.

At the turn of the century, when Filomena and Paula were murdered, patriarchal cultures and legal codifications in Spain, Italy, and Argentina prescribed virtue and obedience for married women, but they also suspected them of infidelity and betrayal. A pervasive grammar of libertine love described the way adultery negatively affected men because it offended honor, betrayed love, and challenged their authority. As noted above, those scripts were profusely used in trials (by defendants, defense attorneys, prosecutors, judges, and medical experts) and had their most telling expression in a legal codification that mitigated or exempted from punishment the husband who, on surprising his wife lying in bed with another man, killed her. Were Filomena and Paula the individualities in which hatred of adultery was personified, and was that why Fiorda and Turero and Miga killed them? It is likely that this hatred, which was social and expressed in the language of moral admonishment and legal sanction, was the ineffable ferment of a mixture made of love, jealousy, anger, and revenge, "evil passions" that had roots in the mind and that spurred their violent impulses.[62]

## Emotional styles

In Chapter III, I pointed out that since Italian and Spanish couples are not proportionally represented in my sources, it was not possible to undertake a comparison of the two groups. Nevertheless, the nuances in the emotional styles of the adulteresses—the protagonists of that chapter—seem pretty apparent, even though with such a small number of cases, it is not easy to establish if those styles were individual or if they responded to widely shared patterns of conduct rooted in emotional learning.

In this section, I will focus on the way the murderers displayed their emotions. The cases of Ángel Fiorda and Joaquín Turero y Miga described above reveal that they resorted to different emotional repertoires and gestures to show their feelings. Their emotional styles are replicated in several other judicial proceedings that also involved Italian and Spanish husbands who killed their wives.[63] Although the circumstances surrounding the murders differ, the affective trajectories of the couples, as well as the reasons claimed by the murderers for committing the crime, show a certain regularity in the way the Spanish, dispassionate and reserved, and the Italians, dramatic and vengeful, expressed their feelings when they evoked their turbulent marital relationships and narrated their bloody endings.

On Christmas Eve 1899, the Spanish bricklayer Antonio Palomares stabbed his wife. The couple had arrived from Spain a few months earlier and had just moved from *El Jardin Florido*, an inn in downtown Buenos Aires, to a tenement house in the San Telmo neighborhood, because Antonio suspected Isabel of having an affair with Sebastian Fernandez, a Spanish confectioner who was a regular at the inn.[64]

As had happened to Turero y Miga, Antonio Palomares was also unable to prove his wife's infidelity, despite the fact that two of the witnesses alluded to some gestures that seemed to reveal that the woman was attracted to Fernández. However, they said that beyond the sympathy she publicly showed for him and the rumors circulating in the inn, they did not know if Isabel had had an intimate relation with Fernandez. Instead, in his statement, Antonio insisted that five days before the crime he had found his wife half-naked in bed with the confectioner. But since no one else than he witnessed this event, in the verdict the judge dismissed the adultery.[65]

When summoned to testify, Fernandez negated having maintained an illicit relationship with Isabel. He said that a couple of weeks before the murder, Palomares invited him to have a lemonade and asked him "to tell the truth because he wanted to reprimand his wife since he was ashamed that she was unfaithful in front of everyone."[66] When Fernandez told him that the adultery he suspected existed only in his imagination, Palomares pulled a knife from his clothes and pounced on him "like a madman" trying to kill him. Until this unfortunate incident, the testimony of Isabel's alleged lover continued, he had a friendly and harmonious relationship with the couple, although he had only known them for a few months. The Palomares arrived from Spain at the end of the winter with a letter of recommendation in which a cousin of Fernández asked him to help them find lodging, so he took them to the *El Jardín Florido*, where he usually had lunch, although he did not live there. Since then, "he has shared the table with Antonio and Isabel every single day."[67]

According to the testimony of one of the waitresses at the inn, a trivial episode would have revealed that Isabel was having an affair with Sebastián. Antonio and Isabel were having lunch when she "had the first evidence" that she was unfaithful to him. Palomares asked the cook to prepare a couple of poached eggs for his wife, but when the waitress took the eggs to the table, Isabel, "with a downcast expression in her face," rejected them refusing to eat, which angered her husband.[68] A few minutes later, Fernández entered the dining room and sat at the table with the couple, who were still arguing over the eggs. Then, the young confectioner tried to reconcile the couple by asking Isabel to eat the eggs, and she "ate them with great pleasure and a cheerful expression, which sharply contrasted with the sad mood she had shown until the moment Fernández walked through the door of the inn."[69]

The witness also pointed out that since that episode, in which Antonio seemed to confirm the adultery in his wife's gestures, his mood changed completely. The quiet, discreet, and cheerful man turned into a distressed and sullen individual who lost his appetite and displayed lunatic attitudes. According to the waitress, "he would sit alone in a corner, crooning songs in Galician, and all of a sudden he would lose his temper and turn pretty much aggressive."[70] The psychiatrists who examined him at the penitentiary reported that Palomares had a nervous temperament, although unlike what happened in Turero y Miga's case, they dismissed any mental or emotional disorder. But regardless of this difference, the report reveals similarities between the two murderers: the parsimonious gestures suddenly interrupted by a burst of anger, the obsessive jealousy, and the feeling of remorse.[71]

Just like his fellow countryman Ángel Fiorda had done a few months earlier, in December 1893, the Italian bricklayer Antonio Pettina tried to escape from the police after killing his wife, Carmen Spinelli.[72] When he was finally captured, he denied that his intention was escaping, and declared that "with the reason clouded, he ran in search of the river or the railway tracks to commit suicide."[73] Instead, Dominga Donnatti, the landlady of the tenement house where he lived and the only witness to the crime, testified that after attacking his wife, Pettina, whose clothes were stained with blood, stopped in the kitchen for a moment and with "much calm" told her that the quarrels with Carmen were over forever, and that "what he had done was for the best."[74] When Dominga peeked in the room, Carmen was lying in a pool of blood, surrounded by three of her children. The youngest, a baby barely twenty days old, slept in the matrimonial bed.

Neighbors in the surrounding houses, who heard Carmen's cries for help as her husband attacked her, alerted the neighborhood watchman that Pettina was trying to escape. Finally, when he was apprehended and confronted with his wife's body, as stated by one of the police officers who was at the crime scene: "cold and unmoved [the murderer] said there was nothing to regret because the crime was already done, and his wife deserved it for her disobedience had ruined his life."[75]

Both the murderer's emotional language and the miserable condition of the family resemble the story of Francisco Debenedetti and Elvira Venezia described in Chapter IV, in which the confluence of misery and rage transformed marital life into a whirlwind of daily quarrels. The testimonies of Carmen's mother and the landlady of the tenement house revealed that the victim's expectations of the migratory project being the solution for the poverty into which the family had been plunged had long vanished. Carmen's mother said that Antonio had forced her daughter to join him in Buenos Aires, although he only had poorly paid temporary jobs and lived in a hellhole. A few weeks after the arrival, Carmen had to find herself a job to feed the children, since her husband brought no money into the house as he had stopped working. She described his son-in-law as an alcoholic and abuser who had pushed his wife into misery and bitterness: "he is a sluggard who spent on alcohol the little money that my sacrificed daughter earned working as a laundress."[76] The woman also told the judge that only two days after Carmen gave birth to her last child, Pettina forced her to leave the bed to wash her customers' clothes even though she was bleeding heavily and suffering from sharp afterpains.[77]

In court, Pettina stated that he was forced to end the life of his wife because she wanted to be the authority of the household, "being that I as a husband and father am the one with the power that certainly does not depend on how much I earn or do not earn."[78] Although four days passed between the murderer and his appearance in court, and three months until the psychiatrists treated him in the penitentiary, Pettina maintained his argument, always displayed the same cold-hearted style, and not only did not show remorse but did not even offer an apology.[79] Furthermore, in his declaration, he stated that he had "very strong" suspicions that his wife was unfaithful. However, when the judge asked him to elaborate on Carmen's adulterous behavior, his clumsy answers uncovered Pettina's fabrication. The invocation of the victim's alleged unfaithfulness was just a shortcut to avoiding a life behind bars.

In their report, the psychiatrists underscored that the murderer only lost his cool when he tried to justify the crime by arguing that Carmen had intended to challenge his authority. While evoking the image of an authoritarian wife who had "tarnished his honor" by attempting to restrict his freedom and to transform him into a submissive person, the accused made gestures that expressed "anger, resentment, and a desire for revenge."[80] In the sentence convicting him to life imprisonment, the judge concluded that the misery and the alcoholism explained the moral degeneration of the accused, his serenity when he contemplated the dead body of his wife, and the contempt with which he evoked the victim.[81]

Admittedly, based on scarce and fragmentary information, it is not possible to formulate a conclusive hypothesis on the interplay between the social and cultural origin of the immigrants involved in judicial proceedings and the performing of a certain emotional style. However, the analogies between the murderers analyzed in this chapter suggest clues to think about the connections between individual autonomy and cultural constrictions, or in other words, about the subject's position in a community and the spatial configurations shaping its emotional conduct.[82]

In the Italian and Spanish murderers' declarations, honor appears to have been a common script available for emotional performance to both ethnic groups. In contrast, it is possible to detect certain nuances in the constellation of feelings that motivated and authorized violence. Among Italians, female disobedience appears to be the most eloquent challenge to male honor.[83] In their verbal and gestural language, the murderers expressed resentment and considered vengeance as the only way to recover their symbolic capital and to vindicate the honor stained by their insubordinate wives. Nevertheless, this does not mean that female infidelity did not affect how these historical actors felt about the honor.[84] In effect, when Italian men claimed that their honor had been injured, they tended to seek vindication by calling into question their dead wives' morality. Whereas among Spaniards, the victim's real or imagined fidelity appeared as the main threat to the moral integrity of the *hombre de bien* (honorable man), and shame as the feeling that mobilized the betrayed husband to commit the homicide.[85]

# 6

# Killing for Love

In her study on domestic homicide, Dawn Keetley argues that the fact that the men who killed their wives in nineteenth-century America justified their homicidal actions in terms of romantic jealousy shows the growing centrality of romantic love in marriage.[1] In contrast, in the cases of marital violence analyzed in the previous chapter, jealousy was part of an emotional configuration linked to the criteria of authority and possession that regulated the patriarchal family.[2] When they killed their wives, husbands presented themselves as the victims of women's disobedience or infidelity. An ungovernable passion made of rancor, anger, and jealousy allegedly pushed them to take the lives of their spouses.

This chapter analyzes the singular story of Ángel Gianoglio, an Italian murderer who distanced himself from this standardized narrative and instead declared that he was a "poor wretch" who killed for love. While in most of the trials, defendants expressed themselves only in their declarations in court, Gianoglio wrote seven letters in his handwriting to the judge trying to prove his love for the victim. Two additional details make this case singular. On the one hand, the victim was a prostitute, a profession to which economic need and family pressures (particularly from husbands) led immigrant women in Argentina.[3] On the other hand, the murderer and the victim were not legally married.[4] In turn-of-the-century Argentina, long-term cohabitation was socially and culturally regarded as marriage. However, the ruling classes defended and promoted the patriarchal family and the middle-class values.[5] When his intention to provoke the judge's sympathy by resorting to the rhetoric of unrequited love and the romantic passion failed, Gianoglio ended up turning to the mainstream notions and values to present the relationship with his victim as a marriage.

## The man who loved too much

On a hot noon in January 1904, two bodies lay in the courtyard of a tenement house in Rincón Street in Buenos Aires. A few minutes later, alerted by the street watchman, the police officers hurried to the scene, making their way through the crowd of nosey neighbors. A curly black-haired woman was lying dead on the floor, dressed in a blue robe and a white nightgown. She had been shot in her throat. Next to her was a man groaning in pain who pressed his hand against his bleeding right ear. The officers requested out loud for the landlord to show up. Diligent and fearful, speaking in a mixture of Italian and Spanish, the man tried to explain what had happened. He said that the woman was called Carmen Moretti and that barely two weeks ago, she had rented a room in which she lived with someone named José Carozzi. However, the landlord was oblivious as to the identity of the injured man. After his testimony, the police searched Carmen's room and partially uncovered the mystery. In the pocket of a man's coat hanging from the back of a chair, they found a passport, two pictures of a woman, and a brief letter written in small and shaky handwriting. The wounded man was Ángel Gianoglio, a 32-year-old Italian bookkeeper. The woman in the photos was the deceased, and the letter had been written by Ángel. It was addressed to the chief of the police station, to whom he begged to pass it on to the Italian consul, so that he could be sure that:

> Everything in room fifty-six in the Savoia Hotel, all the letters, and photographs inside my suitcase and trunk, will be sent to Gianoglio Francesca Felizziana in Italy . . . so my soul will be comforted . . . I am being forced to do this because love has ruined me. May God save the world from passions like mine.[6]

Ángel had shot Carmen twice, and then put the gun to his temple and tried to kill himself. The severity of his wounds prevented him from making a statement and he was immediately taken to the hospital.

The next day, *La Prensa* dedicated much space to the murder in a chronicle pompously titled "Short Novel. Passion Drama: the work of a jealous man" that uncovered the real identity of the victim.[7] She was Carlota Castellari, a 30-year-old Italian immigrant who some time before the crime had ended an eight-year intimate relationship with Ángel because "there were between them great personality differences that might lead to a fatal outcome at any moment." The woman used the alias "Carmen Moretti" when she engaged in prostitution, "a vile and sad journey that was the source of her money, and from which her lover took advantage." Even though after the separation Ángel had returned to Italy, according to *La Prensa* the love and attraction he felt for the prostitute was so intense that he was "unable to forget her." He would regularly write letters to her expressing his feelings, but Carlota was reluctant to respond, and when she did, she seemed to be dispassionate. After spending a year in his homeland, "the intensity of love" drove Ángel back to Buenos Aires believing that "his presence would persuade his ex-partner to return to a life together." However, the reunion confronted him with a cruel reality: Carlota refused to mend the relationship and confessed to him that there was another man in her life. Then, according to the newspaper, jealousy was aroused in him, and he became obsessed with plotting a bloody revenge, because his honor had been insulted in such a manner that no forgiveness was possible. Since without his beloved, Ángel's existence made no sense, the outcome of that plot, devised in a room at the Hotel Savoia, "could not be other than a romantic suicide."[8]

In her testimony before the court, Rosa Amelotti, the madam of the brothel where the victim was employed, declared that after learning about "Carmen's demise" she immediately guessed who might have been the perpetrator of the crime. She said that the victim had a relationship with "a tall individual with a mustache who claimed to be a widower despite being married in Italy, and who was supported by the victim since he did not work at all." Although she ignored whether Carmen had continued providing for him "she was aware that she paid for the fare when he left for Italy, because she had told her so."[9]

The testimony of the brothel's madam was consistent with what José Carozzi, the victim's brand-new partner, had declared at the scene of the crime. Although he had never met Ángel in person, he knew of his existence because Carlota always "blamed him for forcing her into the bordello."[10] He also said that the victim had told him that she had met Ángel in Milan where they had had a love affair, because he was married, but after a while, he proposed to her to migrate to Buenos Aires to start a new life together. José also told the police that after visiting Carlota for a year in the brothel they agreed to move together and rented the room in the tenement house. Just one week after settling there, Carlota left for Olavarría (a town located 370 kilometers southwest of Buenos Aires City). However, José was unaware of the reason for the trip, from where she had returned the day before her death.

In her testimony, the brothel's madam also stated that as a municipal bylaw in force since early 1904 obliged to evict every brothel that, like hers, housed more than two sex workers,[11] she and the victim had traveled to Olavarría intending to set up a bordello, but since the rent for the premises was too high, they agreed to return. While the women were in Olavarría, Carlota received two letters and a telegram from Ángel—who had just returned from Italy—asking her to renew the relationship. When they came back to Buenos Aires, continued the madam's testimony, he was waiting for them. Carlota got off the train and "headed towards him quite thrilled while the declarant went to her home."[12] That was the last time Rosa saw her alive.

When Ángel was interrogated, he was still in the hospital recovering from the suicide attempt. He declared that in the letters that the owner of the brothel mentioned, he had told Carlota that, upon arriving from Italy, "as soon as he got off the steamboat and set foot on Argentine soil, his first fervent desire was to see her and talk to her, as his only wish was to return to her."[13] A few days after he learned Carlota's whereabouts, he decided to set off to Olavarría, and sent her a telegram begging her to grant him a meeting. As Carlota not only agreed but also arrived "to our reencounter behaving so affectionately, [he] dismissed . . . any fear that she might have forgotten him." In that encounter, they agreed that Ángel would travel to Buenos Aires first, and that both would meet three days later at Constitución station.[14]

At five in the afternoon on the appointed day, Ángel was standing on the train station platform. His anxiety increased as the minutes passed. The train had been delayed for almost an hour. When at last Carlota stepped down the passenger car, Ángel—unaware that his expectations were doomed to be "a romantic disillusion"—experienced a combination of "desire and joy."[15] But far from showing "the affection she had displayed in Olavarría," Carlota revealed to him she had a relationship with another man, and that she was determined to live with her new lover. Nevertheless, she offered to pay for Ángel's fare if he would want to return to Italy. The woman's "cold and sincere tone" provoked "an overflowing sorrow in the heart" of Ángel, who "burst into tears in the sight of everyone." His grief grew when Carlota mocked him and "imitating the crying, pretended to cry as well." That afternoon they parted ways. Plunged into loneliness in a hotel room, Ángel "realized he would not be able to live without her." If Carlota did not desist from her intention, he would kill her and then take his own life. That bloody plan was conceived amidst of a deep distress that came from "realizing that she had no desire of resuming the pure and honest loving relationship they once had."[16]

One month later, discharged from the hospital, Ángel was transferred to the penitentiary. The persistent aftereffects of the suicide attempt had seriously deteriorated his health. Since the doctors were unable to remove the bullet from his skull, he suffered "cruel, painful and constant headaches," he had partially lost his sight and was deaf in the right ear. The letters he sent to the judge recreated the physical suffering but also addressed his other affliction: the absence of Carlota, "whose memory causes me unbearable grief."[17]

The prosecutor requested a twenty-year-imprisonment sentence, to which the defense attorney contested resorting to the rhetorical devices of the crime of passion:

When Gianoglio committed the crime, he suffered from a serious mental and emotional disturbance as the result of the profound passion he felt for Carmen Moretti and the disillusion of learning from her own lips that they could not be together because she was engaged to another man. Without doubt, the jealousy excited by such confession was what caused the tragedy.[18]

However, the defendant departed from the semantics of the crime of passion and, complaining about the defense attorney's indolence, he gave up his mediation to assume his own legal representation, addressing the magistrate by correspondence. Love, loss, and bodily suffering are the recurring topics of his seven missives, which he sent between May and October 1904.

In the first letter, the murderer devoted two lengthy paragraphs to express physical suffering. As he could not bear the "hammering in the head and buzzing in the ear," he begged the judge to sentence him to death. He depicted himself as a devastated individual who suffered from excruciating pain and only wished to die, because:

> In addition to physical pain, my soul is also shattered since the tragedy, but if there exists an afterlife, and my beloved Carlota is watching me from heaven, she must be suffering for me. I have loved her so much for she bewitched my heart, and now my soul is buried with her, my thoughts are with her, and my sole desire is to be under the earth that covers her grave. It will not be very long before I join her.[19]

A month later, the murderer wrote another letter requesting to be transferred again to the hospital so "that once and for all I can undergo a procedure to get rid of my pain and ailments." But the doctors refused to perform a surgery that might have fatal consequences. So, once again, Ángel turned to the judge requesting him to apply the death penalty, "since if I had a gun in my possession, I would have already taken my life."[20] However, in the rest of the letter, and in spite of this plea, he set forth an exculpatory argument that contradicted his alleged desire to die:

> When I committed the crime, you must know, believe it or not, that I had been unable to do anything but weep for a week. I believe that you are a man of good heart and therefore I trust that you will have compassion for a man whose only fault was to love that woman too much. I lost her and then I lost myself for love ... I am a poor wretch, a poor wretch and nothing else ... a miserable man who needs Carlota Castellari to continue living. Without that fatal attraction to her that made me a weak man who depended on her to continue living ... without her betrayal I would be an honest man and we would live together happily.[21]

In his following letter, the defendant attached three documents with which he tried to prove his honesty and his love for the victim. The first one was a criminal record "that proves I have not committed any crime in my own country." The second one was a certificate of employment from a trading company in Milan, where he had been a bookkeeper. Behind that anodyne paper lay "the beginning of [his] misfortunes" because, as he noted in the missive, while he was employed there, his boss learned of his affair with Carlota and asked him to leave her if he wanted to keep the job. Faced with this dilemma, Ángel refused to resign his love "and let my boss fire me, I separated from my legal wife, moved in with Carlota, and a few months later we both traveled to Argentina."[22] Finally, he attached a recommendation letter addressed to the head of the National Department of Health, Eduardo Wilde, dated October 1899. There, the foreman of an Italian company where Ángel had got a job a few weeks after arriving in Argentina requested Wilde to help Carlota get urgent medical treatment in a city hospital, as she was seriously ill. According to the explanatory comment that Ángel added to the note:

> This is the most telling evidence that I have always made sacrifices to face any setback that the woman I loved could suffer, like in this circumstance when I not only turned to my social networks but also sold all my belongings just to see her return to full health.[23]

In alignment with his intention to demonstrate his love for Carlota, in the spring of 1904, he wrote again to the judge to share a letter he had received from Italy in which the victim's father forgave him:

> Because my father-in-law is aware of how much I loved Carlota and of all the sacrifices I made for her, and because he always thought of me as his daughter's husband, he agreed with me that she committed a great fault by leaving me for another man.[24]

Ángel, who by that point seemed to have discarded his desire to die, told the judge that in case he did not take Carlota's father's letter as evidence, he would like to have it back because "I shall keep it in my dread misfortune as a reminder of the noble heart that cherished me, and with whom I was so madly in love ... She was the woman I always wanted to spend my life with ... I am certain that in mutual company, we would have been a blissful couple."[25]

The murderer was unable to save this fateful souvenir because it was included in the case file. The letter was the response of Carlota's father to a missive that in mid-March 1904, Ángel himself had sent him informing about the murder. The "father-in-law" replied that, despite the overwhelming distress he was feeling, he understood that "betrayal and disobedience" had led Carlota to her "terrible destiny," and that he forgave his "son-in-law" wishing him "heavenly protection."[26] The court did not question the authenticity of the letter; but rather seemed indifferent to it, and contrary to what was usual when the proof was written in a foreign language, no official translation of it was even requested, nor was the letter mentioned in the verdict which sentenced Ángel to twenty years' imprisonment. However, this letter is a crucial piece for my analysis because it constitutes a turning point in the exculpatory strategy of the accused.

As noted above, pain and grief constitute the two emotions that remain constant throughout the seven letters Ángel penned. In contrast, the notions of guilt and love exhibit a transformation. From the third letter on, Ángel replaced his pretentious request for the death penalty—so that he could reunite with Carlota in the afterlife—with an exculpatory rhetoric that sought to demonstrate the love he felt for the victim by evoking the care he had lavished on her while she was sick. In the letter to the judge in which he evoked the time when Carlota was hospitalized in 1899, Ángel described the relationship he had back then with the victim as "a legal marriage." He argued that it was the desire to mend the marital bond that prompted him to return from Italy. But then, Carlota rejected his love "because she fell into the trap of a dishonest profession, even though I always begged her to leave the brothel."[27]

This way the murderer aligned his arguments with the dominant prescriptions about conjugal life—one of whose sounding boards was the law—entailing monogamous and heterosexual relationships in which husbands' role as protectors and providers combined with a male-dominant position, whereas women remained in the domestic sphere fulfilling their "natural" obligations as mothers and housewives. When Ángel looked for Wilde's intercession, he assumed the role of the protective and responsible husband. Likewise, by asking the judge to take into consideration the letter from the victim's father, he not only reassured that even though Carlota and he were cohabitees, everyone treated them like a married couple, but also drew from his "father-in-law" letter the arguments to justify his crime by blaming it on Carlota's insubordination. The defendant's emotional language reveals the coexistence of two notions of marital love. In the first letters, Ángel presented himself as the victim of intense and idealized love. The longing for the woman he loved was a force beyond his control that had led him to live a wretched life. For the love of Carlota, he had abandoned his wife and lost his job in Milan, he had returned from Italy, he had wept, and he had tried to take his own life. On the other hand, in his last missives, the pompous and sentimental tone gave way to a more standardized self-portrayal: that of a man dishonored by his wife's disobedience and treachery.

The weeping, to which—as noted in the previous chapter—police news reports resorted to describe the desolation felt by Ángel Fiora when Filomena abandoned him to run away with another man, also appears in this case. But this time, it was not the newspaper that described Ángelo Gianoglio weeping but the murderer himself. He narrated it in his declaration in court as well as in one of the letters to the judge, in which he represented himself the days before the crime as an individual plunged into a profound grief that prevented him from managing his emotions. Just as he failed to hold back his tears when Carlota rejected him at the train station, in the loneliness of the room at Hotel Savoia he was unable to control the urge to kill her and then take his own life.

It is not clear if Ángel really wept, or if the tears were a fabrication in the attempt to gain the sympathy of both the judge and the prosecutor. Also, there is no way of knowing if the crying of the other Ángel (Fiora), who stabbed his wife thirty-six times, was real or if it was part of the "fictional tears" present in the commonplace script to which the news stories on passion crimes resorted. Nevertheless, the tearful narration and the portrayal of the sensitive man that, as we will see below, was widespread in feuilletons and serial novels, also suggest the existence of non-normative masculinity represented in some of the most popular cultural circuits in late nineteenth- and early twentieth-century Argentina.[28] On the other hand, the weeping of the sensitive man, which seemed a rather familiar image in the society of that time, did not permeate the judicial system, an emotion-free bastion of reason and normative masculinity. Why did Ángel then portray himself before the court as a poor wretch who wept for his beloved Carlota? His tears, real or fictional, might be interpreted as an expression of the love he felt for the victim, and at the same time, as a rhetorical device to prove the authenticity of the passion he felt.

If we assume that tears express a particular emotion, Ángel would have wept in sorrow. However, it has been pointed out that crying does not necessarily express any emotion at all.[29] In this case, it may be argued that beneath the surface of Ángel's tearful account hides the sense of possession and male-dominance that was at the core of the patriarchal marriage.[30] Frustration was likely the actual cause of the crying. Carlota had left him for another man, so she was no longer his possession, the same thing that happened to Ángel Fiora with Filomena. The autonomous behavior of the two women challenged the male honor and patriarchal notions of power and set a limit to the husbands and partners to possess them and demand submission from them. Devoid of power and full of frustration, both men cried. Thus, weeping was not a mere expression of emotion, but it rather appears to be part of a more complex cultural performance.

Carlota was not legally married to Ángel, and the court record always refers to her as "the mistress." However, from the third letter to the judge, the murderer began to present their relationship as a marriage. His exculpatory arguments shifted from a romantic narrative of love understood as "a mysterious agency beyond human control [that] made the recovery of 'lost' love exceedingly difficult,"[31] to another one in which, resorting to a notion of love based on male authority and female submission, he blamed Carlota for her tragic end. According to the forensic psychiatrists, who made a thorough report on the mental health of the accused, none of these reenactments were truthful. They were only two masks behind which was hidden a man "without morals and sensitivity" who had acted with "ferocity." The doctors doubted both Ángel's declaration in court and everything he said throughout the clinical evaluation:

> The facts show that when talking about honor, care, sensitivity, honesty, etc., Gianoglio speaks about feelings he knows only by name. Otherwise, he cannot explain the kind of life he has led for so many years without the slightest remorse. His crime was not the irresistible urge of a respectable and loving man who feels dishonored by the infidelity of the woman with whom he lives ... He could hardly feel offended now if he has always tolerated the prostitution of the woman he refers to as his 'significant other'.[32]

Moreover, contradicting a social morality that prescribed female virtue and submission, the doctors justified the insubordination of the victim who, aware of the fact that she was being exploited, rebelled "in a gesture of courage" by abandoning her partner, a man who "having lost the habit of working honestly, only wished to continue to live without worrying where the bread he ate came from."[33]

Although the account that romanticizes the crime and the script that justifies it in the disobedience of the victim coexisted in the proceedings, neither of them moved the psychiatrists and the magistrate. The former described Ángel as a "liar, degenerate and amoral, who killed his wife while being completely aware of what he was doing,"[34] while in his verdict, the judge departed from both the sentimental language in which Ángel narrated his love story and presented his version of the events, and from the rhetoric of male honor and female decorum and subordination.[35] He did not directly refer to obedience, but resorted instead to his father-in-law's letter to introduce that notion in his narrative. And although

Carlota's refusal to restart a relationship based on sexual exclusivity (which supposedly had existed before she practiced prostitution) triggered the tragedy, Ángel also made no reference to jealousy, either as proof of love or as a passion that seizes reason at the moment of committing the crime.[36] Instead, the script of jealousy, so common in this kind of trial, was introduced by the public defenders. The first of them—whom Ángel had dismissed in a failed attempt to assume his own defense—invoked it when he contested the punishment requested by the prosecution, and the second, in the appeal of the first-instance sentence, stated that "Gianoglio is not the vulgar and ferocious criminal that is intended to be presented but the victim of a jealous passion that blinds him."[37] Likewise, while in his letters to the judge, the murderer always resorted to the word *amor* (love), that feeling was translated in the court record as *cariño* (affection), a common expression that judicial language relied on to refer to marital love.

However, outside the courtroom, the imaginary of romantic love was widespread in popular culture, not only in the police news about crimes of passion and romantic suicides, but also in feuilletons and serial novels targeting laboring classes.[38] Popular literature resorted to an archetypical image of the sensitive male tormented by unrequited love. The similarity between Ángel's emotional language and that used in the love stories featured in the feuilletons suggests that they might have been his source of inspiration[39] Unlike most of the men who are the protagonists of the stories in this book, who were either illiterate or had a poor command of Spanish, Ángel had a formal education, was able to express himself in Spanish, and according to the psychiatrists, he could articulate his arguments "in a way that indicates he has logical reasoning skills." All this could have facilitated his approach to the romantic stories featured in the feuilletons.

Excess of love, complementarity, and the soul mate metaphor constituted common denominators in both crime news and serial novels. Not only the national press, but also the ethnic newspapers resorted to this love imagery. In the fall of 1902, for example, *La Patria degli Italiani* reported the tragedy caused by adultery in the marriage of Giuseppe de Simone (mentioned in Chapter V), who hammered his wife to death "because he was deeply in love with her."[40] The excessive love that feels like a torment, in which separation cannot be conceived as a possibility, and only death is capable of ending a relationship, was a usual image used by journalism to describe the crime of passion. The murderer was presented as the victim of his love, that prevented him from emotional management and made him fluctuate between hope, anguish, and dejection.[41] According to the chronicle from *La Patria degli Italiani*, Ángel Gianoglio had undergone this "emotional ambiguity until his passion and the urge to kill and die seized him."[42]

As for unrequited love, popular literature—which I hypothesize that Ángel may have read—resorted almost exclusively to the image of a man who suffered for love. *Caras y Caretas*, an extraordinarily popular illustrated weekly created in Buenos Aires in 1898 by a Spanish immigrant, published serial novels and poems featuring lovesick men.[43] The protagonists of these stories used to confess their sorrow to another man, a friend, or an occasional drinking partner in a bar. Women were portrayed as cold, indifferent, materialistic, or treacherous people, who exercised emotional power over their heartbroken suitors. Sexual ardor and sorrow ended up weakening romantic and passionate men living in a city where women were scarce, because the proportion of males in the population had increased due to immigration.

Several poems published in *Caras y Caretas* throughout the first decade of the twentieth century revolved around the misfortunes of weak spirited men driven mad by love. Such was the case of the character of *El loco de los pensamientos* (The Madman of the Pansies), who lost his reason and secluded himself in his garden after being abandoned by the woman he loved. The madman would do nothing but weep and tenderly look at the pansies, which he saw as a reflection of the face of that "frivolous and flirty" woman who had rejected him. Overwhelmed by sorrow, one day, he plucked a flower, squeezed it, dug a small hole in the ground, and buried it while muttering: "If you do not love me, then I hate you, and if I hate you, you shall not live."[44]

In the serial novel *El paraguas misterioso* (The Mysterious Umbrella), love is described as a magic spell, as a force beyond individual control.[45] The lover in the story treasures a lock of his beloved's hair that she gave him while they were happy together. And now that she has left him to marry a wealthy man, he cries while caressing tenderly the lock of hair. Then, his friend and confidant advises him to throw it into the fire to free himself from the spell and avoid being consumed by love.

Although the image of a man in love capable of ending his life in a "romantic suicide,"[46] or killing the woman he loves was widespread in popular cultural circuits, it did not cross the courthouses' threshold. Justice kept a cautious distance from emotions, not only to ensure an impartial judgment but also to fulfill the duty of safeguarding traditional marriage,[47] to whose standards Ángel tried to fit by presenting his relationship with Carlota as lawful. It is paradoxical that he should have chosen that strategy, because if cohabitation and legal marriage would have been regarded as equals by the law, the judge may have sentenced him to life imprisonment, the punishment the Penal Code provided for uxoricides.[48] Instead, he was tried for homicide—since the couple's lack of legal marital status prevented the crime from being typified otherwise—and as a result, he was convicted with a term of imprisonment very close to the maximum, set on twenty-five years.[49] In the verdict, the judge pointed out a mitigating circumstance, by interpreting like insanity the psychiatrist's diagnosis of "physical and mental degeneration."[50] However, the fact that the murderer did not fulfill the expected role of provider, and instead lived off a woman who got her money from what the magistrate characterized as "an irregular life," was regarded as an aggravating factor. Except for the classification of the case as a homicide, all the arguments used during the proceedings—not only by the judge, but also by the prosecutor, the defense attorneys, and the forensic psychiatrists—were virtually indistinguishable from those on which the criminal courts usually relied to judge husbands who would murder their wives.[51]

However, some nuances may be identified in this particular court decision. In the proceedings of bodily harm and uxoricide analyzed above, judges recriminated the victims, casting doubt on their decorum when their husbands suspected them of infidelity, or admonishing them posthumously, as happened with Filomena Maestroestéfano. According to the judge who sentenced Ángel Fiorda to life imprisonment, it was the victim who exacerbated the jealousy of the murderer by confessing that she no longer felt affection for him. It is possible to speculate, then, that if Filomena had not defied her husband in this way, she would have likely saved her life.

In the case of Ángel Gianoglio, instead, the judge expressed sympathy for Carlota—as the psychiatrists had done in their reports. The court decision did not directly refer to prostitution, even though the word had been mentioned on several occasions throughout the proceedings (in the testimonies of the brothel's madam and the victim's new partner, the defendant's declaration, the defense allegations, and the medical report). The judge stated that Carlota's life was "irregular," yet he presented her as a woman having been doubly victimized by Ángel: because this immoral man had exploited her to live at her expense, and because when Carlota, "who was not his wife"—as it is underlined in the sentence—rejected him, he decided to take her life. If Carlota and Ángel had been legally married, it is likely that the judge would have highlighted the victim's moral lapses. But this was not a married couple, nor even a cohabiting couple. This was the case of a poor woman pushed into prostitution by a "moral degenerate."[52] Ángel and Carlota were not legally wed, therefore, the law had nothing to safeguard.

# Conclusion

Thousands of couples met again in turn-of-the-century Argentina to resume a relationship that migration had put on hold. Thousands more migrated together and adapted to living in a foreign country without this experience causing any irreparable rifts in their relationship. In these cases, love and longing prevailed over frustration, anger, grief, and resentment, emotions that these men and women must surely have experienced in different stages of their marital lives, before and after the migration. However, even amidst the vicissitudes, they all managed to realize the promise and fulfill the expectations that the migratory project had awakened. Different ways of asymmetrical exchange and reciprocal care made them feel together during the separation, a lonely vigil that entailed anxious feelings, emotion management, and capacity to maintain conjugal love.[1] In the end, the work of waiting bore fruits and the reunion of the couple in Argentina was a motive of joy and hope, two emotions that made easier the recovering of the languages of intimacy that during the liminal temporality of the wait had confined their expression to the narrow frame of the letters. After passing through the usual stages of the immigrants' life—the narrowness of a room in a tenement house, temporary jobs, frugality and savings—"the land of prosperity" ended up giving them the chance to move along the path of upward mobility that led to the middle classes' social and cultural universe. At this point, their existences disappeared in the anonymity of the happy families. In contrast, for the gloomy and tormented individuals whose stories were narrated in this book, the material and emotional costs of the migratory experience brought about dramatic circumstances that ended up taking them—sometimes abruptly—out of the course of their ordinary existences.

Stories of bigamy show the fragility of love challenged by distance and the passing of time, but also the agency of the women who, overcoming material, legal, and cultural barriers, appeared in cosmopolitan Argentina in search of their forgetful husbands. At the same time, bigamy reveals how these men integrated into the new society following a normative family model that promised them the "happiness" alluded to by *La Prensa* when describing the golden years of marriages that met a tragic end. At the dawn of the twentieth century, Domingo DeBartolo's attorney made a virtue of the bigamist's crime when he pointed out that getting married and forming a family ("an undeniable right for any honorable man after enduring such a prolonged loneliness") had helped his client to take roots in Argentina.[2] Although the lawyer's words should be taken with caution (because he was seeking to obtain a reduction of the punishment), it is suggestive that from the repertoire of possible allegations, he chose to claim that a double marriage had allowed the bigamist not only to overcome the emotional instability that the uprooting and loneliness caused in thousands of male immigrants, but that marrying again, even knowing that he was committing a crime, safeguarded DeBartolo's honor and manliness because he had complied with the prescriptive family model promoted by the Argentine ruling classes of the time.

Honorability was also invoked by husbands who sued their spouses for adultery or defended themselves against accusations of abuse by claiming that their marital authority had been scorned by a disobedient wife. Betrayed husbands' resentment and thirst for retaliation reverberated in the sentences of the judges, who, however, resorted to a more restrained semantical repertoire to avoid exacerbating the bitterness of the vindictive husbands—who represented themselves as the victims of their wives—and to keep the courtroom free of emotions. But despite the judges' neutral language, the notions of male honor and authority and of female obedience and submission resonated in their admonitions to decorum and virtue not only for the living wives, but also for the ones whose lives had been taken by their husbands. This attitude might also explain why the word *amor* (love) is rarely found in the court records, even though love was the emotion at stake in most cases.[3] The judges resorted to the word *cariño* (affection) instead. This is possibly because from the perspective of the law, *amor* was understood as a romantic passion—like the one evoked by Angel Gianoglio in his letters—an intense and overwhelming feeling that was at odds with reason and therefore did not conform to the patriarchal notion of marriage held by the state. The distribution of power in marriage required an emotional stability that love, understood as passion, lacked. Hence, the word *cariño*, more dispassionate, proved to be consistent with turn-of-the-century Argentina's mainstream notions of conjugal and family life.

Female agency, through which women often circumvented the barriers that prevented them from obtaining a passport without marital authorization or forced them to pay the cost of the uprooting responding with obedience and resignation to an unhappy marital relationship, challenged the prescriptive notion of marriage. This was accomplished both when women went to court to thwart their husbands' frauds or to defend themselves from their abuse, and when they were brought to justice to explain why they had "fallen in the arms of another man." Regardless of whether their judicial and extra-judicial battles achieved only ephemeral victories, women's actions were sustained by the idea that the law might help them escape from their husbands' authoritarianism. Their performances in the judicial arena, which rested on repertories and practices that were anchored in the places of origin but also resorted to scripts available in Argentina at that time, reveal how women integrated themselves into a country that many of them would probably not have chosen if it had not been for the mandate that forced them to live wherever their husbands established residence. Viewed from the perspective of the marital conflict and the distribution of power within marriage, the emotional standards and the emotional styles of the places of origin and those of the host society do not appear as discrete units nor as sets of shared norms, but rather as a broad space sharing common (or similar) meanings, in which new languages were interpreted in the light of old webs of significance.

For the protagonists of the stories of this book (and for the couples who, unlike them, never emerged from anonymity), adaptation to the host society used to be a tortuous path that entailed both negative and positive emotions. While many immigrants probably managed to navigate through uncertainty, nostalgia, and forgetfulness for finally reaching the anchorage of love and the joy of the reunion, those who left their traces in the court records were deprived of these affable feelings. Their lives, or rather the fragments of their lives glimpsed through source materials that are often laconic, show them moving through a narrow emotional landscape. Men, treacherous or gloomy and vengeful, looked like individuals consumed with fear, rage, and hatred. And women, who had to control their anger—although they were not always able to do so, as occurred with Rafaela Fioretto when she learned of her husband's bigamy—displayed the burden of resignation, but also the audacity of contempt, although expressing it often would imply losing their freedom and, in some cases, their lives.

Through the analysis of the court records in the light of the contexts in which plaintiffs, defendants, witnesses, and judicial officers were embedded, this book sought to identify both emotions and standards, values, styles, and expectations giving shape to their expression. Which feelings were valued in the various emotional communities where the immigrants' lives unfolded? Which emotions could be expressed openly, and which ones had to be restrained? Although the words (love, jealousy, anger, shame, contempt, vengeance, compassion) were the ones that oriented my search for the emotions in the sources, the eloquence of the gestural language and of the agonizing cries coming from the wounded bodies were—to the extent that it was possible—also considered. Admittedly, words are translations and bodies are portraits made from the cultural perspectives and moral prejudices of third parties (police, witnesses, lawyers, medical experts, and judges). However, this bias did not constitute a disadvantage for the analysis. A reading against the grain of complaints, testimonies, medical reports, and verdicts allowed me to uncover not only the conceptual frameworks of the state officials but also those of the different emotional communities that coexisted—often in tension—in turn-of-the-century Argentina.

In their muddled discourses, where lies and truth are intermingled, men and women who were taken out of their daily existence to have their frauds, their futile hoaxes, and their bloody crimes recorded in the pages of a file, the keys for understanding how immigrants interacted with the state and coped with the emotional standards and mainstream representations may be found. With different levels of detail, each case reveals how poor, illiterate, or semi-literate immigrants understood and made use of the judicial system, relying both on legal counsel and profane wisdom. They were historical actors who resorted to the police station and the court defending their rights, seeking retribution, or trying to find relief for their turbulent marital relationships. Victims and perpetrators used to regard the law as a realm devoid of emotion, in which, nonetheless, they might express their feelings and seek the sympathy of the judges, from whom they expected both compassion and impartial judgment.

In this book, several questions remained unanswered. I have chosen only two of them for these concluding remarks. The first one is to what extent bigamies, adulteries, abuses, and homicides committed by the immigrants differed from those perpetrated by the natives of the Argentina criolla. I should admit that I have no response to this issue since this comparison was not the main motivation for this research, which, less ambitiously, focused only on the impact of migration on conjugal love and on the emotions that used to replace it when the promises were broken, and the expectations remained unfulfilled.

The second question has to do with the bias of the archives. As it was pointed out in the introduction, if we were only to be guided by the marital conflicts that were brought to the courts (or whose records some archivist chose to be preserved), then the French, Jewish, Russians, and Scandinavians would not have committed bigamy and adultery, or would have not abused and murdered their wives. Naturally, this was not so. Rather it has to do with the bias of the archives and of the spatial framing I chose to address the immigrants' emotional experiences. The court records I relied on are faint images of a specific time and place, representing the imbalance of a long immigration process in which Italians and Spaniards had a dominating presence, but also reflect the uneven geographical distribution of the immigrants in Argentina, who mostly settled in the city and the province of Buenos Aires. However, if we shift the focus to the interior of the country, we notice that, for instance, the Arabic-speaking community that established itself in the northern provinces also brought to the courts a myriad of private conflicts. Syrian husbands, whom Hyland's study refers to, perpetrated such merciless uxoricides as the ones committed by Ángel Fiorda, Joaquin Turero y Miga, Antonio Palomares, and Antonio Pettina.[4]

Nevertheless, one would also hypothesize that each ethnic group found its own way of settling marital disputes and that many of them did it without resorting to the court. Probably, the Danes and the Volga Germans living in the rural close-knit communities of the south of the province of Buenos Aires, the Jews settled in the Buenos Aires City or in the agricultural colonies of Carlos Casares, in the northwest of the province of Buenos Aires (ethnic groups of which I did not find traces in the archives) likely would have turned to their pastors, parish priests, or rabbis seeking resolution to their marital conflicts. The churches and synagogues became the courts where the spouses laid out the details of the turbulent conjugal life before a judge with whom they were familiar with and in whom they could trust. However, those improvised "trials" melted into air because nobody registered them. They unfolded in the intimacy of a sacred place where marital disputes could be settled before they escalated to threaten the stability of the marriage or, even worse, endanger the life of one of the spouses.

# Notes

## Introduction

1  This term is used in David Gerber, *Authors of their Lives: The Personal Correspondence of British Immigrants to North America in the Nineteenth Century* (New York: New York University Press, 2006), 92.

2  On immigrant family correspondence, see Samuel Baily and Franco Ramella, *One Family, Two Worlds: An Italian Family's Correspondence across the Atlantic, 1901–1922* (New Brunswick: Rutgers University Press, 1988); Marcelo J. Borges, "For the good of the family: migratory strategies and affective language in Portuguese emigrant letters, 1870s–1920s," *The History of the Family* 21, n°3 (2016): 368–97; Borges, Marcelo, and Sonia Cancian, 'Reconsidering the migrant letter: from the experience of migrants to the language of migrants.' *The History of the Family*, 21, n°3 (2016): 281–90; Sonia Cancian, *Family, Lovers, and their Letters: Italian Postwar Migration to Canada* (Winnipeg, Manitoba University Press, 2010); María L. Da Orden, *Una familia y un océano de por medio. La emigración gallega a la Argentina: una historia a través de la memoria epistolar* (Barcelona: Anthropos, 2010); Bruce Elliot, David Gerber and Suzanne Sinke ed., *Letters Across Borders: The Epistolary Practices of International Migrants* (New York: Palgrave Macmillan, 2006); Emilio Franzina, *Merica, Merica! Emigrazione e colonizzazione nelle lettere dei contadini veneti in America Latina, 1876–1902* (Milán: Feltrinelli, 1979); Gerber, *Authors of Their Lives*; Antonio Gibelli and Fabio Caffarena, "Le lettere degli emigrante", in *Storia dell'emigrazione italiana*, Vol. 1. *Partenze*, ed. Piero Bevilacqua, Andreina De Clementi, and Emilio Franzina (Rome: Donzelli, 2001), 563–74; María Izilda Matos y Oswaldo Truzzi, "Present in absentia: Immigrant letters and requests for Family Reunification," *História Unisinos* 19, n°3 (2015): 348–57; Xosé Manoel Nuñez Seixas and Raúl Soutelo Vázquez. *As cartas do destino* (Vigo: Galaxia, 2005).

3  On the notion of imaginary co-presence see Loretta Baldassar, "Missing Kin and Longing to be Together: Emotions and the Construction of Co-presence in Transnational Relationships", *Journal of Intercultural Studies* 29, n°3 (2008): 247–66.

4  In her study of the contemporary Chinese migration to Korea, Kwon uses the notion of "work of waiting" and argues that the spousal waiting at home forms part of migration as an active attempt to realize a collectively imagined future. See June Hee Kwon, "The Work of Waiting: Love and Money in Korean Chinese Transnational Migration," *Cultural Anthropology* 30, n°3 (2015): 477–500.

5   One of the exceptions is the study undertaken by Steven Hyland of the personal
    experiences and daily interactions of the Arabic-speaking immigrants settled in the
    province of Tucumán in northern Argentina, in the period 1910–1940. The author
    resorts to court records of adultery, domestic abuse, divorce, and uxoricide. The
    content of his sources does not differ from the ones I use in this study; nevertheless,
    my perspective departs significantly from Hyland's. While I intend to shed light on
    how migration affected marital love, and hence the focus is on the intersection of
    migration and emotion, Hyland—who also attempts to understand better some of the
    deeply personal experiences of migrants—illuminates the interactions of Arabic-
    speaking immigrants with the Argentine state through the lens of the judicial system
    during an era of intense economic dislocation and sociopolitical turbulence. See
    Steven Hyland Jr., "Arabic speaking immigrants before the Court in Tucumán,
    1910–1940," *Journal of Women's History* 28, n°4 (2016): 41–64. Available online: https://
    muse.jhu.edu/article/641105 (accessed September 1, 2020). Another notable exception
    is found in the excellent microhistory of the Italian immigrants in Brazil by Maíra Ines
    Vendrame, *Power in the Village: Social Networks, Honor and Justice among Immigrant
    Families from Italy to Brazil*, trans. Miriam Adelman (New York: Routledge, 2020).
6   This trend coincides with the migratory flows of both groups. Except for the period
    1910–1913, the arrival of Italians in Argentina was much more numerous than that
    of Spaniards. In the decades of the 1880s and 1890s, the proportion was fourteen to
    one. On the comparison of the migratory flows, see Blanca Sánchez Alonso, "La
    inmigración española 1880–1914. Capital Humano y Familia," in *Impulsos e Inercias
    del Cambio Económico. Ensayos en Honor a Nicolás Sánchez-Albornoz*, ed. Clara E.
    Lida and José A. Piqueras (Valencia: Fundación Instituto de Historia Social, 2004),
    197–230.
7   The corpus is composed of fifty bigamy court records, thirty trials for adultery, thirty
    for domestic violence, and five trials for uxoricide. The sources were gathered in
    Archivo General de la Nación (National Archives), Archivo Histórico de la Provincia
    de Buenos Aires (Historic Archives of the Buenos Aires Province), and Sección
    Histórica del Departamento Judicial de Dolores (History Division at the Dolores
    Judicial Department).
8   Loretta Baldassar and Paolo Boccagni, "Emotions on the move: mapping the
    emergent field of emotions and migration," *Emotion, Space and Society*, n°16 (2015):
    73–80. Available onlyne: https://www.sciencedirect.com/science/article/abs/pii/
    S1755458615300153 (accessed July 7, 2018).
9   On the language of marital and family love in the immigrant letter see Borges, "For
    the good of the family;" Sonia Cancian, "My dearest love . . . Love, Longing, and
    Desire in International Migration," in *Migrations: Interdisciplinary Perspectives*, ed.
    Michi Messer, Renee Schroeder, and Ruth Wodak (Vienna: Springer Verlag, 2012),
    175–86.

10 According to the 1914 national census of population 930,000 Italians and 830,000 Spaniards were settled in Argentina. Among those of 7 years or more of Italian origin, illiteracy was 36 percent, while among Spaniards it was 26 percent. For further discussion, see Fernando Devoto, *Historia de la Inmigración en la Argentina* (Buenos Aires: Sudamericana, 2003).

11 At the turn of the twentieth century, Argentina—like other countries impacted by transatlantic immigration—was characterized by extraordinary spatial mobility of the male workforce. The phenomenon of "migration within migration" affected millions of men who did not have a fixed residence.

12 This was an excuse usually deployed in court by women accused of adultery.

13 The term "white widow" refers to a married woman whose husband was still alive but due to emigration had been absent for years. See Linda Reeder, *Widows in White: Migration and the Transformation of Rural Italian Women, Sicily, 1880–1920* (Toronto: University of Toronto Press, 2003).

14 Spanish Civil Code of 1889, article 58.

15 On the divergences between court records and personal narratives see Arlette Farge, *Le goût de l'archive* (Paris: Le Seuil, 1989). On the use of court records in the History of Emotions, see Susan J. Matt, "Recovering the invisible. Methods for the historical study of the emotions," in *Doing Emotions History*, ed. Susan J. Matt and Peter N. Stearns (Urbana: University of Illinois Press, 2014), 41–54; Katie Barclay, "Performing Emotions and Reading the Male Body in Irish Courts, 1800–1845," *Journal of Social History* 51, n°3 (2017): 293–312; Laura Kounine, "Emotions, mind, and body on trial: a cross-cultural perspective," *Journal of Social History* 51, n°2 (2017): 219–230; Mark Seymour, "Emotional arenas: from provincial circus to national courtroom in late nineteenth-century Italy," *Rethinking History: The Journal of Theory and Practice* 16, n°2 (2012): 177–197; Gian Marco Vidor, "Rhetorical Engineering of Emotions in the Courtroom: the Case of Lawyers in Modern France," *Rechtsgechichte/Legal History*, n°25 (2017): 286–295.

16 On emotional standards and feeling rules, see Arlie R. Hochschild, "Emotions Work, Feeling Rules and Social Structure," *American Journal of Sociology*, n°85 (1979): 551–75; Hochschild, "Ideology and Emotion Management: A Perspective and Path for Future Research," In *Research Agendas in the Sociology of Emotions*, edited by Theodor D. Kemper, 117–42. Albany: State University of New York Press, 1990; Hochschild, *The Commercialization of Intimate Life: Notes from Home and Work* (Berkeley: University of California Press, 2003); Peter N. Stearns and Caroline Z. Stearns, "Emotionology: Clarifying the History of Emotions and Emotional Standards," *American Historical Review* 90, n°4 (1985): 813–36. On emotional styles see Benno Gammerl, "Emotional Styles: concepts and challenges," *Rethinking History* 16, n°2 (2012): 161–75; Eva Illouz, *Saving the Modern Soul. Therapy, Emotions, and the Cutlure of Self-help* (University of California Press, 2008); Peter N. Stearns,

*American Cool: Constructing a Twentieth-century Emotional Style* (New York and London: New York University Press, 1994).

17  Jean-Claude Passeron and Jacques Revel, "*Penser par cas*. Raisonner à partir de singularités," in *Penser par cas*, ed. Jean-Claude Passeron and Jacques Revel (Paris: Éditions de l'EHESS, 2005), 9–44; Philippe Lacour, "Penser par cas, ou comment remettre les sciences sociales à l'endroit," Espaces Temps.net, 2005. Available online: https://www.espacestemps.net/articles/remettre-les-sciences-sociales-a-endroit (accessed June 16, 2017).

18  For a discussion on the convergences and divergences between historians and judges concerning the treatment of evidence, see Carlo Ginzburg, *The Judge, and the Historian: Marginal Notes on a Late-Nineteenth-century Miscarriage of Justice*, trans. by Anthony Shugaar (London: Verso, 1999).

19  For further discussion on the relevance of the context, see Giovanni Levi, "On Microhistory," in *New Perspectives on Historical Writing*, ed. Peter Burke (Pennsylvania: The Pennsylvania State University Press, 2001), 97–119; Jacques Revel, "Microanalyse et construction du social," in *Jeux d'echelles. La micro-anlyse à l'experience*, ed. Jacques Revel (Paris: Gallimard-Seuil: 1996), 15–36.

20  Victoria Calabrese, "Land of Women: Basilicata, Emigration, and the Women Who Remained Behind, 1880–1914" (Ph.D. diss., The Graduate Center, City University of New York, 2017). Available online: https://academicworks.cuny.edu/gc_etds/2101 (accessed, July 19, 2018).

# 1  The Land Of Prosperity

1  In 1890, after a decade of economic growth, Argentina underwent a severe economic and financial crisis, known as the "Baring Crisis," named after the English institution which was nearly brought down because of Argentina's default on its debt underwritten by Baring. But while Baring was saved thanks to a joint effort of the Bank of England and some private financial houses, Argentina did not receive much help and fell into a deep recession. In 1890, Argentina suspended servicing its external debt, and lost access to world capital market. The GDP fell 11 percent between 1890 and 1891 and the local paper currency (*peso*) was depreciated.

2  For an overview of the history of immigration in Argentina, see Devoto, *Historia de la inmigración*; María Bjerg, *Historias de la inmigración en la Argentina* (Buenos Aires: Edhasa, 2009).

3  Two million Italians and 1.4 million Spaniards arrived over the whole period. Those groups were followed, in far fewer number, by immigrants from France (170,000) and Russia (160,000). The latter were mostly Jewish.

4   In the first three decades of the twentieth century, Buenos Aires harbored more Galicians than any other city in the world. On Galician immigrants in Buenos Aires, see Xosé Manoel Nuñez Seixas ed., *La Galicia Austral. La inmigración gallega en la Argentina* (Buenos Aires: Biblos, 2001); Ruy Farías Iglesias, 'La inmigración gallega en el sur del Gran Buenos Aires 1869–1960' (Ph.D. diss., Programa de doctorado en Historia, Geografía e Historia del Arte, Universidad de Santiago de Compostela, Santiago de Compostela, 2010).

5   One example of the policy oriented to accomplish that aim was the *Ley de Inmigración y Colonización* (Immigration and Colonization Law) enacted in 1876. It was a state instrument to encourage agriculture and stimulate the arrival of European farmers by subsidizing fares and offering land at a reasonable price. This law also provided for the establishment of a department of immigration, an employment office, the immigrant hotel, and the appointment of immigration agents in different points of Europe. On the Immigration and Colonization Law, see Alejandro Fernández, "La ley argentina de inmigración y su contexto histórico," *Almanack Guarulhos*, n°17 (2017): 51–85. Available online: https://doi.org/10.1590/2236-463320171705 (accessed July 5, 2020).

6   In 1914, 74 percent of Spanish and 69 percent of Italian immigrants lived in urban areas. However, although the patterns of settlement were mostly urban, we should bear in mind that immigrants also played a key role in the countryside. Those who had access to arable land—mostly as sharecroppers or tenants—in the littoral and the province of Buenos Aires became the main historical actors of the huge agricultural growth process that turned Argentina into one of the greatest exporters in the world of wheat and corn. For a discussion about the immigrants' access to land, see Julio Djenderedjian, *Gringos en las pampas. Inmigrantes y colonos en el campo argentino* (Buenos Aires: Sudamericana, 2008); Ezequiel Gallo, *La pampa gringa* (Buenos Aires: Sudamericana, 1983); Blanca Zaberio, "Entre deux mondes les agriculteurs européens dans les 'nouvelles terres' de l'Argentine: exploitation agricole et reproduction sociale dans la pampa: 1880–1930" (Ph.D. diss., École des Hautes Études en Sciences Sociales, Paris, 1994).

7   Luis Alberto Romero, *A History of Argentina in the Twentieth Century*, trans. James P. Brennan (Pennsylvania: Pennsylvania State University Press, 2002), 9.

8   Roberto Cortés Conde and Ezequiel Gallo, *La Formación de la Argentina Moderna* (Buenos Aires: Paidós, 1972), 47.

9   Relations between Argentina and Europe increased radically in the last decades of the nineteenth century. France and Great Britain were the main trade partners. French imports were significant in luxury goods, wines, and sugar, while British textiles, hardware, coal, and machinery led the international market for Argentina. In parallel, British investors were crucial for the development of the infrastructure needed to modernize the country, such as railroads and harbors.

10 In 1895 there were 177 men for every 100 women, and 166 for every 100 in 1914. If counted separately by nationality, Spanish immigrants had the highest masculinity rate: 190 men for every 100 women. There were 179 Italian men for every 100 Italian women. On this topic, see Devoto, *Historia de la inmigración*, 265.

11 In the United States, even during the decades with the highest immigration rates, the immigrant population represented only 15 percent of the total population.

12 Only towns with more than 2,000 inhabitants are being considered.

13 Both in 1895 and in 1914, more than 80 percent of the total population lived there.

14 The most important exceptions, however, occurred in the provinces of Tucumán and Mendoza, centered around the production of sugar and wine, respectively. Both provinces prospered by supplying the growing markets of the littoral, thanks to state protective policy of high custom tariffs.

15 On the dream of the homeownership, see Jorge Francisco Leinur, "Radicar y controlar. La estrategia de la casa autoconstruida," in *La casa y la multitud. Vivienda, política y cultura en la Argentina moderna*, ed. Anahí Ballent and Jorge Francisco Leinur (Buenos Aires: Fondo de Cultura Económica, 2014), 173–92.

16 Among immigrants, marriage patterns were mainly endogamic, not only at the national level, but also at the regional and local levels. Nonetheless, this tendency fluctuated according to the sex ratio of each immigrant group, the places of settlement, immigrants' social and cultural backgrounds, and their religious affiliations. Both Spanish and Italian immigrants, as well as some minority groups—such as Danes and Jews—were the most endogamic, whereas the French showed a higher tendency to exogamic marriages. On immigrants' marriage patterns and spouse selection, see Samuel L. Baily, "Marriage patterns and immigrant assimilation in Buenos Aires, 1882–1923," *Hispanic American Historical Review* 60, n°1 (1980): 32–49; Ruth Freundlich de Seefeld, "La integración social de los extranjeros en Buenos Aires según sus pautas matrimoniales: ¿pluralismo cultural o crisol de razas?," *Estudios Migratorios Latinoamericanos*, n°2 (1986): 203–31; Hernán Otero, "Una visión crítica de la endogamia: reflexiones a partir de una reconstrucción de familias francesas (Tandil, 1850–1914)," *Estudios Migratorios Latinoamericanos*, n°15–16 (1990): 343–77.

17 José Luis Moreno, *Historia de la Familia en el Río de La Plata* (Buenos Aires: Sudamericana, 2004),192.

18 On popular classes' housing and the tenement house in Argentina, see Diego Armus and Jorge Hardoy, "Conventillos, ranchos y casa propia en el mundo urbano del novecientos," in *Mundo Urbano y Cultura Popular. Estudios de Historia Social Argentina* ed. Diego Armus (Buenos Aires: Sudamericana, 1990), 155–93; Juan Suriano, "Vivir y Sobrevivir en la Gran Ciudad. Hábitat Popular en la Ciudad de Buenos Aires a Comienzos del Siglo," *Estudios Sociales* 7, n°1 (2005): 49–68.

19 The electrification of the streetcars in Buenos Aires started in 1897, and by 1905 it connected the downtown area with most of the suburban neighborhoods in an

intricate network. Electrification reduced the price of public transportation in the city.

20 The increase of the population in Buenos Aires city was extraordinary. It grew from 177,000 inhabitants in 1869 to almost 1.6 million in 1914.

21 In 1907, several cities of the country were the scene of a tenants' strike demanding a reduction of the rent and an improvement in the living conditions of the tenement houses. The protest was known by the name of "the brooms strike" as women and children took to the streets with brooms in hand to "sweep" the landlords and defend themselves from the police. That same year, the National Department of Labor conducted a survey on twenty-three tenement houses in Buenos Aires, comprising 708 rooms where 3,146 people lived (an average of 136 persons per tenement). See Oscar Yujnovsky, "Políticas de vivienda en la ciudad de Buenos Aires (1880–1914)," *Desarrollo Económico* 14, n°54 (1974): 327–72.

22 At the beginning of the twentieth century, Italians owned 47 percent of the tenement houses and accommodated almost half of the tenants in the city of Buenos Aires, while Spanish immigrants owned 10 percent of the tenements and housed 9 percent of the tenants. See Fernando Devoto, *Historia de la inmigración*, 266.

23 Juan Suriano, "Vivir y sobrevivir en la gran ciudad," 55.

24 Because immigrants would spend some years in the city and then go back to their home countries (a common practice as can be seen in the high return rates mentioned above), or because they migrated from Buenos Aires to other regions of Argentina, where labor force was demanded either during the harvest seasons or in the construction of public buildings, railroads, and ports.

25 Grandi de Stella Anita por adulterio y José Berreta por complicidad, Juzgado del Crimen, G-82-3, 1897, Archivo General de la Nación, 25.

26 Ibid., 29.

27 According to the national census of population of 1914, children under the age of 14 represented 35 percent of tenement houses' dwellers.

28 For a discussion on child labor in Argentina in the late-nineteenth and early-twentieth centuries, see Ricardo Falcón, *El mundo del trabajo urbano (1890–1914)* (Buenos Aires: Centro Editor de América Latina, 1986), 43–58; Juan Suriano, 'Niños trabajadores. Una aproximación al trabajo infantil en la industria porteña de comienzos del siglo', in *Mundo urbano y cultura popular*, ed Armus, 251–79.

29 Intendencia Municipal de Buenos Aires, *Patronato y asistencia de la infancia en la capital de la República Argentina. Trabajos de la comisión especial* (Buenos Aires: El Censor, 1892), 270. Cited in Claudia Freidenraij, "La niñez desviada. La tutela estatal de niños pobres, huérfanos y delincuentes. Buenos Aires c. 1890–1919" (Ph.D. diss., Facultad de Filosofía y Letras, Universidad de Buenos Aires, 2015), 78.

30 School dropout rates were high; they were between 90 percent and 97 percent during the last two decades of the nineteenth century. This was aggravated by the fact that

most children left formal schooling between the first and second year of elementary education.

31 Freidenraij, "La niñez desviada," 88–93.

32 Some authors have pointed out that in turn-of-the-century Argentina, the universalist aspiration of public education coexisted with the skepticism on the part of a wide sector of the intellectual elite about the government's expectation that every child may be included in the public education system. For a discussion on this topic, see Sandra Carli, *Niñez, pedagogía y política. Transformaciones de los discursos acerca de la infancia en la historia de la educación argentina entre 1880 y 1955* (Buenos Aires: Miño y Dávila, 2002); María Carolina Zapiola, "Los niños entre la escuela, el taller y la calle (o los límites de la obligatoriedad escolar). Buenos Aires, 1884–1915," *Cadernos de Pesquisa* 39, n°136 (2009), 69–81.

33 Sandra Gayol, *Sociabilidad en Buenos Aires. Hombres de honor y cafés, 1862–1910* (Buenos Aires, Signo, 2000), 42.

34 Donna J. Guy, *Sex & Danger in Buenos Aires: Prostitution, Family and Nation in Argentina* (Lincoln: University of Nebraska Press, 1991), 24.

35 Pablo Ben, "Historia global y prostitución porteña: El fenómeno de la prostitución moderna en Buenos Aires, 1880–1930," *Revista de Estudios Marítimos y Sociales*, n°5/6 (2012/2013): 13–26.

36 Ben, "La ciudad del pecado: moral sexual de las clases populares en Buenos Aires del 900," in *Moralidad y comportamientos sexuales (Argentina, 1880–2011)*, ed. Dora Barrancos, Donna Guy and Adriana Valobra, Adriana (Biblos: Buenos Aires, 2014), 98.

37 See Chapter IV.

38 On the influence of positivism in Argentina see Kristin Ruggiero, *Modernity in the Flesh: Medicine, Law, and Society in Turn-of-the-Century Argentina* (Stanford, CA: Stanford University Press, 2004); Ricardo Salvatore "Criminología positivista, reforma de prisiones y la cuestión social en Argentina," in *La cuestión social en Argentina, 1870–1943*, ed. Juan Suriano (Buenos Aires: La Colmena, 2000), 127–58.

39 At the beginning of the twentieth century, immigrants' political activism, especially anarchism, affected the financial interests of the elites and provoked fear. Immigrants were regarded as a potential factor of social collapse. The social representation of immigrants began to change with the involvement of Spanish and Italian immigrants in worker unions and socialist and anarchist political movements. At the same time, under these circumstances, the notions of public order and law enforcement grew in importance among the ruling elite, for whom aliens became associated with crime and marginalization. For a discussion on social unrest and the criminalization of the immigrants, see Juan Suriano, "La cuestión social y el complejo proceso de construcción inicial de las políticas sociales en la Argentina Moderna," *Ciclos* XI, n°21 (2001): 123–47; Eduardo Zimmermann, *Los liberales*

*reformistas. La cuestión social en la Argentina 1890–1916* (Buenos Aires: Sudamericana-Universidad de San Andrés, 1994).

40 Created in 1887, by that time, the police statistics system was still embryonic. It is likely, therefore, that the numbers showing an increase in crime at the turn of the century are not reliable. However, even with its shortcomings, police statistics may have contributed to spread the image of social unrest and rising criminality not only among the political elites and the penitentiary authorities, but also among the middle and lower classes. The press may have played a crucial role, as crime statistics were made public monthly by the main national newspapers. On this topic see Lila Caimari, *Apenas un delincuente. Crimen, cultura y castigo en la Argentina* (Buenos Aires: Siglo XXI, 2004); Máximo Sozzo, 'Los exóticos del crimen. Inmigración, delito y criminología positivista en la Argentina (1887–1914)', *Delito y Sociedad*, 2 n°32 (2016): 19–52.

41 These attitudes toward Southern European immigrants—in particular, Italians— among politicians, academics and criminologists were not only a product of Argentina. They echoed racial discourses circulating throughout Italy since unification that depicted southern Italians as uncivilized and barbaric. Alfredo Niceforo, an anthropologist, sociologist, and criminologist wrote in *Italia Barbara*: "There are truly *two Italies* in collision, with completely different moral and social coloration . . . this diversity is also physical, because Italy is formed out of two very different breeds; one of these breeds peoples the north and center, the other the south and the islands." Cited in Linda Reeder, "Men of honor and honorable men: migration and Italian migration to the United States from 1880–1930', *Italian Americana* 28, n°1 (2010), 27. For a discussion on the Mezzogiorno backwardness and the dichotomic way of conceiving north-south relations in the peninsula, see Jane Schneider ed., *Italy's "Southern Question". Orientalism in One Country* (Oxford and New York: Berg Publishers, 1998) as well as the review article about revisionist historiography by Lucy Riall, "Which road to the south? Revisionists revisit the Mezzogiorno," *Journal of Modern Italian Studies* 4, n°1 (2000): 89–100.

42 Cited in Sozzo, "Los exóticos del crimen," 39–40.

# 2  Promise, Wait, and Betrayal

1 The concept refers to the different ways to exchange asymmetrical, reciprocal care and economic support among transnational family members and kin. They bring themselves "together across distance" by dealing with the challenges posed by absence and separation. However, as Kwon has pointed out, unlike waiting and caring for parents, children, and other family members, anticipating the return of a spouse is the condition of a couple-oriented project. In the case of spousal

relationships the work of waiting may lead to anxiety, vulnerability and precariousness in relationships. See Kwon, "The work of waiting," 481. On circulation of care, see Loretta Baldassar and Laura Merla, "Locating Transnational Care Circulation in Migration and Family Studies," in *Transnational Families, Migration, and the Circulation of Care: Understanding Mobility and Absence in Family Life*, ed. Loretta Baldassar and Laura Merla (Londres: Routledge, 2013), 25–58.

2  The notion alludes to the affective relationships of people to the material world, and to the role of objects in shaping emotions and of emotions shaping objects. An official document such as a marriage certificate, may be a sentimentally anodyne thing. Nevertheless, in a particular situation such as bigamy or divorce, it may transfigure into both a representation of the breaking of the marriage bond, and into an emotional object that bears and shape feeling such as sorrow, sadness, and rancor. For a discussion about emotional objects, see Stephanie Downes, Sally Holloway, and Sara Randles, eds. *Feeling Things. Objects and Emotions Through History* (Oxford: Oxford University Press, 2018); Juan Manuel Zaragoza Bernal, "Ampliar el marco. Hacia una historia material de las emociones," *Vínculos de Historia*, n°4 (2015): 28–40.

3  Unzueta v. Serafín por bigamia, Fondo Penal, 183-27-4, 1875, Sección Histórica del Departamento Judicial de Dolores.

4  Ibid., 8.

5  Letter from the chief of the police to the judge, in Unzueta v. Serafín, 42.

6  Parroquia Nuestra Señora de Dolores, Libros de Bautismo 1876–1877. Available online: https://familysearch.org/ark:/61903/1:1:XJ9X-Z56 (accessed May 5, 2018).

7  Barrachina v. Aldaz por bigamia, Juzgado del Crimen de la Capital, 351-2, 1881, Archivo Histórico de la Provincia de Buenos Aires.

8  Ibid, 24.

9  Ibid., 26.

10 Ibid., 27.

11 Ibid., 36.

12 The Justice of the Peace of Juárez to the Investigating Judge. Letter and authenticated copy of marriage certificate attached, August 18, 1881, in Barrachina v. Aldaz, 47.

13 A good example of the resignification of bonds and affection among immigrant couples is found in Maria Brunswig de Bamberg, *Allá en la Patagonia* (Buenos Aires: Javier Vergara, 1999). The book is a compilation of the letters written by a German migrant, Ella Hoffmann, who arrived in Argentina in 1923. After three and a half years of separation, she traveled in the company of her children to reunite with her husband, who was the manager of a sheep ranch in Patagonia. Ella's letters were addressed to her mother. The correspondence from her first year in Patagonia offers insight on the emotional implications of the couple's reunion and the conscious and unconscious effort she and her husband made to re-establish the relationship and the common language of affection.

14 Barrachina v. Aldaz, 50.

15 Baldomero Navacíes to Luis Aldaza. Letter, December 4, 1879, in Barrachina v. Aldaz, 51.

16 Barrachina v. Aldaz., 56.

17 Ibid., 82.

18 A feature of Latin American family and sexuality dating back to colonial times, concubinage was still a widespread practice in nineteenth-century Argentina. The historiography of the family has identified the existence of a double pattern of family organization in which factual unions and illegitimate children (mostly among popular sectors and in the rural areas) coexisted with legally married couples (a more common option among the so-called "decent classes"). People involved in "marriage-like" relationships and assembled families in which children of previous unions converged were common practices, although part of society rejected them. These two kinds of family arrangements have been, very roughly, associated with social stratification and status, settlement patterns, territorial mobility, and church and state control. Among urban upper and middle classes, marriage was valorized while among lower and subaltern classes, sexual unions and children born out of wedlock were much more common. On family and sex in colonial Latin America, see Asunción Lavrín, *Sexuality and Marriage in Colonial Latin America* (Lincoln: University of Nebraska Press, 1989). For Argentina, see Moreno, *Historia de la familia*; Ricardo Cicerchia, ed. *Historia de la vida privada en la Argentina. Desde la Constitución de 1853 hasta la crisis de 1930* (Buenos Aires: Troquel, 2001).

19 Major Paulino Amarante to the Justice of the Peace of Tandil. Letter July 31, 1864, Archivo Histórico Municipal de Tandil.

20 Parroquia Nuestra Señora de los Dolores, Libro de Bautismos 1858–1859. Available online: https://familysearch.org/ark:/61903/1:1:XNMV-426 (accessed August 11, 2016).

21 Melina Yangilevich, "Construir Poder en la Frontera. José Benito Machado," in *Vivir entre dos mundos. Las fronteras del Sur de la Argentina. Siglos XVIII y XIX*, ed. Raúl Mandrini (Buenos Aires: Taurus, 2006), 195–226.

22 His father-in-law's networks likely influenced the improvement of Luis' status from railroad worker to rural policeman.

23 This seems to have been a quite usual practice among upper class women, as the fact of merely appearing in court risked compromising their reputations. An honor/shame system whose centerpiece was men's control over female kin sexual behavior was at stake in this case. However, as I will show in the following chapters, the meaning of female honor differed when the historical actors belonged to the popular classes. In fact, male defense of the reputation of their female kin is notable by its absence. Oftentimes, in the search for redress, men whose honor had presumably been injured intended to tarnish women's honesty. For a discussion on the

intersection of honor, class and gender, see Sueann Caulfield, *In Defense of Honor: Sexual Morality, Modernity and Nation in Early-Twentieth-century Brazil* (Durham and London: Duke University Press, 2000); Sueann Caulfield, Sarah C. Chambers, and Lara Putman eds. *Honor, Status, and Law in Modern Latin America* (Durham and London: Duke University Press, 2005).

24 República Argentina, Segundo Censo Nacional de Población, 1895, Justina Amarante De Aldaz, 1895; Sección 21, Subdivisión 33, Ciudad de Buenos Aires. Available online: https://familysearch.org/ark:/61903/1:1:MWWD-GN9 (accessed September 19, 2016).

25 Atilio Roncoroni, *Historia del Municipio de Dolores* (Dolores: Edición de la Municipalidad de Dolores, 1967), 43–47.

26 On this notion, see Jeremy Boissevain, *Friends of Friends: Networks, Manipulators, and Coalitions* (New York: St. Martin's Press, 1974).

27 Barrachina v. Aldaz, 59.

28 Ibid., 60.

29 Ibid., 61.

30 William M. Reddy, *The Navigation of Feeling: A Framework for the History of Emotions* (New York: Cambridge University Press, 2001), 122–30.

31 República Argentina, Segundo Censo Nacional de Población, 1895, Andresa B. De Aldáz, Sección 01, Población urbana, La Plata. Available online: https://familysearch.org/ark:/61903/1:1:MWW2-PQN (accessed October 28, 2017).

32 Ute Frevert, *Emotions in History Lost and Found* (Budapest and New York: Central European University Press, 2011), 87–88. For a discussion on honor and gender, see also Sandra Gayol, *Honor y duelo en la Argentina moderna* (Siglo XXI: Buenos Aires, 2008); Julian Pitt-Rivers, "La enfermedad del honor," *Anuario IHES*, no.14 (1999): 235–45.

33 See Chapter IV.

34 Conforti por bigamia, Juzgado del Crimen, C28, 1884, Archivo General de la Nación.

35 In 1880, in the baptismal records of the parish Inmaculada Concepción Angela Conforti was registered as the legitimate daughter of Nicola Confori and his second wife María Ingenito. Available online: https://familysearch.org/ark:/61903/1:1:XN89-NHJ (accessed September 17, 2017).

36 Conforti por bigamia, 14.

37 Ibid., 11.

38 Ibid., 26.

39 Parroquia Nuestra Señora de Balvanera, Libro de Matrimonios 1885. Available online: https://familysearch.org/ark:/61903/1:1:V68Q-D2X (accessed September 18, 2017).

40 Fioretto v. DeBartolo por bigamia, Juzgado del Crimen, B89, 1901, Archivo General de la Nación.

41 Rafaela's testimony before the judge, in Fioretto v. DeBartolo, 16.

42 Ibid.

43 Julia's testimony, Fioretto v. DeBartolo, 25.

44 Fioretto v. DeBartolo, 18.

45 Ibid., 51.

46 Farge, *Le goût*, 10.

47 Mario De Filippis, *Storia, società, istituzioni, fede e pietà popolare a Marano Marchesato. La chiesa parrocchiale di Santa Maria del Carmine* (Consenza: Progetto 2000).

48 Marano Marchesato, Civil Records, 1879–1910. Available online: http://www. rootsweb.ancestry.com (accessed August 9, 2016).

49 On transnational conjugal relationships and marital love see Borges, "For the Good of the family."

50 On bigamy in colonial Latin America, see Alexandra Parma Cook and David Noble Cook, *Good Faith and Truthful Ignorance: The Case of Transatlantic Bigamy* (Durham and London: Duke University Press, 1991); Richard Boyer, *The Lives of the Bigamists: Marriage, Family and Community in Colonial Mexico* (Albuquerque: University of New Mexico Press, 1995); Mónica Ghirardi, *Matrimonios y familia en Córdoba. Prácticas y representaciones* (Córdoba: Centro de Estudios Avanzados Universidad Nacional de Córdoba, 2004).

51 Just to mention two examples: drawing on the remarkable records from the trial of a Spanish bigamist in Peru in the sixteenth century, in *God Faith and Truthful Ignorance*, the Cooks delved into the daily life, the relations between the sexes, the social order, the *mentalité* and experience of conquest and settlement of the New World. The story of an unusual man and his two wives is used to illuminate the world of sixteenth-century Spain and Peru. In *The Lives of the Bigamists*, Boyer, in a sort of collective ethnography that describes the processes involved in different life stages (childhood, marriage and family life), studied 200 plebeian individuals prosecuted by the Inquisition to shed light on the texture of the lives of ordinary people in Colonial Mexico, but also to demonstrate the remarkable social internalization of the Catholic notion of marriage. One of the main questions examined in the book is how the Inquisition was able to find and prosecute so many bigamists of the plebeian class.

52 Gayol, *Sociabilidad en Buenos Aires*.

53 Ben, "La ciudad del pecado."

54 On social control and gossip, see among others Robert F. Harney, "Men Without Women: Italian Migrants in Canada, 1885–1930," in *The Italian Immigrant Woman in North America*, ed. Betty Boyd Caroli, Robert F. Harney, and Lydio F. Tomasi (Toronto: Multicultural History Society of Ontario, 1977), 79–102; Borges, "For the Good of the Family."

55 Nicola Ruperto por bigamia, Fondo Penal, 97-133-6-91, 1891, Sección Histórica del Departamento Judicial de Dolores.

56 Birth records, Benevento, Castelvetere in Val Fortore, 1810–1942. Available online: https://familysearch.org/ark:/61903/1:1:QLK5-MR6P (accessed June 15, 2018).

57 Reeder, *Women in White.*

58 Gayol, *Sociabilidad en Buenos Aires.*

59 On the role of women after the migration of their husbands see Calabrese, "Land of Women;" Caroline Brettell, *Men Who Migrate, Women Who Wait: Population and History in a Portuguese Parish* (Princeton: Princeton University Press, 1986); Sally Cole, *Women of the Praia: Work and Lives in a Portuguese Coastal Community* (Princeton: Princeton University Press, 1986); Fortunata Piselli, *Parentela ed emigrazione. Mutamenti e continuità in una comunità calabrese* (Turín, Einaudi, 1981); Reeder, *Widows in White*; Maddalena Tirabassi 'Le emigrante italiane: dalla ricerca locale a quella globale', *Giornale di storia contemporanea* IV, no. 1 (2001): 86–94.

60 The Italian South was characterized by two systems of inheritance. The first system divided the family patrimonies so that sons and daughters would inherit equally. The other one was partible but patrilineal, where the family patrimony passed to male heirs and every effort was made to avoid dividing land into plots that could not guarantee the subsistence of the next generation. In this system, women simply did not inherit land; instead, they received a cash dowry which could be paid on at a later stage if the family had no sufficient cash reserves at the date of the marriage of a daughter. This might have been the case for Rafaela (although we can only speculate, as the sources do not provide enough evidence). On the systems of inheritance in southern Italy, see Andreina De Clementi, "Gender relations and migration strategies in the Rural Italian South: Land, Inheritance and Marriage Market," in *Women, Gender, and Transnational Lives, Italian Workers of the* World, ed. Donna Gabaccia and Franca Iacovetta (Toronto: University of Toronto Press, 2002), 76–105.

61 Reeder, Linda, "When Men Left Sutera: Sicilian Women and Mass Migration, 1880–1920," in *Women, Gender and Transnational Lives*, ed. Gabaccia and Iacovetta, 45–75.

62 See Marcelo J. Borges, *Chains of Gold: Portuguese Migration to Argentina in Transatlantic Perspective* (Leiden: Brill, 2009), 194; Caroline Brettell, *Men who Migrate*; Pilar Cagiao Vila, "Género y emigración: las mujeres inmigrantes gallegas en la Argentina," in *La Galicia Austral*, ed. Nuñez Seixas, 107–36; Reeder, *Women in White.*

63 Women may have tried to work around the law or manipulate officials, but most were unsuccessful when requesting passports without the authorization of their husbands. See Calabrese, "Land of Women."

# 3 Breaking the Sacred Vows

1  On the debate about the consequences of emigration from southern Italy see Reeder, *Women in White*.

2  A divorce law did not exist in any of the three countries.

3  Órdenes del Día, 139–1885, 167–1894, 387–1898 and 1069–1900, Archivo y Museo Histórico del Servicio Penitenciario de la Provincia de Buenos Aires.

4  According to Reedy, this is a freedom not to make rational choices, but to undergo or derail conversion experiences and life-course changes involving numerous contrasting incommensurable factors. See Reddy, *The Navigation of Feelings*, 129.

5  Only two of the sixty-five reports consulted for the period 1880–1900 involved Argentine adult women.

6  Lamar v. Castellani y Nicolas Lamar por adulterio y complicidad, Fondo Pena, 268-142-12-92, 1892, Sección Histórica del Departamento Judicial de Dolores, 8.

7  Ibid., 13.

8  For a discussion on honor in Italy, see Reeder, "Men of Honor.'"

9  On the situation of women in Italy in the era of mass migration, see Donna Gabaccia, *Italy's Many Diasporas* (New York; London: Routledge, 2000); Reeder, *Widows in White*.

10  Lamar v. Catellani y Nicolás Lamar, 13.

11  Ibid., 17.

12  Ibid., 13.

13  Reeder, "Men of Honor," 24.

14  Joaquín Escriche y Martín, *Diccionario razonado de legislation y jurisprudencia* (Madrid: Cuesta, 1874–1875). Cited in Kristine Ruggiero, "Private Justice and Honor in the Italian Community in Late XIXth Century Buenos Aires," *Crime, Histoire & Sociétés/Crime, History & Societies* 13, n°2 (2009); 55–68.

15  This notion of adultery was put forward by the Spanish jurist Joaquín Escriche y Martín. His legal work was a reference in the Argentine law.

16  Lamar v. Castellani y Nicolás Lamar, 45.

17  Solomon, Robert C., "Justice v. Vengeance. On Law and the Satisfaction of Emotion," in *The Passions of Law*, ed. Susan A. Bandes (New York; London: New York University Press, 1999), 127.

18  Solomon maintains that the intensity of passion is not necessarily proportionate to irrationality. See Solomon, "Justice v. Vengeance," 130.

19  Lamar v. Castellani y Nicolás Lamar, 19.

20  When he was a foreigner.

21  In her study on adultery in Argentina at the end of the nineteenth and the beginning of the twentieth century, Donna Guy found that although the crime of adultery was difficult to prove, women were usually incarcerated as the husbands' strategy for

punishment. In the cases studied by Guy, just like Pedro Lamar, men withdrew their complaints as they evaluated that the time in prison had a sufficient deterrent effect to discipline an allegedly unfaithful wife. See Donna J. Guy, "Volviendo del silencio: Divorcio y violencia familiar en la Argentina de fines del siglo XIX y comienzos del XX," *Feminaria* 15, n° 28/29 (2002): 45–46. For further discusión see Dora Barrancos, *Mujeres entre la casa y la plaza* (Buenos Aires; Prometeo, 2008).

22 República Argentina, Segundo Censo Nacional de Población, 1895, Nicolás Lamar, Sección 10, Subdivisión 29, Ciudad de Buenos Aires. Available online: https://familysearch.org/ark:/61903/1:1:MWCV-SPT (accessed January 19, 2018).

23 Gongeiro v. Josefa Blanca Lois y Luis Álverez por adulterio y complicidad, Fondo Penal, 73-152-3-93, 1893, Sección Histórica del Departamento Judicial de Dolores, 5.

24 Caretaker of a section of a ranch.

25 Although shame overlaps with embarrassment, Stearns notes that they are clearly different in principle. Embarrassment, when one has violated group norms or expectations, is simply less intense and noticeably less durable. Shame not only lasts longer but also its sensations can be revived through community pressure. See Peter N. Stearns, *Shame: A Brief History* (Chicago; Springfield, University of Illionis Press, 2017), 1–3.

26 Marianna Muravyeva, "*Vergüenza, vergogne, schande, skam* and *sram*. Litigating for shame and dishonour in Early Modern Europe," in *Shame, Blame and Culpability: Crime and Violence in the Modern State*, ed. Judith Rowbotham, Marianna Muravyeva, and David Nash (London; New York: Routledge, 2013), 17–31.

27 Gongeiro v. Lois y Álvarez por adulterio y complicidad, 27.

28 Ibid., 31.

29 Ibid., 17.

30 Ibid., 20.

31 Ibid., 34.

32 Both in criminal justice and in the justice of the peace, it was usual that husbands ended up withdrawing the charges before the judge's sentence. For a discussion on adultery and the justice of the peace in the province of Buenos Aires, see Yolanda Paz Trueba, "La justicia en una sociedad de frontera: conflictos familiares ante los Juzgados de Paz. El centro sur bonaerense a fines del siglo XIX y principios del XX," *Historia Crítica*, n°36 (2008): 102–23.

33 From my corpus of sources, I selected thirty court records of women accused of adultery to trace them both in the national population censuses and in baptism records from the database "Familysearch." From that universe, I could only trace nineteen defendants. All of them resumed their marital lives after the date on which the case was closed, which usually occurred because the plaintiff dropped the charges.

34 Jan Plamper, "The history of emotions. An interview with William Reddy, Barbara Rosenwein and Peter Stearns," *History and Theory* 49, n°2 (2010), 240.

35 Reedy, *The Navigation of Feelings*, 128–30.

36 On the criticism of Reddy's analytical framework, see among others Jan Plamper, *The History of Emotions: An Introduction* (Oxford: Oxford University Press, 2015); Barbara Rosenwein, "Review of The Navigation of Feeling: a framework for the History of Emotions," *The American Historical Review* 107, nº4, (2002): 1181–82; Peter N. Stearns, "Review of The Navigation of Feeling: a framework for the History of Emotions," *Journal of Interdisciplinary History* 33, nº3 (2003): 473–75. See also Reddy's response to his critics in the interview made by Plamper, "The History of Emotions. An interview," 238–49.

37 For further discussion on the situation of women in Spain, see Mary Nash, *Mujer, familia y trabajo en España, 1875–1936* (Barcelona: Anthropos Editorial, 1983).

38 Antonio Pareja Serrada, *La influencia de la mujer en la regeneración social*, (Guadalajara: Establecimiento Editorial D. Antero Concha, 1880). Cited in Nash, *Mujer, familia*, 19.

39 Mary Nash, "Un-contested identities: motherhood, sex reform and the modernization of gender identity in early-twentieth-century Spain," in *Constructing Spanish Womanhood: Female Identity in Modern Spain*, ed. Victoria Lorée Enders and Pamela Beth Radcliff (New York: State University of New York Press, 1999), 25–49.

40 The same emotional style can be observed in other Spanish women whose stories are told in this book; for example, in the case of Paula Lamas analyzed in Chapter V.

41 Calabrese Salvador v. Teresa Salomone y José Rochart o Rosciano por rapto, adulterio y hurto, Fondo Penal, 137-1-91, 1891, Sección Histórica del Departamento Judicial de Dolores, 8.

42 Ibid., 15. Instead of using *usted*, the formal way of addressing someone, Rosciano used the so-called *tuteo*.

43 Ibid., 34.

44 Ibid., 9.

45 Ibid., 27.

46 Ibid., 21.

47 Letter from the justice of the peace of Juárez to the investigating judge, January 4, 1992, in Calabrese v. Salomone y Rochart o Rosciano, 39.

48 Calabrese v. Salmón y Rochart o Rosciano, 47.

49 Ibid.

50 Ibid., 52.

51 The practice of abandoning children was widespread in Italy in the nineteenth century and turned into a heavily debated social issue. See David I. Kertzer, *Sacrified for Honor: Italian Infant Abondonment and the Politics of Reproductive Control* (Boston: Beacon Press, 1993); Anna-Maria Tapaninen, "Motherhood through the wheel: the care of foundlings in late nineteenth-century Naples," in *Gender, Family*

*and Sexuality: The Private Sphere in Italy, 1860–1945*, ed. Perry Willson (London: Palgrave Macmillan: 2004), 51–70. For a discussion on the role of the Italian press and the debate about the consequences of massive male migration in the late nineteenth and early twentieth century, see Reeder, "Men of Honor."

52 Martha C. Nussbaum, *Upheavals of Thought: The Intelligence of Emotions* (Cambridge: Cambridge University Press, 2001), 337.

53 Calabrese v. Salomone y Rochart o Rosciano, 53.

54 Parroquia Nuestra Señora del Carmen de Juárez, Libro de Bautismos 1890–1892. Available online: https://familysearch.org/ark:/61903/1:1:XNZJ-174 (accessed June 26, 2017).

55 Calabrese v. Salomene y Rochart o Rosciano, 47.

56 Ibid., 48.

57 Bugni, Mateo v. Olinda Bértola y Franciso Mélica por adulterio y complicidad, Fondo Penal, 158-14-94, 1894, Sección Histórica Departamento Judicial de Dolores, 24.

58 Ibid., 11.

59 Ibid.

60 Ibid., 13.

61 Ibid., 25.

62 Ibid., 28.

63 Ibid, 49.

64 Ibid., 54.

65 Katie Barclay, *Love, Intimacy and Power: Marriage and Patriarchy in Scotland, 1650–1850* (Manchester; New York: Manchester University Press, 2011).

66 On negotiation in the patriarchal structure see Deniz Kandiyoti, "Bargaining with Patriarchy," *Gender & Society* 2, n°3 (1988): 274–90; Margaret Ezell, *The Patriarch's Wife: Literary Evidence and the History of the Family* (Chapel Hill: North Carolina University Press, 1987).

67 On this notion as well as on the theoretical challenges of the persistence of patriarchy, see the contribution of the feminist historian Judith Bennett, *History Matter:. Patriarchy and the Challenge of Feminism* (Philadelphia: University of Pennsylvania Press, 2006), 54–81.

68 Barclay, *Love, and Intimacy*, 9.

69 Kandiyoti, "Bargaining," 278–79.

70 Susan A. Bandes, "Introduction," in *The Passions*, ed. Bandes, 9.

71 Nussbaum, *Upheavals of Thought*, 348.

72 Domenico Rizzo, "Marriage on trial: adultery in nineteenth-century Rome," in *Gender, Family, and Sexuality*, ed. Willson, 20–36.

73 However, it is worth noting that apart from the evocation of "need," in my sources there are no other allusions to the role religion might have played in the way in

which adulterous and abandoned spouses coped emotionally with the collapse of their marital bonds and expectations. The reason for this silence may obey to the nature of the sources and the space in which the marital conflicts were settled, namely the court. The judicial system was one of the powers of a new liberal and secular state. The relation between the Catholic Church and the Argentine State underwent a period of conflict due to the enactment of the *leyes laicas* (lay laws) such as the law of civil marriage in the 1880s. In only one of the cases analyzed in the previous chapter—that of Andresa Barrachina—is there a reference to the role of the church, since it was a priest who opened the way for Barrachina to sue her bigamous husband.

74 Calabrese v. Salomone y Rochart o Rosciano.

75 Nussbaum maintains that it is not possible to feel "compassion for the sufferings of mortals without an awareness of sharing the same possibilities and vulnerabilities." See Nussbaum, *Upheavals of Thought*, 327.

76 Reeder, "Men of Honor," 24–25.

77 Historians have proved that the statistics of illegitimate birth and child abandonment did not change in a substantial manner because of the massive migration of men. However, it is also true that statistics furnish data and numbers which do not allow a comprehensive estimation. For example, in post-unification Italy, infanticide was often calculated as a part of the overall tally of homicides, or else lumped in with parricides, so it is a phenomenon whose real extent is for the most part still unknown. The same applies to abortion and the abandonment of infants outside foundling hospitals, the common strategies used by women to circumvent the codes imposed by society and by the law. See Silvia Chiletti, "Infanticide and the Prostitute: Honour, Sentiment and Deviancy between Human Sciences and the Law," in *Italian Sexualities Uncovered, 1789–1914*, ed. Valeria P. Babini, Chiara Beccalossi and Lucy Riall (London: Palgrave, 2015), 143–61.

78 Maddalena Tirabassi, "Bourgeois Men, Peasant Women: Rethinking Domestic Work and Morality in Italy," in *Women, Gender, and Transnational Lives*, ed. Gabaccia and Iacovetta, 106–30.

79 The Spanish Penal Code from 1870 provided the punishment of expatriation for the husband who killed his wife and/or her accomplice instantly or caused them serious bodily injures when he discovered her committing adultery. Whereas, if he caused them minor injuries, he would be acquitted. In Italy, uxoricide in the occasion of adultery was part of the so-called *delitto d'onore*. The so-called "Zanardelli Code" eliminated the death penalty, which allowed for greatly reduced punishments for those who killed female family members surprised in flagrant adultery or intercourse. In Argentina, the so-called *Código de Tejedor*, which was in force between 1874 and 1886, punished with imprisonment for up to three years the husband who killed his wife and/or her accomplice upon discovering her

committing adultery. When in 1886 a new Criminal Code entered into force, the uxoricide of an adulterous wife discovered in *flagrante delicto* exempted the betrayed husband from criminal responsibility. For further discussion, see Eva Cantarella, "Homicides of honor: the development of Italian adultery law over two millennia," in *The Family in Italy from Antiquity to the Present*, ed. David I. Kertzer and Richard P. Saller (New Haven: Yale University Press, 1991), 229–44; Steven C. Hughes, "Honourable murder: The *delitto d'onore* and the Zanardelli code of 1890," *Journal of Modern Italian Studies* 25, n°3 (2020): 229–51. Available online: https://doi: 10.1080/1354571X.2020.1750786 (accessed September 5, 2020); Alicia Rodríguez Nuñez, "El parricidio en la legislación española," *Boletín de la Facultad de Derecho*, n°5 (1993–1994): 145–71; Raúl Eugenio Zaffaroni and Miguel Alfredo Arnedo, *Digesto de Codificación Penal Argentina* (Buenos Aires: AZ Editora, 1996) vol. I, 320; vol. II, 198; vol. III, 161.

80 Mark Seymour, "Keystone of the patriarchal family? Indissoluble marriage, masculinity and divorce in Liberal Italy," *Journal of Modern Italian Studies* 10, n°3 (2005): 297–313.

81 On religious and civil marriage in Spain, see Javier Ferrer Ortiz, "Del matrimonio canónico como modelo al matrimonio civil deconstruido: la evolución de la legislación española," *Revista Ius et Praxis* 17, n°2, (2011): 391–418. On adultery and divorce in Spain, see Francisco Checa Olmos and Concepción Fernández Soto, "Adulterio femenino, divorcio y honor en la escena decimonónica española. El debate social en la recepción de El nudo gordiano de Eugenio Sellés (1842–1926)," *Revista de Dialectología y Tradiciones Populares*, LXIX, n°1 (2014): 155–69.

82 On the escape, "illicit relationships" and sexuality in the pampa, see Carlos Mayo, *Estancia y Sociedad en la pampa, 1740–1820* (Buenos Aires: Biblos, 1995).

# 4 The Anatomy of Everyday Hatred

1 For a discussion on family and violence in Europe, see among others Benoît Garnot, "La violence dans la France moderne: une violence apprivoisée?," in *Violence, Conciliation et Répresion, Recherches sur l'histoire du crime, de l'Antiquité au XXIe siècle*, ed. Aude Musin, Xavier Rousseaux, and Frédéric Vesentini (Louvain: Presses Universitaires de Louvain, 2008). Available online: http://books.openedition. org/pucl/723 (accessed 14 May, 2018); Jacques Goody, *The European Family* (London: Blackwell, 2000); George Vigarello, *Histoire du viol, XVIe–Xxe siècles* (Paris: Seuil, 1998).

2 For a discussion on domestic violence in late nineteenth- and early twentieth-century Argentina, see Mónica Ghirardi, "Disciplinamiento familiar y nuevos dispositivos de dominación en tiempos de modernización. Córdoba, Argentina, fines

del siglo XIX," in *Trayectorias familiares. Identidades y desigualdad social*, ed.
Francisco Chacón Jiménez (Murcia: Ediciones Universidad de Murcia, 2018), 58–79;
Yolanda Paz Trueba, "Violencia física y efectos simbólicos. El caso de Tres Arroyos a
fines del siglo XIX y principios del XX,, *Anuario del Instituto de Historia Argentina*,
n°8 (2008), 173–92. For the colonial period and the first half of the nineteenth
century, see Mónica Ghirardi, "Familia y maltrato doméstico. Audiencia Episcopal de
Córdoba, 1700–1850," *História Unisinos* 8, n°1 (2008): 17–33; Viviana Kluger, *Escenas
de la vida conyugal. Los conflictos matrimoniales en la sociedad virreinal rioplatense*
(Buenos Aires: Quórum, 2003).

3  This uxoricide is analyzed in the next chapter.

4  "Morbosidad," *El Correo Español*, May 11, 1889, 8.

5  According to Barbara Rosenwin, "emotional communities are largely the same as
social communities—families, neighborhoods, syndicates, academic institutions,
monasteries, etc—factories, platoons, princely courts. But the researcher looking at
them seeks above all to uncover systems of feeling, to establish what these
communities (and the individuals within them) define and assess as valuable or
harmful to them; the emotions that they value, devalue, or ignore; the nature of the
affective bonds between people that they recognize; and the modes of emotional
expression that they expect, encourage, tolerate, and deplore." See Barbara H.
Rosenwein, "Problems and Methods in the History of Emotions," *Passions in Context*,
n°1 (2010), 11. As for the term "moral community," Weisman used it in his study of
the emotion of remorse and shows how the moral community exerts pressure on its
members both to show remorse and not to show remorse. See Richard Weisman,
*Showing Remorse: Law and the Social Control of Emotions* (London; New York:
Routledge, 2014), 12–13.

6  "Marito arrabiatto,'" *La Patria degli Italiani*, March 28, 1902, 4.

7  "Comida insípida," *La Prensa*, January 24, 1902, 5.

8  "Furia de una Moglie," *La Patria degli Italiani*, July 15, 1899, 4.

9  For a discussion on women's anger see Frevert, *Emotions in History*, 89–100; Linda
Pollock, "Anger and the negotiation of relationships in Early Modern England," *The
Historical Journal* 47, n°3 (2004): 567–90.

10  Debenedetti, Francisco por maltrato y lesiones a su esposa, Juzgado del Crimen,
D93,1906, Archivo General de la Nación, 2.

11  Ibid., 11.

12  Ibid., 12.

13  Ibid., 29.

14  Ibid., 18.

15  Ibid.

16  Ibid., 31.

17  Ibid.

18 The amended Argentine Criminal Code of 1903 provided a prison sentence of six months to one year when the injury did not cause a permanent impairment to the victim. However, if the impairment of health, organs, or senses endangered the victim's life or prevented him or her from working for more than a month, the aggressor would be punished with imprisonment of one to six years. See Zaffaroni and Arnedo, *Digesto de Codificación*, vol. II, 213 and vol. III, 174.
19 Debenedetti por maltrato y lesiones, 51.
20 Ricardo Salvatore, "Sobre el surgimiento del estado médico legal en la Argentina (1890–1940)," *Estudios Sociales*, n°20 (2001): 81–114.
21 Teresa Brasca v. Mariano Darbano por lesiones, Juzgado del Crimen, D94-1908, Archivo General de la Nación, 3–4.
22 Ibid., 8.
23 Ibid., 9.
24 Ibid., 20.
25 Lila Caimari, ed. *La ley de los profanos. Delito, justicia y cultura en Buenos Aires (1870–1940)* (Buenos Aires: Fondo de Cultura Económica, 2007).
26 Código Civil de la República Argentina, 1869, article 187.
27 Marinelli v. Schiavo por adulterio y hurto, Juzgado del Crimen, S-61, 1891, Archivo General de la Nación.
28 Ibid., 11.
29 Ibid., 14.
30 Ibid., 8.
31 Ibid., 15.
32 Underlined in the original.
33 Marinelli v. Schiavo, 27.
34 Letter from Marinelli to the judge in Marinelli v. Schiavo, 37.
35 Ibid., 49.
36 Vigo v. Guardamagna por lesiones e intento de homicidio, Juzgado del Crimen G-123, 1902, Archivo General de la Nación, 14.
37 Ibid., 15.
38 Ibid., 8.
39 Ibid., 21.
40 Ibid., 27.
41 Ibid., 31.
42 Ibid., 32.
43 Ibid., 480.
44 Bretell, *Men who Migrate*; Pilar Cagiao Vila, *Muller e Emigración* (Santiago de Compostela: Xunta de Galicia, 1997); Andreina de Clementi, *L´assalto al cielo. Donne e uomini nell'emigrazione italiana* (Rome: Donzelli, 2014); Gabaccia and Iacovetta, eds. *Women, Gender and Transnational Lives*; Reeder, *Widows in White*.

45 See Borges, "For the good of the family."
46 See Chapter II.
47 Kwon, "The work of waiting," 495.
48 Cesare Pavese, *The Moon and the Bonafires*, trans. Louise Sinclair (London, Lehmann, 1963), 58. Available online: https://archive.org/details/in.ernet. dli.2015.149109 (accessed August 16, 2020)
49 For a discussion on the moral and social meanings of money, see Johnathan Parry and Maurice Bloch, eds. *Money and Morality of Exchange* (Cambridge: Cambridge University Press, 1989); Viviana Zelizer, *The Social Meaning of Money: Pin Money, Paychecks, Poor Relief & Other Currencies* (New York: Basicbooks, 1994); Ariel Wilkis, *Las Sospechas del Dinero. Moral y Economía en la Vida Popular* (Buenos Aires, Paidós, 2013).
50 Vigo v. Guardamagna, 32.
51 Myriam Jimeno, *Crimen Pasional. Contribución a una Antropología de las Emociones* (Bogotá: Universidad Nacional de Colombia, 2004), 37.
52 Ariel Wilkis, "El poder moral del dinero. Una perspectiva sociológica," *Diferencia(s)*, n°5 (2017), 46.
53 In his studies on the moral power of money, Wilkis sustained that earned money is transformed in safeguarded money through negotiations despite the resistance of certain members of the family. Thus, safeguarded money is attained through concessions, tensions, and strategies to protecting it. See Wilkis, "El poder moral."
54 Vigo v. Guardamagna, 43.
55 Ibid., 54.
56 Barclay, *Love, Intimacy and Power*, 1.

# 5 The Passion of Jealousy

1 I do not use the expression "crime of passion" because neither the court records nor the press chronicles on which I have relied use that denomination when alluding to men who killed their wives. Uxoricide, homicide, and tragedy were the most common words used in the sources. Moreover, from the analytical perspective, "crime of passion" is an ambiguous category because—as noted by Benoît Garnot— crimes of passion are not always conjugal, and conjugal crimes are not always passionate. See Benoît Garnot, *Une histoire du crime passionnel. Mythes et archives* (Paris: Belin, 2014).
2 "Marito bestiale," *La Patria degli Italiani*, April 4, 1902, 10. In his analysis of domestic violence among Syrian immigrants in the province of Tucumán, Hyland noted that social crimes of passion touched a sensitive chord in Argentine society. Hyland draws on Eusebio Gómez, an important Argentine legal scholar, who at the

beginning of the twentieth century asserted that "public opinion was excessively tolerant with crimes related to amorous passion that justified the murderer and denigrated the victim." Notwithstanding, it seems relevant to underscore that in my research I found that although the notion "crimes of passion" was present in the public discourse, also expressed as "romantic crimes" or "romantic suicide"— particularly in the press—attorneys, prosecutors, and judges would not evoke it in the court. Nevertheless, this did not necessarily mean that the judicial authorities did not show sympathy for the defendants when the wives were allegedly unfaithful. See Hyland, "Arabic-Speaking Immigrants."

3   *El Correo Español*, September 15, 1893, 6.

4   For a discussion on the place of emotions in law, see Bandes, "Introduction," in *The Passions*, ed. Bandes, 1–15.

5   Fiorda, Ángel por uxoridicio de Filomena Mastrostefano, Juzgado del Crimen, F-38-1892, Archivo General de la Nación, 2–3.

6   Ibid., 14. In Argentina, having a *macho* is a vulgar way to describe having a lover.

7   *La Prensa*, August 6, 1892, 5.

8   Ibid.

9   Código Penal de la Nación Argentina de 1886, article 250.

10  Although in both 1891 and 1903 the committees in charge of drafting the projects aimed at reforming the Penal Code proposed to no longer consider adultery as a crime, this proposal was not adopted on either occasion.

11  Rodolfo Moreno (hijo), *Ley Penal Argentina Estudio Crítico* (La Plata: Editores Sesé y Larrañaga, 1903), 160.

12  Only three of the thirty cases of adultery from which I drew information to write Chapter III went through the entire judicial process and resulted in the conviction of the adulteress.

13  If we were to follow Solomon's arguments, we could affirm that Fiorda lacked the rationality required by the feeling of vengeance, to which we refer in Chapter III, when I presented the case of Pedro Lamar and his adulterous wife. Undoubtedly, by murdering his wife, Fiorda sought retribution for the suffering that her unfaithfulness had caused him; however, as Solomon states, not all forms of retribution are vengeful because vengeance is reflective and rational, at least in its instrumental sense.

14  Fiorda por uxoricidio, 11.

15  Ibid., 18.

16  *Palermo* refers to a neighborhood of the city of Buenos Aires where, back then, the National Penitentiary was located.

17  Fiorda por uxoricidio, 62.

18  Steven C. Hughes, "Honourable murder;" Eva Cantarella, "Homicides of Honor."

19  Fiorda por uxoricidio, 24.

20 The tragedy of the Fiordas was reported in a similar moral tone by *La Prensa* and *La Nación*, two of the Argentine newspapers with the largest circulation, as well as by the ethnic paper *La Patria degli Italiani*.

21 Fiorda por uxoricidio, 63.

22 Ibid. 65.

23 Ibid., 66.

24 Ibid., 69.

25 See Terry A. Maroney, "The persistent cultural script of judicial dispassion," *California Law Review* Vol. 99, n°2 (2011): 629–81; Vidor, "Rhetorical engineering of emotions," 288.

26 Hyland, "Arabic-speaking immigrants," 48–49.

27 Fiorda por uxoricidio, 29.

28 Garnot, *Une histoire du crime passionnel*, 94.

29 Fiorda por uxoridicio, 83.

30 The Penal Code of 1886 provided the death penalty for anyone who killed his/her father, mother, siblings, or spouse. If attenuating circumstances were proved, the punishment would be life imprisonment.

31 These are the words of the judge of the first instance. Fiorda por uxoridicio, 63.

32 Fiorda por uxoricidio, 29.

33 Ibid., 36.

34 Mark Seymour, "Keystone to the patriarchal family?."

35 Fiorda por uxoricidio, 91.

36 On the general paralysis of the insane, see Olga Villasante Armas, "Introducción del concepto de parálisis general progresiva a la psiquiatría decimonónica española," *Asclepio* 52, n°1, (2000): 53–72; Juan Manuel Pérez Trullen, Álvaro Giménez Muñoz, Isabel Campello, and Luis Chárlez, "La parálisis general progresiva o enfermedad de Bayle," *Neurosciences and History* 3, n°4 (2015): 147–53.

37 Fiorda por uxoricidio, 84.

38 Turero y Miga, Joaquín por el uxoridicio de Paula Lamas, Juzgado del Crimen, T-15B-1889, Archivo General de la Nación, 4.

39 Ibid., 11.

40 Ibid., 12.

41 *La Prensa*, November 11, 1889, 6.

42 Turero y Miga, 17.

43 Ibid., 19.

44 The article 81 of the Argentine Penal Code of 1886, in force when Turero y Miga killed his wife, exempted from punishment defendants suffering from a mental infirmity.

45 Turero y Miga por uxoricidio, 34.

46 Ibid., 39.

47 Ibid.

48 For a discussion on male nervous character and the role of reason and feelings in men's behavior, see Luiz Fernando Dias Duarte, *Da vida nervosa nas clases trabalhadoras urbanas* (Río de Janeiro: Jorge Zahar, 1986).

49 Turero y Miga por uxoricidio, 45.

50 Ibid., 54.

51 Ibid., 56, emphasis in the original.

52 Ibid, 55.

53 Ibid.

54 Ibid., 69.

55 Scheer had termed "emotional practices," doings and sayings such as speaking, gesturing, remembering, manipulating objects, and perceiving sounds, smells, and spaces. According to her, "emotional practices" build on the embodied knowledge of the habituated links that form complexes of mind/body actions. See Monique Scheer, "Are Emotions a kind of practice (and is that what makes them have a history?) A Bourdieuian approach to understanding emotion," *Theory and History* 51, n°2 (2012): 209.

56 Fiorda por uxoricidio, 14.

57 Ibid., 24.

58 Arlie R. Hochschild, "Emotions work;" Ibid. *The Comercialization*; Stearns and Stearns, "Emotionology."

59 Weisman, *Showing Remorse*, 3–17.

60 On hate crimes see Sarah Ahmed, *The Cultural Politics of Emotions* (Edinburgh: Edinburgh University Press, 2004); Mari J. Matsuda, "Public response to racist speech: considering the victim's story," in *Words that Wound: Critical Race Theory, Assaultive Speech, and the First Amendment*, ed. Mari J. Matsuda, Charles R. Lawrence, and Richard Delgado (Boulder: West View Press, 1993), 17–51.

61 Ahmed, *The Cultural Politics*, 49.

62 On the role of emotions in explaining and demonstrating insanity in legal debates during the nineteenth and early twentieth centuries, see Daphne Rozenblatt, "Legal insanity: towards an understanding of free will thorough feeling in modern Europe," *Rechtsgeschichte/Legal History*, n°25 (2017): 263–75.

63 I analyzed twenty-two court records kept in the Archivo General de la Nación in Buenos Aires.

64 Palomares Antonio por uxoricidio, Juzgado del Crimen, P-51, 1890, Archivo General de la Nación, 2–3.

65 Ibid., 18.

66 Ibid., 28.

67 Ibid., 28.

68 Ibid., 20.

69 Ibid., 26.

70 Ibid., 22.

71 According to the report of the medical experts, Palomares also expressed remorse during the observation. Nevertheless, unlike Turero y Miga, he was sentenced to life imprisonment as his insanity was not proven.

72 Antonio Pettina por uxoridicio, Juzgado del Crimen, P-66, 1893, Archivo General de la Nación.

73 Ibid., 4.

74 Ibid., 30.

75 Ibid., 20.

76 Ibid., 40.

77 Ibid., 41.

78 Ibid., 14.

79 Although the scholarly literature tends to view remorse and apology as synonyms, as noted by Weisman, offering an apology is not functionally and semiotically equivalent to the showing of remorse. While apology may convey in words meanings that are consistent with what is expressed in the showing of remorse, displays of feeling (breaking down, losing control, having fits) have a greater weight than words to infer that the self that condemns the act is more real than the self that had committed the act. See Weisman, *Showing Remorse*, 9–10.

80 Pettina por uxoricidio, 49.

81 Ibid., 56.

82 In the cases analyzed here the special configuration affects the person's emotional performance as the court is a social space where "dominant and subordinate" emotional styles intersect. For further discussion see Gammerl, "Emotional styles;" William Reddy, William M., "Emotional styles and modern forms of life.'" In *Sexualized Brains: Scientific Modeling of Emotional Intelligence from a Cultural Perspective*, edited by Nicole C. Karafyllis and Gotlind Ulshöfer (Cambridge, MA: MIT Press, 2008), 81–100; Stearns, *American Cool*.

83 Although occasionally disobedience and infidelity tended to overlap, as in the case of Ángel Fiorda, for example.

84 For a discussion on how historical actors felt about honor and on the relation between their feelings and their sense of honor's meanings, see Carolyn Strange, Robert Cribb, Christopher E. Forth (ed.), *Honour, Violence and Emotions in History* (London; New York: Bloomsbury, 2014).

85 In Spain, the nineteenth century was a period in which honesty became a basic element for the social esteem of individuals. The so-called "hombre de bien" articulated the sense of male honor and that man was becoming the prototype of reference of the society of the time. For a discussion on honor and honesty, see Pablo Ortega del Cerro, "Del honor a la honradez: un recorrido por el cambio de valores

sociales en el España de los siglos XVIII y XIX," *Cuadernos de Ilustración y Romanticismo Revista Digital del Grupo de Estudios del Siglo XVIII*, no. 24 (2018): 597–618.

# 6  Killing for Love

1  Dawn Keetley, "From Anger to Jealousy: Explaining Domestic Homicide in Antebellum America," *Journal of Social History* 42, n°2 (2008): 269–97.

2  In the emotional configuration interact thoughts and feelings which are socially shared and culturally constructed. The configuration is made up of social and individual habitus that operate as a mark of unity in the face of a particular theme of social life: the couple's loving relationships. On emotional configuration related to crimes of passion, see Jimeno, *Crimen Pasional*, 48.

3  According to official statistics, however, prostitutes constituted a small minority of the immigrant women in Buenos Aires. For example, between 1889 and 1901, there were 6,413 women selling sex registered in the city, and only 25 percent were Argentines. In contrast, Russian, Romanian, German, and Austro-Hungarians totaled 36 percent. The next largest groups came from Italy (19 percent) and France (9 percent). See Guy, *Sex and Danger in Buenos Aires*, 17.

4  As noted in Chapter I, several studies relying on censuses and vital records had shown that in the late nineteenth and early twentieth century, cohabitation was not a widespread practice among immigrants in Argentina. In the popular classes marriage rates were higher among foreigners than among Argentines. See María Cristina Cacopardo and José Luis Moreno, *La familia italiana meridional en la emigración a la Argentina* (Napoli: Edizione Scientifiche Italiane, 1994).

5  On the middle-class family in turn-of-the-century Argentina, see Eduardo Míguez, "Familias de clase media: la formación de un modelo," in *Historia de la vida privada en Argentina. La Argentina plural (1870–1930)*, ed. Fernando Devoto and Marta Madero (Buenos Aires: Santillana, 1999), 21–46.

6  Ángel Gianoglio por homicidio de Carlota Castellari (alias Carmen Moretti), Juzgado del Crimen, G 131, 1904, Archivo General de la Nación, 2.

7  *La Prensa*, January 18, 1904, 5.

8  Ibid.

9  Gianoglio por homicidio, 19.

10  Ibid., 5.

11  In 1904, the municipality of Buenos Aires restricted the exercise of the sex trade forcing brothels to have no more than two prostitutes, one maid, and one janitor. The new provision also increased penalties and fines for clandestine prostitution, and provided that even those brothels that operated in accordance with the law were

liable for temporary or permanent closure in the event of public disturbance. See Guy, *Sex and Danger in Buenos Aires*, 80.

12  Gianoglio por homicidio, 20.

13  Ibid., 24.

14  Ibid.

15  Ibid., 25.

16  Ibid.

17  Letter from Ángel Gianoglio to the investigating judge, May 5, 1904, in Gianoglio por homicidio, 40.

18  Gianoglio por homicidio., 34.

19  Letter from Gianoglio, May 5, 1904, 40. Emphasis in the original.

20  Letter from Gianoglio to the investigating judge, June 1, 1904, in Gianoglio por homidicio, 52.

21  Ibid.

22  Letter from Ginoglio to the investigating judge, July 6, 1904, in Gianoglio por homicidio, 54.

23  Ibid.

24  Letter from Gianoglio to the investigating judge, September 3, 1904, in Gianoglio por homicidio, 59.

25  Ibid.

26  Letter from the victim's father to Gianoglio, August 14, 1904, in Gianoglio por homicidio, 64.

27  Letter from Gainoglio, July 6, 1904, 54.

28  On the role of tears and weeping, see Anne Vincent-Buffault, *Histoire des larmes: XVIIIe–XIXe siècles* (Marseille, Rivages, 1986); Anne Coudreuse, *Le goût des larmes au XVIIIe siècle* (Paris: Presses Universitaires de France, 1999); Tom Lutz, *Crying: The Natural and Cultural History of Tears* (New York; London: Norton, 1999); Marco Menin, "'Who Will Write the History of Tears?' History of Ideas and History of Emotions from Eighteenth-Century France to the Present," *History of European Ideas* 40, n°4 (2014): 516–523; Thomas Dixon, "The Tears of Mr Justice Willes,'" *Journal of Victorian Culture* 17, n°1 (2012): 1–23. Available online: https.//doi.org.10.1080/1355 5502.2011.611696 (accessed May 20, 2020).

29  Thomas Dixon points out that tears only became expressions of emotions during the nineteenth century. Even then, they continued to be also expressions of thoughts and of sensations. Not only, then, did crying not necessarily express a particular emotion such as grief or sorrow; it did not necessarily express any emotion at all. See Dixon, "The tears," 5.

30  However, possession may also be related to the morality of romantic love that demanded exclusivity and complete devotion on the part of the female partner. See Frevert, *Emotions in History*, 71.

31 Karen Lystra, *Searching the Heart: Women, Men and Romantic Love in Nineteenth-century America* (Oxford: Oxford University Press, 1992), 206.

32 Gianoglio por homicidio, 106.

33 Ibid., 107.

34 Ibid., 108.

35 On crimes of passion and madness, see Lisa Appignanesi, *Trials of Passion: Crimes in the Name of Love and Madness* (London: Virago, 2014).

36 On love and jealousy, see among others Aaron Ben-Ze'ev, "Jealousy and Romantic Love," in *Handbook of Jealousy: Theory, Research and Multidisciplinary Approaches,* ed. Sybil L. Hart and Maria Legerstee (Oxford: Blackwell, 2010), 40–54; Ronald de Sousa, "Love, Jealousy and Compersion," in *The Oxford Handbook of Philosophy of Love,* ed. Christopher Grau and Aaron Smuts (Oxford: Oxford University Press, 2017). Available online: https//doi.org/10.1093/oxfordhb/9780199395729.013.30 (accessed April 19, 2020).

37 Gianoglio por homicidio, 119.

38 On the social circulation of the serialized novel, see Alejandra Laera, "Novelas argentinas (circulación, debates y escritores en el último cuarto del siglo XIX)", in *Historia crítica de la literatura argentina,* Vol. 3. *El brote de los géneros,* ed. Noé Jitrik (Buenos Aires: Emecé Editores, 2010), 95–118.

39 Several studies have analyzed the historical, philosophical, and literary forms of romantic love in different social and cultural contexts. The authors agree on the relevance of literature, music, and the press as the main cultural circuits through which the notion of romantic sentiment was expanded. On the history of the romantic emotion see, among others, Claire Langhamer, *The English in Love: The Intimate Story of an Emotional Revolution* (Oxford: Oxford University Press, 2013); Oliva López Sánchez and Edith Flores, "Reflexiones iniciales para una genealogía del amor romántico en clave de emociones," in *Pensar los Afectos. Aproximaciones desde las Ciencias Sociales y las Humanidades,* ed. Ana Abramowski and Santiago Canevaro (Los Polvorines: Ediciones UNSG, 2017), 191–206; Simon May, *Love: A History* (New Haven: Yale University Press, 2011); Sarah Pinto, "Researching Romantic Love," *Rethinking History* 21, n°4 (2017): 567–85; William Reddy, *The Making of Romantic Love* (Chicago: The University of Chicago Press, 2012).

40 "Marito bestiale," *La Patria degli Italiani,* April 3, 1902, 10.

41 Benoît Garnot, *Une histoire du crime passionnel.*

42 "Ha ucciso la prostituta e tentó il suicidio," *La Patria degli Italiani,* January 16, 1904, 5.

43 For a discussion on the cultural and social role of *Caras y Caretas* in early twentieth-century Argentina, see Geraldine Rogers, *Caras y Caretas. Cultura, política y espectáculo en los inicios del siglo XX argentino* (La Plata: Editorial de la Universidad de la Plata, 2008).

44 "El loco de los pensamientos," *Caras y Caretas*, October 8, 1898, 9.

45 "El paraguas misterioso," *Caras y Caretas*, August, 1901, 11.

46 That was the way the press referred to suicides committed due to unrequited love. For example, in 1901, *Caras y Caretas* reported the suicide of two young men who had taken their lives for that reason, pointing out that "in the last few years a wave of suicides has been committed mostly by men who experienced love in the dramatic style depicted by romantic novels." It seems paradoxical that the same weekly journals published fictions narrating stories of unrequited love with tragic denouements, while alerting about them in the police news section when they occurred in real life.

47 The notion of family and marriage (monogamous and heterosexual) prescribed by the Catholic Church, namely a patriarchal institution based on the indissolubility of the marital bond and the obedience of wife and children to the authority of the husband/father, was adopted without any significant change by the civil marriage law enacted in Argentina in 1888. See Nancy Calvo, "Cuidar la familia, forjar la nación. La institución matrimonial y el modelo de familia. Argentina, Siglos XIX–XX', *Prohistoria*, n°27 (2017): 37–54.

48 The death penalty for uxoricide was abolished in 1903, and was replaced by life imprisonment.

49 The amended Penal Code of 1903 provided a term of imprisonment from ten to twenty-five years for the crime of homicide.

50 Gianoglio por homicidio, 117.

51 For a discussion on the treatment received by the cohabitees in the judicial system, see Stephen Parker, *Informal Marriage, Cohabitation, and the Law, 1750–1989* (New York: St. Martin's Press, 1990); Ginger Frost, "He Could Not Hold His Passions": Domestic Violence and Cohabitation in England (1850–1905)," *Crime, Histoire & Sociétés/Crime, History & Societies* 12, n°1 (2008): 45–63.

52 Gianoglio por homicidio, 107.

# Conclusion

1 On the notion of circulation of care, see Baldassar and Merla, "Locating Transnational Care," 40.

2 Fioretto v. DeBartolo por bigamia, 52.

3 In their various ways and expressions, from which neither love nor money were excepted.

4 On the Arabic-speaking immigrants' interactions with the justice system in northern Argentina, see Hyland Jr, "Arabic-speaking immigrants."

# Bibliography

Ahmed, Sarah. *The Cultural Politics of Emotion*. Edinburgh: Edinburgh University Press, 2004.

Appignanesi, Lisa. *Trials of Passion: Crimes in the Name of Love and Madness*. London: Virago, 2014.

Armus, Diego, and Jorge Hardoy. "Conventillos, ranchos y casa propia en el mundo urbano del novecientos." In *Mundo Urbano y Cultura Popular. Estudios de Historia Social Argentina*, edited by Armus, Diego 155–93. Buenos Aires: Sudamericana, 1990.

Baily, Samuel, and Franco Ramella. *One Family, Two Worlds: An Italian Family's Correspondence across the Atlantic, 1901–1922*. New Brunswick: Rutgers University Press, 1988.

Baldassar, Loretta. "Missing kin and longing to be together: emotions and the construction of co-presence in transnational relationships." *Journal of Intercultural Studies* 29, n°3 (2008): 247–66.

Baldassar, Loretta and Laura Merla. "Locating transnational care circulation in migration and family studies." In *Transnational Families, Migration, and the Circulation of Care: Understanding Mobility and Absence in Family Life*, edited by Baldassar, Loretta and Laura Merla, 25–58. London: Routledge, 2013.

Baldassar, Loretta and Paolo Boccagni. "Emotions on the move: mapping the emergent field of emotions and migration." *Emotion, Space, and Society*, n°16 (2015): 73–80, https://www.sciencedirect.com/science/article/abs/pii/S1755458615300153

Bandes, Susan A. "Introduction." In *The Passions of Law*, edited by Bandes, Susan A., 1–15. New York; London: New York University Press, 1999.

Barclay, Katie. *Love, Intimacy and Power: Marriage and Patriarchy in Scotland, 1650–1850*. Manchester; New York: Manchester University Press, 2011.

Barclay, Katie. "Performing emotions and reading the male body in Irish courts, 1800–1845." *Journal of Social History* 51, n°3 (2017): 293–312.

Barrancos, Dora. *Mujeres entre la casa y la plaza*. Buenos Aires: Prometeo, 2008.

Brunswig de Bamberg, María. *Allá en la Patagonia*. Buenos Aires: Javier Vergara, 1999.

Ben, Pablo. "Historia global y prostitución porteña: El fenómeno de la prostitución moderna en Buenos Aires, 1880–1930." *Revista de Estudios Marítimos y Sociales*, n°5/6 (2012/2013): 13–26.

Ben, Pablo. "La ciudad del pecado: moral sexual de las clases populares en la Buenos Aires del 900." In *Moralidades y comportamientos sexuales. Argentina 1880–2011*, edited by Barrancos, Dora, Donna Guy, and Adriana Valobra, 95–113. Buenos Aires: Biblos, 2014.

Bennett, Judith. *History Matters: Patriarchy and the Challenge of Feminism*. Philadelphia: University of Pennsylvania Press, 2006.

Ben-Ze'ev, Aaron. "Jealousy and romantic love." In *Handbook of Jealousy: Theory, Research and Multidisciplinary Approaches*, edited by Hart, Sybil L. and Maria Legerstee, 40–54. Oxford: Blackwell, 2010.

Bjerg, María. *Historias de la inmigración*. Buenos Aires: Edhasa, 2009.

Boissevain, Jeremy. *Friends of Friends: Networks, Manipulators and Coalitions*. New York: St. Martin′s Press, 1974.

Borges, Marcelo J. *Chains of Gold: Portuguese Migration to Argentina in Transatlantic Perspective*. Leiden: Brill, 2009.

Borges, Marcelo J. "For the good of the family: migratory strategies and affective language in Portuguese emigrant letters, 1870s–1920s." *The History of the Family* 21, n°3 (2016): 368–397.

Borges, Marcelo J. and Sonia Cancian. "Reconsidering the migrant letter: from the experience of migrants to the language of migrants." *The History of the Family* 21, n°3 (2016): 281–90.

Boyer, Richard. *The Lives of the Bigamists: Marriage, Family and Community in Colonial Mexico*. Albuquerque: University of New Mexico Press, 2001.

Brettell, Caroline. *Men Who Migrate, Women who Wait: Population and History in a Portuguese Parish*. Princeton: Princeton University Press, 1986.

Cacopardo, María Cristina and José Luis Moreno. *La familia italiana meridional en la emigración a la Argentina*. Napoli: Edizione Scientifiche Italiane, 1994.

Cagiao Vila, Pilar. *Muller e Emigración*. Santiago de Compostela: Xunta de Galicia, 1997.

Cagiao Vila, Pilar. "Género y emigración: las mujeres inmigrantes gallegas en la Argentina." In *La Galicia Austral. La inmigración gallega en la Argentina*, edited by Nuñez Seixas, Xosé Manoel, 107–36. Buenos Aires: Biblos, 2001.

Caimari, Lila, ed. *La ley de los profanos. Delito, Justicia y Cultura en Buenos Aires (1870–1940)*. Buenos Aires: Fondo de Cultura Económica, 2007.

Caimari, Lila. *Apenas un delincuente. Crimen, cultura y castigo en la Argentina*. Buenos Aires: Siglo XXI, 2004.

Calabrese, Victoria. "Land of women: Basilicata, emigration, and the women who remained behind, 1880–1914." Ph.D. diss., The Graduate Center, City University of New York, 2017, https://academicworks.cuny.edu/gc_etds/2101.

Calvo, Nancy. "Cuidar la familia, forjar la nación. La institución matrimonial y el modelo de familia. Argentina. Siglos XIX–XX." *Prohistoria*, n°27 (2017): 37–54.

Cancian, Sonia. *Family, Lovers, and their Letters: Italian Postwar Migration to Canada*. Winnipeg: Manitoba University Press, 2010.

Cancian, Sonia. "*My Dearest Love* . . . Love, longing and desire in international migration." In *Migrations: Interdisciplinary Perspectives*, edited by Messer, Michi, Renee Schroeder, and Ruth Wodak, 175–86. Vienna: Sprinter Verlag, 2012.

Cantarella, Eva. "Homicides of honor: the development of Italian adultery law over two millennia." In *The Family in Italy from Antiquity to the Present*, edited by Kertzer, David I., and Richard P. Saller, 229–44. New Haven: Yale University Press, 1991.

Carli, Sandra. *Niñez, pedagogía y política. Transformaciones de los discursos acerca de la infancia en la historia de la educación argentina entre 1880 y 1955*. Buenos Aires: Miño y Dávila, 2002.

Caulfield, Sueann. *In Defense of Honor: Sexual Morality, Modernity and Nation in Early-Twentieth-century Brazil*. Durham; London: Duke University Press, 2000.

Caulfield, Sueann, Sarah C. Chambers, and Lara Putman, eds. *Honor, Status, and Law in Modern Latin America*. Durham; London: Duke University Press, 2005.

Checa Olmos, Francisco, and Concepción Fernández Soto. "Adulterio femenino, divorcio y honor en la escena decimonónica española. El debate social en la recepción de El nudo gordiano, de Eugenio Sellés (1842–1926)." *Revista de Dialectología y Tradiciones Populares* LXIX, n°1 (2014): 155–69.

Chiletti, Silvia. "Infanticide and the prostitute: honour, sentiment and deviancy between human sciences and the law." In *Italian Sexualities Uncovered, 1789–1914*, edited by Babini, Valeria P., Chiara Beccalossi, and Lucy Riall, 143–61. London: Palgrave Macmillan, 2015.

Cicerchia, Ricardo, ed. *Historia de la vida privada en la Argentina. Desde la Constitución de 1853 hasta la crisis de 1930*. Buenos Aires: Troquel, 2001.

Cole, Sally. *Women of the Praia: Work and Lives in a Portuguese Coastal Community*. Princeton: Princeton University Press, 1986.

Cortés Conde Roberto, and Ezequiel Gallo. *La Formación de la Argentina Moderna*. Buenos Aires: Paidós, 1972.

Coudreuse, Anne. *Le goût des larmes au XVIIIe siècle*. Paris: Presses Universitaires de France, 1999.

Da Orden, María Liliana. *Una familia y un Océano de por medio. La emigración gallega a la Argentina: una historia a través de la memoria epistolar*. Barcelona: Anthropos, 2010.

De Clementi, Andreina. "Gender relations and migration strategies in the rural Italian South: land, inheritance and marriage market." In *Women, Gender, and Transnational Lives: Italian Workers of the World*, edited by Gabaccia, Donna and Franca Iacovetta, 76–105. Toronto: University of Toronto Press, 2002.

De Clementi, Andreina. *L´assalto al cielo. Donne e uomini nell'emigrazione italiana*. Rome: Donzelli, 2014.

De Filippis, Mario. *Storia, società, istituzioni, fede e pietà popolare a Marano Marchesato. La chiesa parrocchiale di Santa Maria del Carmine*. Consenza: Progetto 2000, 2000.

de Sousa, Ronald. "Love, jealousy and compersion." In *The Oxford Handbook of Philosophy of Love*, edited by Grau, Christopher and Aaron Smuts. Oxford: Oxford University Press, 2017, https//doi.org/10.1093/oxfordhb/9780199395729.013.30.

Devoto, Fernando. *Historia de la Inmigración en la Argentina*. Buenos Aires: Sudamericana, 2003.

Dias Duarte, Luiz Fernando. *Da vida nervosa nas clases trabalhadoras urbanas.* Rio de Janeiro: Jorge Zahar, 1986.

Dixon, Thomas. "The tears of Mr. Justice Willes." *Journal of Victorian Culture* 17, n°1 (2012): 1–23, https.//doi.org.10.1080/13555502.2011.611696

Djenderedjian, Julio. *Gringos en las pampas. Inmigrantes y colonos en el campo argentino.* Buenos Aires: Sudamericana, 2008.

Downes, Stephanie, Sally Holloway, and Sara Randles, eds. *Feeling Things: Objects and Emotions Through History.* Oxford: Oxford University Press, 2018.

Elliot, Bruce, David Gerber, and Suzanne Sinke, eds. *Letters Across Borders: The Epistolary Practices of International Migrants.* New York: Palgrave Macmillan, 2006.

Ezell, Margaret. *The Patriarch's Wife: Literary Evidence and the History of the Family.* Chapel Hill: North Carolina University Press, 1987.

Falcón, Ricardo. *El mundo del trabajo urbano (1890–1914).* Buenos Aires: Centro Editor de América Latina, 1986.

Farge, Arlette. *Le Goût de l'archive.* Paris: Seuil, 1989.

Farías Iglesias, Ruy. "La inmigración gallega en el sur del Gran Buenos Aires 1869–1960." Ph.D. diss., Programa de doctorado en Historia, Geografía e Historia del Arte, Universidad de Santiago de Compostela, Santiago de Compostela, 2010.

Fernández, Alejandro. "La ley argentina de inmigración y su contexto histórico." *Almanack Guarulhos,* n°17 (2017): 51–85, https://doi.org/10.1590/2236-463320171705

Ferrer Ortiz, Javier. "Del matrimonio canónico como modelo al matrimonio civil deconstruido: la evolución de la legislación española." *Revista Ius et Praxis* 17, n°2 (2011): 391–418.

Franzina, Emilio. *Merica, Merica! Emigrazione e colonizzazione nelle lettere dei contadini veneti in America Latina (1876–1902).* Milan: Feltrinelli, 1979.

Freidenraij, Claudia. "La niñez desviada. La tutela estatal de niños pobres, huérfanos y delincuentes. Buenos Aires c. 1890–1919." Ph.D. diss., Facultad de Filosofía y Letras, Universidad de Buenos Aires, 2015.

Freundlich de Seefeld, Ruth. "La integración social de los extranjeros en Buenos Aires según sus pautas matrimoniales: ¿pluralismo cultural o crisol de razas?." *Estudios Migratorios Latinoamericanos,* n°2 (1986): 203–31.

Frevert, Ute. *Emotions in History Lost and Found.* Budapest; New York: Central European University Press, 2011.

Frost, Ginger. "He could not hold his passions': domestic violence and cohabitation in England (1850–1905)." *Crime, Histoire & Sociétés/Crime, History & Societies* 12, n°1 (2008): 45–63.

Gabaccia, Donna. *Italy's Many Diasporas.* New York; London: Routledge, 2000.

Gallo, Ezequiel. *La pampa gringa,* Buenos Aires, Sudamericana, 1983.

Gammerl, Benno. "Emotional styles—concepts and challenges." *Rethinking History* 16, n°2 (2012): 161–75.

Garnot, Benoît. "La violence dans la France moderne: une violence apprivoisée?." In *Violence, Concialtion et Répresion, Recherches sur l'histoire du crime, de l'Antiquité au*

*XXIe siècle*, edited by Aude, Musin and Xavier y Frédéric Vesentini, 289–97. Lovaina: Presses Universitaires de Louvain, 2008, http://books.openedition.org/pucl/725.

Garnot, Benoit. *Une histoire du crime passionnel. Mythes et archives*. Paris: Belin, 2014.

Gayol, Sandra. *Sociabilidad en Buenos Aires. Hombres, honor y cafés, 1862–1910*. Buenos Aires: Del Signo, 2000.

Gayol, Sandra. *Honor y duelo en la Argentina moderna*. Buenos Aires: Siglo XXI, 2008.

Gerber, David. *Authors of their Lives: the Personal Correspondence of British Immigrants to North America in the Nineteenth Century*. New York: New York University Press, 2006.

Ghirardi, Mónica. *Matrimonios y familia en Córdoba. Prácticas y representaciones*, Córdoba, Centro de Estudios Avanzados Universidad Nacional de Córdoba, 2004.

Ghirardi, Mónica. "Familia y maltrato doméstico. Audiencia Episcopal de Córdoba, 1700–1850." *História Unisinos* 8, n°1 (2008): 17–33.

Ghirardi, Mónica. "Disciplinamiento familiar y nuevos dispositivos de dominación en tiempos de modernización. Córdoba, Argentina, fines del siglo XIX." In *Trayectorias familiares. Identidades y desigualdad social*, edited by Chacón Jiménez, Francisco, 58–79. Murcia: Ediciones Universidad de Murcia, 2018.

Gibelli, Antonio, and Fabio Caffarena. "Le lettere degli emigrante." In *Storia dell'emigrazione italiana*, t. I *Partenze*, edited by Bevilacqua, Piero, Andreina De Clementi, and Emilio Franzina, Emilio, 563–774. Roma: Donizelli, 2001.

Ginzburg, Carlo. *The Judge, and the Historian: Marginal Notes on a Late-Nineteenth-century Miscarriage of Justice*. Translated by Anthony Shugaar. London: Verso, 1999.

Goody, Jacques. *The European Family*. London: Blackwell, 2000.

Guy, Donna J. *Sex & Danger in Buenos Aires: Prostitution, Family and Nation in Argentina*. Lincoln: University of Nebraska Press, 1991.

Guy, Donna J. "Volviendo del silencio: Divorcio y violencia familiar en la Argentina de fines del siglo XIX y comienzos del XX." *Feminaria* 15, n°28/29 (2002): 45–50.

Harney, Robert F. "Men without women: Italian migrants in Canada, 1885–1930." In *The Italian Immigrant Woman in North America*, edited by Boyd, Betty, Robert Caroli, Robert F. Harney, and Lydio F. Tomasi, 79–101. Toronto: Multicultural History Society of Ontario, 1977.

Hochschild, Arlie R. "Emotions work, feeling rules and social structure." *American Journal of Sociology* 85, n°3 (1979): 551–575.

Hochschild, Arlie R. "Ideology and emotion management: a perspective and path for future research." In *Research Agendas in the Sociology of Emotions*, edited by Kemper, Theodor D., 117–42. Albany: State University of New York Press, 1990.

Hochschild, Arlie R. *The Commercialization of Intimate Life: Notes from Home and Work*, Berkeley: University of California Press, 2003.

Hughes, Steven C. "Honourable murder: The delitto d'onore and the Zanardelli code of 1890." *Journal of Modern Italian Studies* 25, n°3 (2020): 229–51, https://doi.org/10.10 80/1354571X.2020.1750786.

Hyland Jr., Steven. "Arabic speaking immigrants before the court in Tucumán, 1910–1940." *Journal of Women's History* 28, n°4 (2016): 41–64, https://muse.jhu.edu/article/641105

Illouz, Eva. *Saving the Modern Soul: Therapy, Emotions, and the Culture of Self-help.* Berkeley; Los Angeles; London: University of California Press, 2008.

Jimeno, Myriam. *Crimen Pasional. Contribución a una Antropología de las Emociones.* Bogotá: Universidad Nacional de Colombia, 2004.

Kandiyoti, Deniz. "Bargaining with patriarchy." *Gender & Society* 2, n°3 (1988): 274–90.

Keetley, Dawn. "From anger to jealousy: explaining domestic homicide in Antebellum America." *Journal of Social History* 42, n°2 (2008): 269–97.

Kertzer, David I. *Sacrified for Honor: Italian Infant Abandonment and the Politics of Reproductive Control.* Boston: Beacon Press, 1993.

Kluger, Viviana. *Escenas de la vida conyugal. Los conflictos matrimoniales en la sociedad virreinal rioplatense.* Buenos Aires: Quórum, 2003.

Kounine, Laura. "Emotions, mind, and body on trial: a cross-cultural perspective." *Journal of Social History* 51, n°2 (2017): 219–30.

Kwon, June Hee. "The Work of Waiting: Love and Money in Korean Chinese Transnational Migration." *Cultural Anthropology* 30, n°3 (2015): 477–500.

Lacour, Philippe. "Penser par cas, ou comment remettre les sciences sociales à l'endroit." *Espaces Temps.net*, Livres, 2005, https://www.espacestemps.net/articles/remettre-les-sciences-sociales-a-endroit

Laera, Alejandra. "Novelas argentinas (circulación, debates y escritores en el último cuarto del siglo XIX)." In *Historia crítica de la literatura argentina*, Vol. 3. *El brote de los géneros*, edited by Jitrik, Noé, Vol. 3, 95–118. Buenos Aires: Emecé Editores, 2010.

Langhamer, Claire. *The English in Love: The Intimate Story of an Emotional Revolution*, Oxford: Oxford University Press, 2013.

Lavrín, Asunción. *Sexuality and Marriage in Colonial Latin America.* Lincoln: University of Nebraska Press, 1989.

Leirnur, Jorge Francisco. "Radicar y controlar. La estrategia de la casa autoconstruida." In *La casa y la multitud. Vivienda, política y cultura en la Argentina moderna*, edited by Ballent, Anahí and Jorge Francisco Leinur, 173–92. Buenos Aires: Fondo de Cultura Económica, 2014.

Levi, Giovanni. "On microhistory." In *New Perspectives on Historical Writing*, edited by Burke, Peter, 97–119. Pennsylvania: The Pennsylvania State University Press, 2001.

López Sánchez, Oliva and Edith Flores. "Reflexiones iniciales para una genealogía del amor romántico en clave de emociones." In *Pensar los Afectos. Aproximaciones desde las Ciencias Sociales y las Humanidades*, edited by Abramowski, Ana, and Santiago Canevaro, 191–206. Los Polvorines: Ediciones UNSG, 2017.

Lutz, Tom. *Crying: The Natural and Cultural History of Tears.* New York; London: Norton, 1999.

Lystra, Karen. *Searching the Heart: Women, Men, and Romantic Love in Nineteenth-century America.* Oxford: Oxford University Press, 1989.

Maroney, Terry A. "The persistent cultural script of judicial dispassion." *California Law Review* 99, n°2 (2011): 629–81.

Matos, María Izilda, and Oswaldo Truzzi. "Present in absentia: immigrant letters and requests for family reunification." *História Unisinos* 19, n°3 (2015): 348–357.

Matsuda, Mari J. "Public response to racist speech: considering the victim's story." In *Words that Wound: Critical Race Theory, Assaultive Speech, and the First Amendment*, edited by Matsuda, Mari J., Charles R. Lawrence, and Richard Delgado, 17–51. Boulder: West View Press, 1993.

Mat, Susan J. "Recovering the invisible. Methods for the historical study of the emotions." In *Doing Emotions in History*, edited by Stearns, Peter N. and Susan J. Matt. Champaign, University of Illinois Press, 2014.

May, Simon. *Love: A History*. New Haven: Yale University Press, 2011.

Mayo, Carlos. *Estancia y Sociedad en la pampa, 1740-1820*. Buenos Aires, Biblos, 1995.

Menin, Marco. "'Who will write the history of tears?' History of ideas and history of emotions from eighteenth-century France to the present." *History of European Ideas* 40, n°4 (2014): 516–23.

Míguez, Eduardo. "Familias de clase media: la formación de un modelo." In *Historia de la vida privada en Argentina. La Argentina plural (1870-1930)* edited by Devoto, Fernando and Marta Madero, 21–46. Buenos Aires. Santillana, 1999.

Moreno, José Luis. *Historia de la Familia en el Río de La Plata*. Buenos Aires: Sudamericana, 2004.

Moreno, Rodolfo (hijo). *Ley Penal Argentina Estudio Crítico*. La Plata: Editores Sesé y Larrañaga.

Muravyeva, Marianna. "*Vergüenza, vergogne, schande, skam and sram*. Litigating for shame and dishonour in early modern Europe." In *Shame, Blame and Culpability: Crime and Violence in the Modern State*, edited by Rowbotham, Judith, Marianna Muravyeva, and David Nash, 17–31. London; New York, Routledge, 2013.

Nash, Mary. *Mujer, familia y trabajo en España, 1875-1936*. Crítica: Barcelona, 1983.

Nash, Mary. "Un-contested identities: motherhood, sex reform and the modernization of gender identity in early-twentieth-century Spain." In *Constructing Spanish Womanhood: Female Identity in Modern Spain*, edited by Lorée Enders, Victoria and Pamela Beth Radcliff, 25–49. New York: State University of New York Press, 1999.

Núñez Seixas, Xosé Manoel. *La Galicia Austral. La inmigración gallega en la Argentina*. Buenos Aires: Biblos, 2001.

Nuñez Seixas, Xosé Manoel and Raúl Soutelo Vázquez. *As cartas do destino*. Vigo: Galaxia, 2005.

Nussbaum, Martha C. *Upheavals of Thought: The Intelligence of Emotions*. Cambridge: Cambridge University Press, 2001.

Ortega del Cerro, Pablo. "Del honor a la honradez: un recorrido por el cambio de valores sociales en el España de los siglos XVIII y XIX." *Cuadernos de Ilustración y Romanticismo Revista Digital del Grupo de Estudios del Siglo XVIII*, n°24 (2018): 597–618.

Otero, Hernán. "Una visión crítica de la endogamia: reflexiones a partir de una reconstrucción de familias francesas (Tandil, 1850–1914)." *Estudios Migratorios Latinoamericanos*, n°15–16 (1990): 343–77.

Parker, Stephen. *Informal Marriage, Cohabitation, and the Law, 1750–1989*. New York: St. Martin's Press, 1990.

Parma Cook, Alexandra and David Noble Cook. *Good Faith and Truthful Ignorance: The Case of Transatlantic Bigamy*. Durham: Duke University Press: 1991.

Parry, Jonathan and Maurice Bloch, eds. *Money and the Morality of Exchange*. Cambridge: Cambridge University Press, 1989.

Passeron, Jean-Claude and Jacques Revel. "*Penser par cas*. Raisonner à partir de singularités." In *Penser par cas*, edited by Passeron, Jean-Claude and Jacques Revel, 9–44. Paris, Éditions de l'EHESS, 2005.

Pavese, Cesare. *The Moon and the Bonfires*. Translated by Louise Sinclair. London: Lehmann, 1963, https://archive.org/details/in.ernet.dli.2015.149109

Paz Trueba, Yolanda. "La justicia en una sociedad de frontera: conflictos familiares ante los Juzgados de Paz. El centro sur bonaerense a fines del siglo XIX y principios del XX." *Historia Crítica*, n°36 (2008): 102–23.

Paz Trueba, Yolanda. "Violencia física y efectos simbólicos. El caso de Tres Arroyos a fines del siglo XIX y principios del XX." *Anuario del Instituto de Historia Argentina*, n°8 (2008): 173–92.

Pérez-Trullen, Juan Manuel, Álvaro Giménez-Muñoz, Isabel Campello, and Luis Chárlez. "La parálisis general progresiva o enfermedad de Bayle." *Neurosciences and History* 3, n°4 (2015): 147–53.

Pinto, Sarah. "Researching romantic love." *Rethinking History*, 21 n°4 (2017): 567–85.

Piselli, Fortunata. *Parentela ed emigrazione. Mutamenti e continuità in una comunità calabrese*. Turín, Einaudi, 1981.

Pitt-Rivers, Julian. "La enfermedad del honor." *Anuario IHES*, n°14 (1999): 235–45.

Plamper, Jan. "The history of emotions. An interview with William Reddy, Barbara Rosenwein, and Peter Stearns." *History and Theory* 49, n°2 (2010): 237–65.

Plamper, Jan. *The History of Emotions: An Introduction*. Oxford: Oxford University Press, 2015.

Pollock, Linda. "Anger and the negotiation of relationships in early modern England." *The Historical Journal* 47, n°3 (2004): 567–90.

Reddy, William M. *The Navigation of Feeling: A Framework for the History of Emotions*. Cambridge: Cambridge University Press, 2001.

Reddy, William M. "Emotional styles and modern forms of life." In *Sexualized Brains: Scientific Modeling of Emotional Intelligence from a Cultural Perspective*, edited by Karafyllis, Nicole C. and Gotlind Ulshöfer, 81–100. Cambridge: MIT Press, 2008.

Reddy, William M. *The Making of Romantic Love*. Chicago: The University of Chicago Press, 2012.

Reeder, Linda. "When men left Sutera. Sicilian women and mass migration, 1880–1920." In *Women, Gender, and Transnational Lives: Italian Workers of the World*, edited by

Gabaccia, Donna, and Franca Iacovetta, 45–75. Toronto: University of Toronto Press, 2002.

Reeder, Linda. *Widows in White: Migration and Transformation of Rural Italian Women, Sicily, 1880–1920*, Toronto: Toronto University Press, 2003.

Reeder, Linda. "Men of honor and honorable men: Migration and Italian migration to the United States from 1880–1930." *Italian Americana* 28, n°1 (2010): 18–35.

Revel, Jacques. "Microanalyse et construction du social." In *Jeux d´echelles. La micro-anlyse à l´experience*, edited by Revel, Jacques, 15–36. Paris: Gallimard-Seuil, 1996.

Riall, Lucy. "Which road to the south? Revisionists revisit the Mezzogiorno." *Journal of Modern Italian Studies* 4, n°1 (2000): 89–100.

Rizzo, Domenico. "Marriage on trial: adultery in nineteenth-century Rome." In *Gender, Family, and Sexuality: The Private Sphere in Italy, 1860–1945*, edited by Wilson, Perry, 20–36. New York: Palgrave Macmillan, 2004.

Rodríguez Nuñez, Alicia. "El parricidio en la legislación española." *Boletín de la Facultad de Derecho*, n°5 (1993–1994): 145–71.

Rogers, Geraldine. *Caras y Caretas. Cultura, política y espectáculo en los inicios del siglo XX argentino*. La Plata: Editorial de la Universidad de la Plata, 2008.

Romero, Luis Alberto. *A History of Argentina in the Twentieth Century*. Translated by James P. Brennan. Pennsylvania: Pennsylvania State University Press, 2002.

Roncoroni, Atilio. *Historia del Municipio de Dolores*. Dolores: Edición de la Municipalidad de Dolores, 1967.

Rosenwein, Barbara. "Review of The Navigation of Feeling: a framework for the History of Emotions." *The American Historical Review* 107, n°4, (2002): 1181–82

Rosenwein. "Problems and methods in the History of Emotions." *Passions in Context*, n°1 (2010): 1–33.

Rozenblatt, Daphne. "Legal insanity: towards an understanding of free will thorough feeling in modern Europe." *Rechtsgeschichte/Legal History*, n°25 (2017): 263–75.

Ruggiero, Kristin. *Modernity in the Flesh: Medicine, Law, and Society in Turn-of-the-Century Argentina*. Stanford: Stanford University Press, 2004.

Ruggiero, Kristin. "Private justice and honor in the Italian community in late XIXth century Buenos Aires." *Crime, Histoire & Sociétés/Crime, History & Societies* 13, n°2 (2009): 55–68.

Salvatore, Ricardo. "Criminología positivista, reforma de prisiones y la cuestión social en Argentina." In *La cuestión social en Argentina, 1870–1943*, edited by Suriano, Juan, 127–58. Buenos Aires: La Colmena, 2000.

Salvatore, Ricardo. "Sobre el surgimiento del estado médico legal en la Argentina (1890–1940)." *Estudios Sociales*, n°20 (2001): 81–114.

Sánchez Alonso, Blanca. "La inmigración española 1880–1914. Capital Humano y Familia." In *Impulsos e Inercias del Cambio Económico. Ensayos en Honor a Nicolás Sánchez-Albornoz*, edited by Lida, Clara E. and José A. Piqueras, 197–230. Valencia: Fundación Instituto de Historia Social, 2004.

Scheer, Monique. "Are emotions a kind of practice (and is that what makes them have a history?) A Bourdieuian approach to understanding emotion." *Theory and History* 51, n°2 (2012): 193–220.

Schneider, Jane, ed. *Italy's "Southern Question". Orientalism in One Country.* Oxford and New York: Berg, 1998.

Seymour, Mark. "Keystone of the patriarchal family? Indissoluble marriage, masculinity and divorce in Liberal Italy." *Journal of Modern Italian Studies* 10, n°3 (2005): 297–313.

Seymour, Mark. "Emotional arenas: from provincial circus to national courtroom in late nineteenth-century Italy." *Rethinking History: The Journal of Theory and Practice* 16, n°2 (2012): 177–97.

Solomon, Robert C. "Justice v. Vengeance. On law and the satisfaction of emotion." In *The Passions of Law*, edited by Bandes, Susan A., 123–48. New York; London: New York University Press, 1999.

Sozzo, Máximo. "Los exóticos del crimen. Inmigración, delito y criminología positivista en la Argentina (1887–1914)." *Delito y Sociedad*, 2 n°32 (2016): 19–52.

Stearns, Peter N. *American Cool: Constructing a Twentieth-century Emotional Style.* New York: New York University Press, 1994.

Stearns, Peter N. "Review of The Navigation of Feeling: a framework for the History of Emotions." *Journal of Interdisciplinary History* 33, n°3 (2003): 473–75

Stearns, Peter N. *Shame: A Brief History.* Chicago; Springfield: University of Illinois Press, 2017.

Stearns, Peter N. and Carol Z. Stearns. "Emotionology. Clarifying the history of emotions and emotional standards." *The American Historical Review* 90, n°4 (1985): 813–36.

Strange, Carolyn, Robert Cribb, and Christopher E. Forth, eds. *Honour, Violence and Emotions in History.* London; New York: Bloomsbury, 2014.

Suriano, Juan. "Niños trabajadores. Una aproximación al trabajo infantil en la industria porteña de comienzos del siglo." In *Mundo Urbano y Cultura Popular. Estudios de Historia Social Argentina*, edited by Armus, Diego, 251–279. Buenos Aires: Sudamericana, 1990.

Suriano, Juan. "Vivir y sobrevivir en la Gran Ciudad. Hábitat popular en la ciudad de Buenos Aires a comienzos del siglo." *Estudios Sociales* 7, n°1 (1994): 49–68.

Suriano, Juan. "La cuestión social y el complejo proceso de construcción inicial de las políticas sociales en la Argentina Moderna." *Ciclos* XI, n°21 (2001): 123–47.

Tapaninen, Anna-Maria. "Motherhood through the wheel: the care of foundlings in late nineteenth-century Naples." In *Gender, Family and Sexuality: The Private Sphere in Italy, 1860–1945*, edited by Wilson, Perry, 51–70. London: Palgrave Macmillan, 2004.

Tarello, Giovanni. *Cultura jurídica y política del derecho.* Fondo de Cultura Económica: México DF, 1995.

Tirabassi, Maddalena. "Le emigrante italiane: dalla ricerca locale a quella globale." *Giornale di storia contemporanea* IV, n°1 (2001): 86–94.

Tirabassi, Maddalena. "Bourgeois men, peasant women: rethinking domestic work and morality in Italy." In *Women, Gender, and Transnational Lives: Italian Workers of the World*, edited by Gabaccia, Donna and Franca Iacovetta, 106–130. Toronto: University of Toronto Press, 2002.

Vendrame, Maíra Inés. *Power in the Village: Social Networks, Honor and Justice among Immigrant Families from Italy to Brazil*. Translated by Miriam Adelman. New York: Routledge, 2020.

Vidor, Gian Marco. "Rhetorical engineering of emotions in the courtroom: the case of lawyers in modern France." *Rechtsgechichte/Legal History*, n°25 (2017): 286–95.

Vigarello, Georges. *Histoire du viol, XVIe–Xxe siècles*. Paris: Seuil, 1998.

Villasante Armas, Olga. "Introducción del concepto de parálisis general progresiva a la psiquiatría decimonónica española." *Asclepio* LII, n°1 (2000): 53–72.

Vincent-Buffault, Anne. *Histoire des larmes: XVIIIe–XIXe siècles*. Marseille: Rivages, 1986.

Weisman, Richard. *Showing Remorse: Law and the Social Control of Emotions*. London; New York: Routledge, 2014.

Wilkis. Ariel. *Las Sospechas del Dinero. Moral y Economía en la Vida Popular*. Buenos Aires, Paidós, 2013.

Wilkis, Ariel. "El poder moral del dinero. Una perspectiva sociológica." *Diferencia(s)*, n°5 (2017): 39–60.

Yangilevich, Melina. "Construir Poder en la Frontera. José Benito Machado." In *Vivir entre dos mundos. Las fronteras del Sur de la Argentina. Siglos XVIII y XIX*, edited by Mandrini, Raúl, 195–226. Buenos Aires: Taurus, 2006.

Yujnovsky, Oscar. "Políticas de vivienda en la ciudad de Buenos Aires (1880–1914)." *Desarrollo Económico* 14, n°54 (1974): 327–372.

Zaffaroni, Raúl Eugenio and Miguel Alfredo Arnedo. *Digesto de Codificación Penal Argentina*. Buenos Aires: AZ Editora, 1996.

Zapiola, María Carolina. "Los niños entre la escuela, el taller y la calle (o los límites de la obligatoriedad escolar). Buenos Aires, 1884–1915." *Cadernos de Pesquisa* 39, n°136 (2009): 69–81.

Zaragoza Bernal, Juan Manuel. "Ampliar el marco. Hacia una historia material de las emociones." *Vínculos de Historia*, n°4 (2015): 28–40.

Zeberio, Blanca. "Entre deux mondes les agriculteurs européens dans les 'nouvelles terres' de l'Argentine: exploitation agricole et reproduction sociale dans la pampa: 1880–1930." Ph.D. diss., Ecole des Hautes Études en Sciences Sociales, Paris, 1994.

Zelizer, Viviana. *The Social Meaning of Money: Pin Money, Paychecks, Poor Relief & Other Currencies*. New York: Basicbooks, 1994.

Zimmermann, Eduardo. *Los liberales reformistas. La cuestión social en la Argentina 1890–1916*. Buenos Aires: Sudamericana-Universidad de San Andrés, 1994.

# Index

Page numbers: Notes are given as: [page number] n. [note number]

spatial mobility 42, 127n.11
Stearns, Peter N. 51
Stella, Mauro 18
street life 18–19, 20, 40, 41
subordination 55, 62
suicide 80, 98, 100–1, 104, 110, 116–17,
    155n.46
sustenance, duty to provide 64
syphilis 97
Syrian immigrants 123, 147n.2

tears 100–1, 114, 153n.29
    *see also* weeping
tenement housing 16–19, 21, 83, 98,
    131n.21, 131n.22
    *see also conventillos*
trade partners, Argentina 129n.9
Tucumán province 130n.14, 147n.2
Turero y Miga case 70, 87, 98–104

United States 38, 130n.11
unrequited love 117, 155n.46
urban areas 14, 129n.6
    *see also* cities
urbanization 13–14
uxoricide (wife killing) 3, 5
    for adultery 143n.79
    archives' bias 123
    jealousy 87–106
    judicial records 6, 9
    life sentences 118, 155n.48
    newspaper sources 7, 87–8
    *see also* murder/uxoricide

vengeance 47–50, 106, 148n.13
Verne, Jules, *France Ville* 13
victims
    hatred of 102
    news portrayal 88

violence
    everyday 69–86
    marital conflict 89
    money and 83
    women against men 72
    *see also* domestic violence/abuse
Volga German communities 123

waiting 2, 23–4, 32, 82, 119, 125n.4, 133n.1
weeping 114–15
    *see also* tears
Weisman, Richard 101
"white widows" 5, 41, 43, 66, 127n.13
"widowers of the living" 39–43
"widows of the living" 5, 41, 43, 66,
    127n.13
Wilde, Eduardo 112
women
    agency 120–1
    deception 39
    home management 42
    honor system 31–2, 33, 92–3, 135n.23
    illiteracy 59
    marriage chances 15
    money 78–86
    passports 138n.63
    patriarchal control 43
    in popular literature 117
    remittances to 23, 26
    sexuality 47–8
    Spanish ideals 55
    subordination 62
    tenement life 17
    violence against men 72
words as translations 122
"work of waiting" 2, 23–4, 32, 82, 119,
    125n.4, 133n.1

"Zanardelli Code" 143n.79

www.ingramcontent.com/pod-product-compliance
Lightning Source LLC
Chambersburg PA
CBHW050515280326
41932CB00014B/2327